Iconoclasm and
Poetry in the
English Reformation

Iconoclasm and Poetry in the English Reformation

Down Went Dagon

Ernest B. Gilman

The University of Chicago Press
Chicago and London

Ernest B. Gilman, associate professor of English at New York University, is the author of *The Curious Perspective: Literary and Pictorial Wit in the Seventeenth Century.*

The University of Chicago Press, Chicago 60637
The University of Chicago Press, Ltd., London
© 1986 by The University of Chicago
All rights reserved. Published 1986
Printed in the United States of America

95 94 93 92 91 90 89 88 87 86 54321

Publication of this work has been supported, in part,
by a grant from the Abraham and Rebecca Stein Faculty
Publications Fund of New York University,
Department of English.

Library of Congress Cataloging-in-Publication Data

Gilman, Ernest B., 1946–
   Iconoclasm and poetry in the English Reformation.

   Includes index.
   1. English poetry—Early modern, 1500–1700—History
and criticism. 2. Iconoclasm in literature. 3. Art
and literature—England. 4. Reformation—England.
5. Ut pictura poesis (Aesthetics). I. Title.
PR545.I25G55 1986 821'.3'09 85-28837
ISBN 0-226-29382-3

For Lois, Seth, and Eve Gilman

Contents

Illustrations

Acknowledgments

I am grateful to the University of Virginia for its support of this project by a Sesquicentennial Associateship in 1981, and to New York University for a Presidential Fellowship in 1983. Publication of this work has been supported in part through the generosity of the Abraham and Rebecca Stein Faculty Publications Fund of New York University. In an earlier version, a substantial part of Chapter 4 first appeared as "Word and Image in Quarles' Emblemes," in *Critical Inquiry* 6, 3 (1980), © 1980 by The University of Chicago. A version of Chapter 5 appeared as "'To adore, or scorne an image': Donne and the Iconoclastic Controversy," in the *John Donne Journal* 4, 2 (Winter 1985). For permission to publish the illustrations, I acknowledge the following with thanks: The Folger Shakespeare Library (figs. 1 and 2 [STC 18966], 4 [BD 500 F4 1617b Cage], 6-8 [STC 18602], 9, 10, 12–17 [STC 20540.2], 11 [BV 4515 H8 1628 copy 1 Cage—plate identical to 1624 ed.], 18 [E 272]); Rare Books and Manuscripts Division, The New York Public Library, Astor, Lenox and Tilden Foundations (fig. 3); Musées Nationaux, Paris (fig. 5); Bayerische Staatsbibliothek (fig. 19 [2° A.gr.b.432h]); and the Avery Architectural and Fine Arts Library, Columbia University in the City of New York (fig. 20).

At every stage I have had the benefit of shrewd advice and warm encouragement from many people. Some deserve far more credit than a brief acknowledgment can confer. Martin Elsky continues to be a learned and generous friend. My former doctoral students at the University of Virginia—Nahla Hashweh, David Radcliffe and especially David Loewenstein, for whose scrupulous commentary on chapter 6 I am grateful—helped to create a climate of ideas for which any instructor trying to come up with a few of his own would be glad. James Nohrnberg, Robert Langbaum, and James Mirollo were there for me when I needed them, as was my most therapeutic critic, William Kerrigan. I would like to add a note of particular thanks to Enid Stubin, and to my colleagues in Renaissance studies at New York University who as readers, advisors, and friends have been invaluable to me during the two years in which this work was finally pulled together: Roger Deakins, Richard Harrier, Daniel Javitch, and Anthony Low. My wife Lois Gilman remains my one temptation to idolatry.

Introduction

This book is about the impact of Reformation iconoclasm on some of the major poetry written during the English Reformation. "Impact" may strike the reader as a critical cliché, but in the study of an age when disputes over sacred art were as likely to be settled with the hammer as with the pen, the term has a more forceful application. For more than a century, from the time of the Henrician reforms of the 1530s to the Restoration in 1660, religious paintings, statues, rood screens, and stained glass all over England fell to successive waves of iconoclastic zeal. During those same years, Protestant enemies of idolatry filled thousands of pages with arguments against the abuse of "images" in devotion, while their opponents—recusant Catholics, moderate Anglicans, Laudians—filled thousands more in reply. My theme will be that both the phenomenon of iconoclasm itself and the body of controversy it provoked are sharply etched in the literature of the period—indeed, that they pose a crucial dilemma for the literary imagination of the sixteenth and seventeenth centuries.

By nearly every precept of Renaissance aesthetic theory, the poet was encouraged to assume the deep affiliation of literary and pictorial art. Poetry, he knew, was a "speaking picture," its figures and structures designed by creative acts as fully visual as verbal. Yet he also knew, on the authority of the Reformation's attack on idolatry, that not only devotional images in churches but the very imaging power of the mind was tainted by the pride and sensuality of fallen humanity and open to the perils of worship misdirected from the Creator to the creation. From the one point of view, *pictura* and *poesis* were companionable sisters in the service of the poet's art; from the other, the word was the bulwark of the spirit against the carnal enticements of the image.

Put in its bluntest terms, this dilemma may seem to be a formula for poetic paralysis. It can lead Sidney, in a moment of bitter reflection on the iconographic tradition in which his own sonnets are set, to observe that "what we call *Cupid's* dart, / An image is, which for our selves we carve; / And, fooles, adore in temple of our hart." Poets and lovers alike, swerving from heaven's (Protestant) rule that "eyes are formed to serve / The inward light," "strive for their own smart."[1] Nearly a hundred years later, it can lead Milton, in *Samson*

Agonistes, to write a "blind" tragedy that culminates in the destruction of a theater. Focused in the urgencies of the Reformation debate over images, such moments also reveal a more general conflict between the constructive, formal dimension of compositions "seen" or spatialized on the analogy with the visual arts, and the kinetic impulse of language toward temporal flow and the subversion of fixed structures. Together this split intention constitutes a major internal drama of Reformation literary texts—and, not incidentally, a focus in our own time for competing modes of literary interpretation. But as the examples of Sidney and Milton may suggest, it is also at such moments of great internal pressure, when poets are forced by the Reformation critique to grapple with the means and motives of their own art, that diamonds are formed.

The poet's "imagination" has of course been the abiding subject of critical concern. By narrowing, and yet in some respects deepening, the word to indicate the poet's engagement with what the Reformation called "images," I hope to make some connections between areas of study that have tended to be fenced off by the enclosure laws of academic specialization. Historians of religion, social historians, and art historians have all contributed to an important body of scholarship on Reformation iconoclasm. Their evidence has been put to occasional good use by literary critics interested in the theological and specifically Protestant foundations of Renaissance literature, and my indebtedness to their work will appear below. There have however been only a handful of literary studies attempting as this one does to get at the meaning of iconoclasm to a body of deeply iconic Renaissance poetry.[2]

From a neighboring field, meanwhile, has come a diverse and growing number of studies in Renaissance literature and the visual arts—studies in the "structure" and "imagery" of poems, in the allusions poems make to artists and works of art, in iconography, emblematics, masquing and spectacle, and so on. Again, some are richly illuminating, but few make the reader aware that there were opposing forces at work in the period to put the very assumptions of the "pictorial" poet under severe strain. The canonical studies of the "sister arts," all of them indebted to Rensselaer W. Lee's original monograph in *The Art Bulletin* in 1940, typically follow the procedure set out there in which the English arts are treated as the reflection of Italian Renaissance theory and example. Works centered in England—Jean Hagstrum on "literary pictorialism," John Dixon Hunt on gardens, Stephen Orgel and Roy Strong on Inigo Jones, Peter Daly on the emblem—still face toward Italy as they assess the importance of Serlian stage design on the English theater or of Alciati for the iconography of English poetry.[3] Such works tend to move, like Lee's, toward a final chapter which exposes the late absurdities of *ut pictura poesis* in Dryden's pronouncements, and then declares the sisterhood of the arts at an end, for better or worse, with the publication of Lessing's *Laocoon* in 1766. In this scheme, what I take to be most interesting and revealing about the relationship of the arts in the English Renaissance—the modifications forced on Italian assumptions by the Reformation—is short-circuited. What echoes in the poetic record of the age is not so much the inheritance of Renaissance theory in pure form as the continuous interplay, and the occasional major collision, between strongly iconic and strongly iconoclastic impulses.

If the present study were a Renaissance emblem book, the pictorial device to be elaborated by the chapters that follow would be the "crossroads" at which these collisions take place. Chapters 1 and 2 survey its dimensions, and the remaining chapters, on Spenser, Quarles, Donne, and Milton, interrogate four poets who pass through it between 1569 and 1671. Although other figures will be observed in the same vicinity, I have not tried to compile an exhaustive census but rather to center the inquiry on a manageable sample of exemplary texts. Still, the book tries to raise, if not answer, a set of more general questions provoked by its topic. How does any age, but the English Renaissance in particular, conceive of the relationship between the word and the image, writing and drawing, linguistic and visual perception? What conditions permit such connections between the arts to be asserted, and what cultural pressures limit them or shape them into characteristic patterns as they come to be imbedded in works of art? What processes govern the nature of the change in such relationships over time?

I

At the Crossroads: The Poetics of the Sister Arts

The battered image that would have made the ideal frontispiece for a book on iconoclasm and literature in the English Reformation itself fell victim to an iconoclastic attack. A large crucifix had stood in London's West Cheap Cross since 1486. Topped by a dove, it was supported below by sculptures of the Virgin and Child, Edward the Confessor, and the Resurrection. It was defaced in 1581; repaired in 1600, but now with a pyramid substituted for the idolatrous crucifix and a partially clad Diana for the Virgin; altered again, at Elizabeth's order, to include a new crucifix mounted on the pyramid; and again, shortly after, by the restoration of the Virgin's statue; but ruined again less than two weeks later when the Virgin lost her infant, her crown, and most of her head.[1]

The conflicts of theology and passion that we may imagine to have been swirling around this one unfortunate crucifix are symptomatic of the wider and more protracted confrontation in England between a growing tradition in the visual arts and the challenge to those arts posed by the Reformation. In some ways there is nothing unique in the particular English version of this debate. The despoiling of images in England in the 1530s and 1540s followed hard upon similar waves of more or less disorderly iconoclasm in Strasbourg, Zurich, Basel, and other northern cities where the reform had taken hold, and was justified—however much we might want to distinguish the political context of the Tudor reform from that in Germany or Switzerland—on the same few points of doctrine that had been defined by Calvin or Zwingli. Yet the debate over sacred imagery in England was to smolder and spark until the Restoration, far longer than on the Continent and at times far more violently. The sixteenth century witnessed the controversy between Tyndale and More in the 1520s over the propriety of images in worship, the antipapal campaign orchestrated for Henry VIII by Thomas Cromwell in the 1530s, the Royal Visitations and iconoclastic Orders of Council promulgated under Cranmer in the 1540s and again under the Elizabethan bishops in the 1560s. All these accusations and investigations that had characterized the early reform were renewed a century later, after a period of fragile Anglican compromise, in the parliamentary opposition to Laud, in the individual zeal of Puritan officers during the Civil War, and then in the organized activity of the county committees established for the abolition of monuments of superstition, and finally in the dispersal of the royal collections.

The Philistine idol Dagon—who was discovered by his worshipers miraculously "fallen upon his face to the ground before the ark of the Lord," his head and the palms of his hands cut off so that "only the stump of Dagon was left to him" (1 Sam. 5:4)—supplied a durable slogan for the iconoclastic campaign. In *Bartholomew Fair*, Jonson's Zeal-of-the-land Busy, the paranoid Puritan for whom "Idolatry peepeth out on euery side" (3.6.45–46), has his moment of triumph when he breaks up a play with the cry: "Downe with *Dagon*, downe with *Dagon*; 'tis I, will no longer endure your prophanations" (5.5.1–2).[2] In *Paradise Lost*, Dagon "mourn'd in earnest, when the Captive Ark / Maim'd his brute Image" (1:458–59); both his followers and the spectacle staged in his honor would be maimed again by the captive Samson as that iconoclastic hero of Milton's tragedy carries on the work of reformation:

> those two massy Pillars
> With horrible convulsion to and fro
> He tugg'd, he shook, till down they came, and drew
> The whole roof after them with burst of thunder
> Upon the heads of all who sat beneath.
>
> (1648–52)[3]

Looking back on the Civil War from a perspective quite different from Milton's, Aubrey recalls that when he "came to Oxford crucifixes were common in the glass in the studies' windows; and in the chamber windows were cannonised saints. . . . But after 1647 they were all broken. Down went Dagon. Now no religion is to be found."[4] The same sentiments on either side might well have been voiced a century before, when the images in St. Paul's and many other London churches were pulled down. Five generations of controversy would unfold in the consequences of Cranmer's charge to the new king at the coronation of Edward VI, "to see, with your predecessor Josias, God truly worshipped and idolatry destroyed, the tyranny of the Bishops of Rome banished from your subjects, and images removed."[5]

The history of English iconoclasm in its sociological and political dimensions has been extensively documented, and it should prove as interesting to psychohistorians as it has to historians of theology. John Phillips, in *The Reformation of Images*, offers the best general account of the period from 1535 to 1660.[6] Such a survey moves through a panorama of events, some tragic, some tragicomic and even bizarre. The dissolution of the monasteries in the 1530s, followed, after the accession of Edward VI in 1547, by an official program for the wholesale removal of images, left untouched only a small fraction of the painting, sculpture, and stained glass that had adorned every English church on the eve of the Reformation. The Royal Visitors' Injunctions, published in July 1547, warned the clergy against "the most detestable offence of idolatry" and directed incumbents to remove and "utterly extinct and destroy" all paintings and other monuments of superstition, not only on the walls or in the windows of churches, but in private houses as well.[7] By 1550, as Laurence Stone notes, "whole shiploads of religious statuary were being exported to France."[8] During the brief reign of Mary, from 1553 to 1558, the destruction was halted and some efforts at restoration were begun. But with her death and the return from their Genevan exile of a new generation of Calvinist enthusiasts, the purification of the church was avidly resumed under Elizabeth. Although mob actions were discouraged, particularly when it came to the property of the nobility, the Royal Visitors supervised a demolition job reaching throughout the kingdom, and including, in London itself, the burning of wooden rood images in two huge bonfires on the night of August 24, 1559. This public immolation—which must have struck some observers as a strange parody of a Marian martyrdom—was perhaps the most spectacular display of a program that went on more quietly elsewhere. In 1560 the accounts of Eton College record the payment "To Glover and his Laborer for two daies brekinge downe Images and filling there places with stone and plaister juxta xxd.– iij˙iiij d."[9] Images were condemned at length in the official *Homilie against perill of Idolatrie* issued in 1563. Their place in the church would now be filled by scriptural verses painted on the walls and altar cloths, and by the literary monuments of the Reformation, the English Bible and Foxe's "Book of Martyrs," *The Acts and Monuments of the Church.*

Other more specialized studies supplement Phillips's work by noting the local impact of the reformation of images on Tudor life. From the time of the early Henrician reforms through the Elizabethan settlement, many unprincipled churchwardens in Essex— driven though they were to substantial outlays for whitewashing, reglazing, "making good the holes in the wall where the image did stand," or for "Writing certain scriptures on the walls"—showed no hesitation in obeying the royal commands: "they pulled down rood-lofts and altars, wrote texts on walls to cover religious paintings, knocked saints' pictures out of windows, and chained Bibles in churches with the same alacrity as they restored altars, rood-lofts, and saints and removed Bibles when the orders came."[10] In 1536, John Henshaw, a Lancashire schoolmaster of more forceful convictions, encouraged his pupils to mock the images in the chapel, whereupon one boy is reported to have been so moved that he seized a sword from the image of St. George and broke it over the saint's head, shouting, "Let me see now how thou canst fight again!" Lancashire was, however, a more conservative county than Essex. The ecclesiastical reforms attempted there in the 1530s were met with armed resistance, and neither the Royal Visitations of 1547– 48 nor those of 1563 had a lasting effect where the clergy to be visited were willing to risk concealing offensive images in their houses or burying them in the vicarage garden.[11] Still, when the spirit of reform seemed to cool, a notorious abomination could always be produced to heat it up again. When the monastery at Boxley in Kent was defaced in 1538, one of the images found there, the Rood of Grace, was discovered to have tricked the faithful into superstitious awe by means, says Foxe, of a "hundred wires to make the image goggle with the eyes; to nod with the head; to hang the lip; to move and shake his jaws, according to the value of the gift which was offered."[12] This rood was paraded through the streets of London and subjected to a sermon against idolatry preached by the bishop of London himself before it was smashed and fed to the flames.

In London such events had their place as interludes among the grander official spectacles of the Tudor court which were themselves affected by the Reformation in ways that suggest a shifting and newly competitive relationship between image and text. Compared with the elaborate civic pageantry staged earlier in Henry's reign—Anne Boleyn's triumphal entry into London in 1533 boasted its own portable Mount Parnassus designed by Holbein—court spectacle in the later 1530s became at once more overtly polemical and more spare as several of its chief devisers were reassigned from visual to verbal propaganda. To take advantage of a technology that could extend the power of the word into the most idolatrous corners of Lancashire, John Rastell and Clement Urmiston were thus drawn into Cromwell's service as pamphleteers. But Urmiston also proposed to circulate a talismanic image of Henry that would—like the Ditchley portrait of Elizabeth or the engraving of Charles I in the frontispiece of the *Eikon Basilike*—impress those to be protected from popish superstition with the monarch's own superior magic. As Frances Yates observes of the cult of Elizabeth, "The bejewelled and painted images of the Virgin Mary had been cast out of churches and monasteries, but another bejewelled and painted image was set up at court, and went on progress through the land for her worshippers to adore."[13] Since, however, much of the king's spiritual authority was symbolized by his having sponsored the English Bible, the motif of the book as a stage prop was to become a main concern of subsequent pageantry. A pageant devised for the entry of Mary and Philip II into London showed Henry holding a volume labeled *Verbum Dei*. For this gaffe the painter was reprimanded by the Catholic queen, but at Elizabeth's coronation pageant the new queen insisted upon being handed the Bible in a gesture clearly reminiscent of her father's role, imaged in the frontispiece of the Bibles he commissioned, as recipient and guardian of the sacred text.[14]

The Civil War brought a new burst of iconoclasm in the 1640s. Archbishop Laud had already been impeached by the Long Parliament in 1640. One of the main charges against him, pressed home at his trial with great vehemence by William Prynne, was that he had countenanced "the setting up of images in churches, church-windows, and other places of religious worship." In the early months of the conflict Colonel Sandys led his troops in an exemplary foray against Canterbury Cathedral. Among the many idols destroyed that day in August 1642, twelve saints over the west door of the quire "were all cast doune headlong and some fell on their heads and their Myters brake their necks."[15] Similar depredations followed, at the hands of equally zealous commanders like Sir William Waller, at Winchester, Exeter, and other cathedrals. The response was a predictable attempt to fan popular resentment by exaggeration and libel. The Royalist broadsheet *Mercurius Rusticus* accused the parliamentary armies of perpetrating "more outrages than the

Goths in the sack of Rome."[16] A satire of 1644 offered the boast of a base mechanic named Anarchus ("the Churches *Scourge*"), that "Wee'l breake the windowes which the Whore / of Babilon hath painted":

> What ere the Popish hands have built
>   Our Hammers shall undoe;
> Wee'l breake their Pipes and bruise their Copes,
>   And pull downe Churches too.[17]

Cromwell himself—tied by the propagandists to the vicious reputation of his ancestor Thomas Cromwell—was charged with having personally supervised deeds of heartless vandalism all over England, including the ruining of the tower of Ely Cathedral which was known to have fallen in the fourteenth century.[18] Although many such reports were undoubtedly baseless, in 1643 Parliament did enact an ordinance reconstituting committees of visitors to put the business of defacement on a more thoroughgoing and methodical footing. William Dowsing, appointed visitor of East Anglican churches, kept a diary which reflects his astonishing dedication to the task. Hammering and smashing his way around Suffolk and Cambridgeshire, he paused long enough to record not only his own exploits but those of his colleagues. From Dowsing we learn of one Edward Partheriche, a member of the committee for Kent, who no sooner discovered pictures of the Crucifixion and the Resurrection in the house of his wife's uncle than he skewered the offensive images on his sword.[19] The uncle's reaction is not recorded, but he would have been shortsighted to suppose that Partheriche and his confederates were possessed by a "strange insensate fury, utterly divorced from its historical context."[20] Depending on one's doctrinal sympathies, Partheriche must be seen to have played out a late and minor role as either the agent of a chronic social pathology, or the physician fiercely devoted to cutting away what one iconoclast earlier in the century had diagnosed as the "gangrene" of idolatry "spread over the whole body of Israel."[21]

This brief chronicle of a hundred years of English iconoclasm can do no more than evoke a complex and pervasive phenomenon. It may yet serve to sketch in the background for what follows, and to suggest at least one probable fact of imaginative life in those years. Few people are likely to have envisioned an "image"—certainly in its most narrowly proscribed form as a representation of the Trinity, of Christ or his cross, of the Virgin or the saints—without at the same time, perhaps for a fleeting instant charged with horror or glee, envisioning that image destroyed. Such speculations are not of exclusive interest to historians of sacred art. They also impinge on the literary imagination in ways I will want to explore broadly in this chapter, and more specifically afterward in the essays on individual poets. It is important to realize that "iconoclasm" is something that can happen to texts and within texts written during this period, and that the most compelling texts often betray a consciousness of the image-debate that reflects on the process of their own composition. The scene of such writing is set at the crossroads where a lively tradition of image-making confronts a militantly logocentric theology armed not only with an overt hostility to "images" in worship but with a deep suspicion of the idolatrous potential of the fallen mind and its fallen language. My assumption will be that the persistent clichés of literary history have tended to assess this confrontation all too crudely as the stifling impact of a dour Puritanism on an exuberant Renaissance imagination. My point will be rather to show how the creative power of sixteenth- and seventeenth-century literature is released at crucial moments when the visual resources of the poet are challenged by a conception of language disinfected, in its blind and often violent purity, of any appeal to the eye.

When Bess of Hardwick acquired the copes from Lillishall Abbey, she had the saints' heads cut out and replaced with classical heads before installing the copes as hangings at Chatsworth.[22] Idolatrous books, if they were not destroyed, were similarly liable to be defaced. A great many devotional works were methodically scoured of both images and text. Caxton's illustrated translation of the *Legenda Aurea*, published in 1483, was soon after on view in parish churches as a "layman's book" open to the understanding of the unlettered; with the Reformation it came under attack as a collection of superstitions. Like the copes and the statuary, it was also to be replaced by Foxe's Protestant hagiography and by authorized translations of the Word, but not before at least one reformer had taken the trouble to mutilate it:

> In one copy of *The Golden Legend*, a mid-Tudor radical revised Caxton's incipit: "Here begynneth the noble historye of thexposicion of the masse." With the striking out of the word "noble," the altered title reads "Here begynneth the most abomynall historye of thexposicion of the popyshe

11

masse moste to be aborryd of all Cristianes." The expur-
gator crossed out the entire legend of the mass with its illustration of two priests carrying the host in the Corpus
Christi procession. Crude crosshatching and the tearing
out of scattered leaves badly damages the surviving text.
The removal of woodcuts for the Nativity and Epiphany
may reflect the radical Protestant conviction that artistic
representation of those events in Christ's life undermines
emphasis on his preachings and passion which constitute
gospel truth.[23]

Protestant writers at the crossroads were also given to revealing
moments of self-censorship in their own work, moments of subtle
expurgation corresponding to the bolder crosshatching and torn
leaves of the *Golden Legend*. Sidney's letters written from Venice in
1573–74 are examples of what Katherine Duncan-Jones calls the
Elizabethans' commonly "schizoid responses to Italian culture":
they "saw the Italians at once as monsters of ingenious depravity
and as paragons of aesthetic taste, good manners, and creativity."[24]
In the letters Sidney portrays himself as a man indifferent, even hos-
tile, to the charms of Venice. He virtually suppresses what must
have been a lasting impression made on him by the Venetian painters, especially by Titian, whose influence is stamped on the ekphrastic style of the *Arcadia*. Duncan-Jones observes that Sidney
never mentions Titian in the correspondence, most likely because
those to whom his letters were addressed, "headed by [Hubert]
Languet, were to a man earnest Protestant diplomats and scholars
who would have been horrified to learn that the subject of their
hopes had been stirred by imagery both Catholic and sensual."[25]
That Languet had in fact himself sat for a portrait by Titian, and
that Sidney had promised to have his own portrait taken in Italy
and sent to Languet, only complicates the issue. Sidney's apparent
need to deny the undeniable is dramatized in *Astrophil and Stella*,
where Astrophil insists that he "NEVER drank of *Aganippe* well,/
Nor ever did in shade of *Tempe* sit" (Sonnet 74) even as nearly every
other sonnet in the sequence makes it clear that Astrophil's creator
drank deep and sat long. Sidney regards the Petrarchan tradition
that generates his sonnet sequence with the same crossed feelings
of attraction and repulsion, and he speaks of it in the language of
Protestant iconoclastic polemics. Since it is "most true, that eyes are
form'd to serve / The inward light," we should understand that
"what we call *Cupid's* dart, / An image is, which for our selves we

carve; / And, fooles, adore in temple of our hart" (Sonnet 5). All this is "True, and yet true that I must *Stella* love" (Sonnet 5). The idolatrous poet convicts himself of idolatry before plunging back into it, his "Stella" at once defaced and restored as the central "image" of the poem. A sharply Calvinist irony reflects from here on Sidney's famous opening sonnet, since it will evidently do little good to cast aside "others' leaves" and "looke in thy heart and write" (Sonnet 1) when thy heart has become a temple of idolatry.[26]

At the same time that Sidney was grappling with the seductive idols of Petrarchan poetry, Thomas Twyne was translating the *De remediis utriusque fortunae*, which contains Petrarch's longest statement on art. There Petrarch had said, "To take delight also in sacred images, which may remind the beholder of the grace of heaven, is often a devout thing and useful in arousing our minds." Faced with this blasphemy, the "translator" adopted the same expedient with others' leaves as Caxton's corrector, now in effect crosshatching Petrarch's text and silently reforming it along safer Protestant lines. In Twyne's version, Petrarch is misrepresented as saying:

> To take delight also in the images and statues of godly and vertuous men, the beholding of which may stirre us up to have remembrance of their manners and lives is reasonable, and may profite us in imitating ye same.[27]

As a translator, Richard Haydocke was at least more straightforward when it came to expurgating Lomazzo's *Trattato dell'arte de la pittvra*. Lomazzo's final two books, though they are listed in the table of contents of Haydocke's work, are simply omitted. The English reader is thus spared, among other things, the account of "How the Trinitie is vsually painted," of "the Forme of the Hierarchies, and the nine order of Angels," and of the "Celestial Ministers" and the "Blessed Soules."[28] Exception might also be taken to passages in the early pages of the original, particularly where Lomazzo declares in praise of sacred painting that "St. Luke made the portrait of the blessed Mother of Christ with his own hand," that by "infinite and astonishing miracles" sinners are frequently struck with guilt at the sight of an image of Christ or Mary, and that few can see a holy image and "not feel an ardent desire kindled within themselves to follow the supreme felicity."[29] At this point, Haydocke bluntly reports: "Here the author entreth into a large discourse of the use of Images, which because it crosseth the doctrine of the reformed

Churches, and his greatest warrant thereof is his bare assertion, I haue thought it good to omitte."[30] A text about images has suddenly become the image of what it contains, and it must be struck down. It must have seemed only just to Haydocke that a text which "crosseth" the teaching of the English church on idolatry should itself be crossed out of the English language.

These isolated bits of translation are symptomatic of wider strategies deployed to appropriate, or misappropriate, the monuments of Italian Renaissance culture. Haydocke expurgating Lomazzo would offer one piece of evidence for a more general account, which others have begun to pursue, of the anxieties as well as the pleasures of *imitatio*.[31] Here I am concerned with perhaps the most unassimilable, and yet for poets at least, one of the most attractive doctrines of the Italian humanists—the set of assumptions about the indissoluble bond between language and the visual image that were compressed into the old Horatian phrase, *ut pictura poesis*. What are the implications for English poetry when the road from Italy is guarded by the doctrine of the reformed churches, and when the ideal of the poem as a "speaking picture" can be exposed as the idol of the poet's heart, like the Rood of Grace made to "goggle with the eyes" and "shake his jaws" by the manipulation of a hundred wires attached ultimately to the Antichrist?

By the late sixteenth century, and with an increasingly avid interest in the seventeenth, England had begun to acquire all the paintings and emigré painters it could afford. As early as 1531 Sir Thomas Elyot, following Castiglione, had advised the aspiring courtier to master the rudiments of painting and sculpture as well as versifying. A small but steady stream of instructional manuals and gentlemen's handbooks—Hoby's translation of the *Courtier* in 1561, Nicholas Hilliard's "Arte of Limning" in the 1590s, Henry Peacham's *Arte of Drawing* in 1606, Edward Norgate's *Miniatura* in the 1620s—encouraged this aspect of aristocratic training, and the sketchbook became a necessary, if not always expertly utilized, piece of equipment on the grand tour. The obscure limners and portrait painters of the Elizabethan period were replaced by Van Dyck, Rubens, Orazio Gentileschi, and other artists of international stature who were persuaded to come to England for more or less extended visits. Under the patronage of Prince Henry and then of Charles, the great collectors like Arundel and Buckingham pursued their wholesale acquisitions of Italian art, an effort capped by Charles's own purchase of the cabinet of Vincenzo Gonzaga, the duke of Mantua. The Mantuan collection would be added to the expanding galleries at Whitehall, and would be sold off along with the rest of the royal collection by order of Parliament in 1650. One monument that remained was the Rubens ceiling installed in the Banqueting House at Whitehall in the 1630s. It had marked the Stuarts' late but magnificent entry into the ranks of the Hapsburgs and the Medici as rulers glorying in, and being glorified by, the most spectacular canvases of the age.[32]

The English had also succeeded in absorbing the main points of the doctrine of the "sister arts," whose formulas about poetry and painting, everywhere invoked, are summarized almost as commonplace material in Sidney's *Apologie*: "Poesie therefore is an arte of imitation, for so Aristotle termeth it in his word *Mimesis*, that is to say, a representing, counterfetting, or figuring foorth: to speak metaphorically, a speaking picture: with this end, to teach and delight."[33] Whether from Alberti, Lomazzo, Ripa, the neo-Vitruvians, from Cartari, Conti, and the other mythographers, from the emblematists and imprese-writers, or from their own reading of the ancients guided by such authorities, the English poets were given to understand that the literary and visual arts shared, as sisters, the same descent, subject matter, techniques, and ends. In such texts as the *Greek Anthology*, Philostratus' *Imagines*, or the *Table of Cebes*, they could admire the most prestigious examples of classical ekphrastic writing, supplemented by at least one modern virtuoso performance in the painterly mode, Francesco Colonna's *Hypnereotomachia Poliphili* (1499), available in a partial English translation of 1592.[34] The consequences for poetry were not merely that the poet, in his descriptions and figurative "colors," might emulate the painter in a *paragone* between two rivals in the same field. More fundamentally, just as the artist could conceive of himself as a master of rhetoric or of the rules of drama visually presented, so the poet could imagine his own activity as a kind of painting, and his works as somehow constituting visual artifacts.

These assumptions are perhaps most clearly displayed in the composite verbal and pictorial form of the Renaissance emblem. Contemporary descriptions of the emblematist's art asserted that the image and the word—the "body" and the "soul" of the emblem as they are commonly regarded—join to create an effect more powerful than that of either component alone. As Geffrey Whitney announces on his title page, "herein, by the office of the eie, and the eare, the minde maye reape double delights through holsome preceptes, shadowed with pleasant deuises."[35] Thomas Blount, translating Estienne's *L'Art de faire les devises*, is typical of the emblem writers in his belief that the two parts should "be so strictly united together, that being considered apart, they cannot explicate themselves distinctly the one without the other."[36] Henry Hawkins is equally typical in his appeal to the ancient formula inherited from Simonides, to "eye well and marke these silent Poesies, give ear to these speaking pictures."[37] The emblematist's woodcut or engraving does not, as we might otherwise suppose from our own experience of picture books, merely "illustrate" its text. As the Renaissance conceives it, the bond between the image as a *poesia tacens* and the word as a *pictura loquens* is far stronger. As a kind of script for a synaesthetic performance, the sequence of plates and their appended texts in the emblem book generates two complementary codes attuned to "the eie, and the eare," each holding the key to deciphering the other. In Jakobson's terms the bond between image and word is, potentially, both metonymic and metaphoric: metonymic in that the two adjoined forms signify and complete each other as parts of a whole, metaphoric in that each translates into the other's medium. Ideally, the image melts into speech, speech recrystallizes the immediacy of the image.

In its own terms the Renaissance had several models by which such a relationship could be understood. One, allied to the role of the emblem book as an educational tool, is the process of "double translation" proposed by Roger Ascham for the sixteenth-century schoolroom, an exercise in which the student is given a text to render "out of Latin into English and out of English into Latin again."[38] Ascham does not advise his pupils to read emblem books. But under him and his successors in England at least, the Renaissance schoolboy was encouraged to master the kind of bilingual fluency of translation that would lead him to read his emblems as he had construed his Tully, shifting dexterously between two registers of meaning. It was a skill he might also bring to the various programs of "spiritual exercises" devised by Ignatius or by Francis de Sales, for the art of meditation would lead him first to compose the imagined scene of his devotions ("I am on my deathbed," "I am at the foot of the cross") and then to engage the voices of reason and will to make the picture speak. Indeed, a number of Jesuit emblem books of the seventeenth century were designed to follow a meditative sequence. But a more fundamental model for joining word and image is suggested in the hermeneutic resonance of the phrase quoted above from Thomas Blount, that the two parts of the emblem mutually "explicate themselves." If we apply the typological language of folding and unfolding that in the Renaissance universally governs the interpretation of the Bible, we will understand that the pictorial body and the verbal soul of the emblem stand in relation to each other as the Old Testament stands to the New: the text is implicated in the picture, the picture explicated in the text.

The conception of the visual image as concealing a language finds support in a number of Renaissance traditions, among them, as Wittkower and others have shown, the odd fascination with Egyptian hieroglyphs that runs undiminished from the discovery of the Horapollo manuscript in 1419 through Alberti, Ficino, Valeriano, and Ripa, to the speculations of Athanasius Kircher in the late seventeenth century.[39] The Egyptian priests had preserved their arcane wisdom in ideograms, which they had perhaps first discovered, as the record of Adam's language, on an obelisk outside the gates of Eden. Here was a "mute and symbolic language of ideas" (Valeriano) at once more universal and indelible than other tongues, and more directly expressive of divine wisdom than written language. In the hieroglyphic image, meaning presented itself purely and instantaneously in the lexicon of things—in rebus rather than in verbis—without the mediation of words. For, as Ficino notes in his commentary on Plotinus, the Egyptians "did not use individual letters to signify mysteries, but whole images of plants, trees, and animals; because God has knowledge of things not through a multiplicity of thought processes but rather as a simple and firm form of the whole thing." Thus they "presented the whole of the discursive argument as it were in one complete image."[40] So conceived, hieroglyphic or pseudo-hieroglyphic images were absorbed into the iconography of the emblem. Francis Quarles, who would later publish an emblem book entitled *Hieroglyphicks of the Life of Man* (1638), instructs the reader of his *Emblemes* of 1635 that "Before the knowledge of letters God was known by *Hieroglyphicks*: And, indeed, what are the heavens, the Earth, nay every Creature, but *Hieroglyphics* and *Emblemes* of his Glory?"[41] The hapless little woodcuts in many emblem books would seem to fall far short of such an exalted sense of the image (and, indeed, some writers distinguished between the emblematic "figure" and the more complex "symbol"), but the aura of hieroglyphic mysteries hovers even over them, reinforcing the impression that the plate is meant to contain a dense and, some would say, inexhaustible pack of significance to be drawn out into discursive argument by the accompanying poem.

This effect extends beyond the emblem to the art of the frontispiece or the illustrated title page in relation to the text in Renaissance printed books. George Sandys—who also traces the origin

of painting to the "Hieroglyphicall Figures on the Aegyptian Obe-
lisques, which were long before the invention of Letters"—ushers
the reader into his translation of Ovid through the portico of an
elaborately engraved title page (fig. 1) showing the four elements
brought into harmony by the power of love and wisdom, and displaying the motto, "Ex his oriuntur cuncta" ("All things take their
origin from these").[42] There follows a brief poem called, as such
poems often are, "The Minde of the Frontispeece, And Argument
of this Worke," a poem that not only clarifies the allegory but further suggests by its title that the frontispiece is itself the image of a
"Minde," of the integral idea of the *Metamorphosis* now unfolding
into the sequential "Argument" of Sandys's text. On the same principle, Sandys explains in a preface "To the Reader" that he has
"contracted the substance of every Booke" of Ovid's poem "into as
many Figures," each figure condensing all the fables to be told in
that book into what Ficino would call "one complete image." So the
illustration to Book 3 (fig. 2) shows Actaeon, Narcissus, Semele,
Tiresias, and so on, the narrative in which they will be positioned
linearly for the reader here contracted beforehand into a display
inviting the viewer to apprehend at a glance the whole network of
their interrelationships. (It might be noted, for example, that if we
follow the gaze of the goddess Diana at the lower left, exposed in
her cave to the gaze of the mortal Actaeon, we will find the mortal
Semele at the upper right, exposed in her house to the consuming
flames of Jove's passion.) Ovid's text is thus reconstituted in a process of double translation all its own, from Ovid's Latin back, by
contraction, into the pictorial script where, we might suppose, its
ancient wisdom was recorded "before the invention of Letters,"
and out again, by expansion, into Sandys's English. In this format
the poem becomes a collection of large-scale emblems asking us not
just to read the narrative but to read it out of a series of engravings
in which (to misread Sandys's own motto slightly) "all things take
their origin."

In this light we can see more clearly how, for example, Holbein's
famous design for the title page of the Coverdale Bible (1535) con-
tracts scriptural history from the Creation to the Last Judgment
into a prefatory visual synopsis (fig. 3), or how the title page to the
first volume of Robert Fludd's *Utriusque cosmi majoris* (1617) not only
illustrates the idea of a universe in microcosm, but itself figures as a
microcosm of Fludd's treatise (fig. 4). Fludd's title page even offers
an emblem of the process I have been describing: a winged creature symbolizing Time is shown striding "off" the plate and "into"

Figure 1. George Sandys,
Ovid's Metamorphosis (1632),
title page

Figure 2. George Sandys,
Ovid's Metamorphosis (1632),
illustration to Book 3

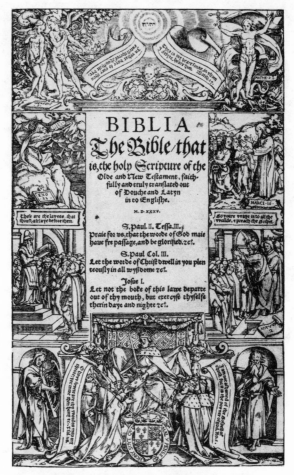

Figure 3. Hans Holbein, title page for the Coverdale
Bible (1535)

Figure 4. Robert Fludd, *Utrius-que Cosmi Majoris*, vol. 1 (1617), title page

Figure 5. Nicholas Poussin, *Fall of the Manna in the Wilderness* (1638)

the book, in his hand the end of a rope coiled around the central diagram like a string around a top. As he pulls on the rope he must be imagined to set the diagram in motion, uncoiling it into the temporal flow of the text.[43]

Apart from such speculations about the quasi-magical properties of the image as a pictorial language, it has been observed that the very possibility of making a reproducible, black-and-white graphic book-illustration tended to merge the image into the medium of the printed word whose technology it shared. It is for this reason among others, perhaps, that the champions of the Word in the early Reformation could publish broadside cartoons and illustrated Bibles even as they condemned devotional paintings and statues as idolatrous. But the Renaissance concept of the image as a readable language is wider than its sometime affiliation with the printed book. It was Rensselaer Lee who first called attention to the importance of Poussin's remark in a letter about his painting of the *Fall of the Manna in the Wilderness* (1638): "Lisez l'histoire et le tableau, afin de connaître si chaque chose est appropriée au sujet."[44] As the artist characterizes his work, the painting (fig. 5) becomes a parallel text to be "read" next to the scriptural account. It moves our eye forcefully from left to right through a series of what art historians conventionally call "passages," from the Israelites' earlier hunger to their later gathering of the manna. Its figures signify their state of mind through a series of oratorical gestures—a raised palm, for instance, as the sign of astonishment—that must be decoded with the help of Quintilian. The painting also imbeds its own typological stratum in that the rainbow-like formation in the upper left, empty in the middle like the Israelites' stomachs, is at the same time a type looking forward, like the Old Testament manna, to our spiritual satisfaction in Christ, adumbrated in the large rock at the upper right.

The procedures of biblical interpretation here reflected in Poussin's painting are doubly relevant because the biblical text itself, unlocked by means of the visual terminology of "figures" and "shadows," could be taken as inherently pictorial.[45] As the exemplar of all the artistic kinds, the Bible, as Barbara Lewalski has shown, offers the Renaissance not only the most prestigious models of lyric or pastoral, but also of the drama, the history painting, and notably—in the case of the "book" of the Apocalypse "sealed with seven seals" (Rev. 5)—the emblem book.[46] The emblematic unfolding of the image into the word, then, first reveals the language compacted in the image; but, reciprocally, the enfolding of the text into the image discloses the latent visual dimension of the text. To "see" a Renaissance text in this way is to gain a large perspective—to borrow from Ficino again—on the "firm form of the whole thing." We profit by what we have heard from William Spanos or Stanley Fish about the engagement and surprise where poems exist as flickers in time. But prospectively and retrospectively "seen," the Renaissance text can assume a kind of spatial or architectural unity. We see the overall design of Herbert's volume as a temple; we see the explicitly or implicitly emblematic shape of many Renaissance lyrics; we see the Phoenix in the middle line of Donne's "Canonization" as the center of the "patterne" celebrated in the poem itself; we see, or are meant to see, the figure of St. Teresa drawn in the swirling colors of Crashaw's hymns more vividly than in the "Picture of the seraphicall saint . . . as she is usually expressed" by the "cold Pencil" of the artist; and through Milton's inward eyes as we see the vast cycles of recurrence in *Paradise Lost* "prepared," as by the compasses in the hands of the Son, to "circumscribe / This Universe, and all created things" (7: 225–27).

For the Renaissance this crucial sense of textual patterning is very far removed from what we may have come to regard, more in reaction to New-Critical commentaries than to Renaissance texts themselves, as an "arid formalism." To see in this pictorial fashion is to apprehend the "idea" or "foreconceit" of the poem, which for Sidney is that unitive and lively prevision of the whole to be bodied forth sequentially, and secondarily in language. The reader's task then is to reverse the procedure by using "the narration" of a poem "but as an imaginatiue groundplot of a profitable inuention."[47] The key term here, borrowed from the vocabulary of architecture, suggests an "imaginative" conception of the text as a floor plan on which the writer constructs—and from which the reader reconstructs—the full "spatial" volume of the work. The power to move and delight is not carried by the flow of words moment to moment but by their cumulative potential to project or release a richly compacted spatial "image" of which language itself is only the signifier. Like his contemporaries, Sidney seems to speak more than metaphorically when he distinguishes poetry from history or philosophy on the grounds of its pictorial charge: "[W]hatsoever the Philosopher sayth should be doone," the poet "giueth a perfect picture of it. . . . A perfect picture I say, for hee yeeldeth to the powers of the minde an image of that whereof the Philosopher bestoweth but a woordish description: which dooth neyther strike, pierce, nor pos-

sesse the sight of the soule so much as that other dooth."[48] In the
same spirit, Spenser outlines the plan of his own work in the letter
to Raleigh prefacing *The Faerie Queene*: "the knight of the Red-
crosse, in whom I expresse Holynes . . . Sir Guyon, in whom I set
forth Temperaunce, . . . Britomartis a Lady Knight, in whom I
picture chastity." More than mere stylistic variations, the parallel
phrases here ask to be taken seriously as synonyms. To "set forth"
an invention is, in the intertranslatable languages of the arts, to express it by picturing it.

On these assumptions we can better appreciate why George Chapman should have chosen to English the description of Achilles'
shield in Book 18 of the *Iliad*, which he published separately as "an
Homericall Poeme" in its own right thirteen years before his complete translation of the epic appeared in 1611. For the Renaissance
this passage supplied not only the most prestigious of ancient ekphrases, but the very key to Homer. What is "here prefigurde by
our miraculous Artist," declares Chapman, "but the universall
world, which being so spatious and almost unmeasurable, one
circlet of a Shield representes and imbraceth."[49] Far from any conception of the epic as oral performance, Chapman envisions the
shield as a pictorial *microcosmos* within the larger world of the poem,
yet of so "spatious" a scope as to contain the whole poem. The
"circlet" of the shield, then, comes to "represent" the circular shape
of the entire epic, with which it is congruent. In reading Homer on
this plan—or Virgil, who goes Homer one better by balancing the
shield of Aeneas in Book 8 of his own epic against the marvelous
paintings adorning Dido's temple in Book 1—we would follow the
linear unfolding of the narrative only to attend, finally, to the "embracing" pattern by which the end of the poem circles back to, and
completes, its beginning. We will not have read the words of the
text until, with the model of the shield before us, we have seen their
configuration.

Sidney's architectural "groundplot" and Sandys' monumental
title page—as well, it might be added, as the role of music in Herbert's *Temple* and the special importance, for the Renaissance, of
Achilles' shield as the *locus classicus* of the cosmic dance—all may
serve to remind us that the sisterhood between poetry and painting
was imagined to extend to all the other arts. A Palladian villa was
laid down on the system of proportions underlying not only the
fabric of the human body, according to Vitruvius, but, according to
the Pythagorean tradition, the harmony of the world. Because we
are thus "attuned" to the building we enter, we can detect a dis-

proportioned room even if its faculty measurements—say 19 feet by 40 instead of the perfect 1:2 ratio—are too small to be seen; by a kind of sympathetic vibration we will respond to, and in a sense "hear," the resultant discord.[50] This explains why the musician GaFurio was called in as a consultant on the construction of the cathedral of Mantua in 1590.[51] In the Wisdom literature God had "ordered everything by measure and number and weight" (Wisd. of Sol. 11:20), as Andrew Marvell recalls when he commends Milton's epic for its congruence with the creation itself: "Thy verse created like thy *Theme* sublime, / In Number, Weight, and Measure, needs not *Rhime*." Marvell similarly "designs / Those short but admirable Lines" of his own poem "Upon Appleton House"—lines by which "Things greater are in less contain'd"—to reflect the "*holy* Mathematicks" embodied in the house and in its owner as well as in the text.[52] The rational substratum of all things provides a standard of comparability to all human products; on it, and as the manifestations of it in the various media, all the arts are constructed, from the *stanza* in a villa to the stanza in a Renaissance poem—"one little roome," as Donne calls it, punning on the Italian—to the perspective scheme of a Renaissance painting.

Within this system of parallels, it is clear that the influence of Poesis on Pictura, like that of a stronger sister on the weaker, was the most deeply felt. Alberti advises the painter in search of an "invention" to associate with poets and orators. His suggestion that the painter read "the description of Calumny which Lucian recounts was painted by Apelles" proposes an important theme in the rhetorical tradition as the promising subject for a painting, and a *Calumny of Apelles*—in effect, a stunning piece of epideictic rhetoric visually conceived—was duly carried out by Botticelli in 1495.[53] Alberti's treatise *On Painting* also leans heavily on literary and rhetorical analysis when it locates the pleasure of a composition in the *copia* and *varietas* of the subject represented.[54] With only a few surviving fragments of classical commentary on painting itself to work with, the Renaissance devised an aesthetics of the visual arts by analogy to the verbal arts, freely appropriating the dicta of Plato, Aristotle, Cicero, Horace, and Quintilian whenever there seemed to be the faintest hope that these authorities might have had painting in mind: *ut pictura poesis erit*. In *Giotto and the Orators*, Michael Baxandall argues that on a more basic level, the very grammar and rhetoric of the humanists' Latin affected "their manner of describing and, then, of attending to pictures"—that for them especially, "observation was linguistically enforced."[55] Thus Alberti's definition of the *compositio* of a painting is "a very precise metaphor transferring to painting a model of organization derived from rhetoric itself," the four-level hierarchy of forms by which a painting is constructed (plane, member, body, picture) derived from the four-level hierarchy of verbal elements (word, phrase, clause, period) that go into the making of a Ciceronian sentence. Within this scheme, when Alberti recommends that two "planes" should "be so joined that pleasant lights flow into agreeable shades and there are no *asperitates* of angles," he is similarly applying to painting Quintilian's rule that the orator should avoid the *structura aspera*, or the "disagreeable conjunction of two 'rough' consonants between the end of one word and the beginning of the next."[56]

Baxandall's theme, as he says, is that any "language, not only humanist Latin, is a conspiracy against experience in the sense of being a collective attempt to simplify and arrange experience into manageable parcels." The force of his evidence is to suggest that for the investors of Renaissance artistic theory—confronted by the enormous prestige of the verbal tradition and immersed, many of them, in a professional and passionate engagement with the study of language—the "field" of painting was heavily overlaid by the "structure" of the language used to describe it.[57] By a kind of linguistic imperialism, paintings themselves were comprehended as a form of language because only in that form could language make them comprehensible to itself. The result, for Italian painting, was the deeply literary sensibility that has been recovered by iconographic research. For Panofsky and his followers, the "meaning" of a Renaissance image is a discursive one, and it lies below the level of the pictorial surface in a substructure of texts to which the image (indifferently, a rough sketch or a finished masterpiece) merely gives access.[58]

But if in Italy *pictura* was so thoroughly appropriated by *poesis*, in England what might be called the image of language was also colored by its theoretical association with painting. In 1568, Sir Thomas Smith began his treatise on the reform of English spelling by "maintaining that writing is as much a picture of speech, or sound, as painting is a picture of the body or features—*ut pictura, orthographia.*"[59] He advocated a system of phonetic orthography that would represent speech in the same manner as bodies are represented in painting—and that would, incidentally, produce a printed page decorated with sprigs of dots, dashes, and circumflexes. Smith's conception of writing as the picture of speech was

shared by John Hart, whose *Orthographie* of 1569 offered to show
"howe to write or paint thimage of mannes voice, most like to the
life or nature."[60] So keen was the desire to develop a stable orthographic picture of English that the wayward irregularities of spelling common in Elizabethan texts could be seen as an iconoclastic
mutilation, the true image of language "Defaced, patched, mar'd,
and made a skorn."[61] On the other hand, that image might be enshrined in a polyglot dictionary that, because its entries in four languages were imagined to fit together in a kind of verbal marquetry,
could advertise itself as "an inlaid piece of Art."[62] For Lomazzo,
"Painting," like writing, "is an instrument vnder which the treasury
of memory is contained, insomuch as writing is nothing else, but a
picture of *white* and *black*."[63]

The campaign for orthographic reform—together with the tendency of both Elizabethan grammar books and Ramist logics to deploy their materials in patterns and paradigms—thus contributed
to the wider impact of print technology. Print emphasized the
visual arrangement of words on the page and left open the implication that its format was an index of the spatialized nature of
thought.[64] These were the dimensions of language that poets were
also urged to explore with all the ingenuity at their command. Puttenham illustrates "the placing and scituation of your measures and
concords" by "ocular example," presenting the reader of *The Arte of
English Poesie* (1589) with a series of diagrams abstracting the various rhyme schemes and stanza forms into purely visual patterns
(pp. 88–95).[65] These prepare the way for a discussion of "proportion in figure," where Puttenham displays a collection of shaped,
"Geometricall," poems—pyramids, lozenges, pilasters, roundels,
Anacreontic eggs and others taken from the *Greek Anthology*—
offered as instances of a particularly subtle art because they yield
"an ocular representation" (pp. 95–105). Such designs enhance
that "qualitie the Greeks called *Enargia*, of this word *argos*, because
it geueth a glorious lustre and light," supplying a tool "wherewith
we burnish our language" and give it "gloss" (p. 148). Although, as
a species of poetical ornament decorating the surface of language,
these figures are to be distinguished from figures of sense "inwardly working a stirre to the mynde" (p. 148), when Puttenham
praises the "instinct diuine" that fired the first poets, he makes it
clear that the inner life of poetry is the life of the eye:

> [I]n all holines of life, and in continuall studie and con-
> templation, [poets] came by instinct diuine, and by deepe

> meditation, and much abstinence (the same assubtiling and
> refining their spirits) to be made apt to receaue visions,
> both waking and sleeping, which made them vtter proph-
> esies and foretell things to come. So also were they the first
> Prophetes or seears, *Videntes*, for so the Scripture tearmeth
> them. . . . (p. 7)

In this light, the visible shape of a poem must be seen as no mere
ornament, but as the lustrous afterimage of a sacred vision prior
to the poem's utterance and preserved in the poem's capacity for
"ocular representation."

In the preface to *Ouids Banquet of Sense* (1595), Chapman expands Puttenham's notion of a painterly *Enargia* in a manner suggesting that, to him, the sister art offers far more than a casual analogy for the vocabulary of poetic ornament:

> That, *Enargia*, or cleerenes of representation, requird in
> absolute Poems is not the perspicuous deliuery of a lowe in-
> uention; but high, and harty inuention exprest in most sig-
> nificant, and vnaffected phrase; it serues not a skilfull
> Painters turne, to draw the figure of a face onely to make
> knowne who it represents; but hee must lymn, giue luster,
> shaddow, and heightning; which though ignorants will es-
> teeme spic'd, and too curious, yet such as haue the iudiciall
> perspectiue, will see it hath motion, spirit, and life.

Those "searching spirits, whom learning hath made noble" will
understand (if their studies have included the art of perspective)
that the writer's palette of "dark" conceits gives his thought as well
as his language the depth and vitality of a skillful portrait: his "philosophical conceits" will be fashioned, like the artists's colors, from
"rich Minerals . . . digd out of the bowels of the earth." The implication that thought itself is a visual process, and that language is
its translation, became a firm principle for John Hoskins, who declares in a sentence quoted verbatim in Jonson's *Discoveries*: "The
conceits of the mind are Pictures of things, and the tongue is the
Interpreter of those Pictures."[66] Like Chapman's own version of
Homer, a heightened text might ideally complete the circuit back
from language to thought by restoring as a visual artifact what had
been "translated," and thus de-pictorialized, by the tongue. In the
case of *Ouids Banquet of Sense*, Raymond B. Waddington has shown
that the 1595 edition represents just such a "high, and harty inuention" whose appeal to the mind through the eye is inseparable from

its appeal through the ear: "The poem extends beyond its verbal text, incorporating such typographic features as title page, prefatory matter, illustrations, headings, notes, glosses and spatial arrangement as a visual rhetoric, ultimately working to make the poem coterminous with the book that contains it."[67]

Yet Chapman is not alone among the advocates of the painterly poem to acknowledge the snares of delusions and sensuality laid for the reader by such a text. *Ouids Banquet* is at once a satire on, and an occasion for, sensual gluttony—the eye feeding to excess on the rich embellishment of a poem warning against excess. The title page sets out a preliminary warning in the form of an emblem about optical illusion: in water, a straight stick will seem bent by the tricks of refraction. The motto, *sibi conscia recti*, cautions that the mind must be vigilant to correct the false impressions of the senses.[68] The emblem embodies an ancient skeptical topic, but in other terms it may also be said to enact the drama of a fall into temptation. The viewer must see, and be taken in by, the crooked stick before his understanding can be rectified by the conviction of his error.

The stronger the confidence placed in sight, not only as a dimension of literary perception but as an avenue of knowledge and a model of knowing, the greater the peril of being captivated by the eye. Bacon declares, almost as an article of methodological faith, that he withdraws his intellect "no further [from "the facts of nature"] than may suffice to let the images and rays of natural objects meet in a point, as they do in the sense of vision." The language of scientific inquiry thus becomes a kind of retinal screen on which "nature" is projected in perfect focus, as if in a camera obscura where the mind stands in place of the aperture or the lens: "words are . . . the images of matter." This last phrase, however, is imbedded in Bacon's attack on "the first distemper of learning, when men study words and not matter":

> And how is it possible but this should have an operation to discredit learning, even with vulgar capacities, when they see learned men's works like the first letter of a patent or limned book, which though it hath large flourishes, yet it is but a letter? It seems to me that Pygmalion's frenzy is a good emblem or portraiture of this vanity, for words are but the images of matter, and except they have life of reason and invention, to fall in love with them is all one as to fall in love with a picture.[69]

Although writing is still associated with limning and words with portraits (and Bacon himself can enjoy the momentary satisfaction of having illuminated his own text with a "good emblem"), still if words are "but" lifeless images, if the dead image is taken for the animate force it only mimics, then words can provoke the superstitious veneration of idolatry. In this passage "reason and invention" figure as the Word behind the words, without whose inspiriting power letters are no more than stocks and stones, however gaudily they may be decorated with lifelike "flourishes." Bacon's emblem of "Pygmalion's frenzy" sets the passage in a classical context, but this besotted maker can be read as the type of the idol worshiper, and the context of the iconoclastic debates is not far below the surface. This "vanity," like the "Idols of the Market Place"—the "names of things which do not exist" except by "fantastic suppositions," or names "confused and ill defined and hastily and irregularly derived from realities"—must be cast out of the temple of the mind before the true reformation of learning can begin.[70] It is probably not coincidental that in the paragraph of the *Advancement of Learning* just before the diagnosis of "Pygmalion's frenzy," Bacon should have had in mind Luther's rebellion against "the degenerate traditions of the church," even though he rather perversely chose to hold Luther solely responsible for the Renaissance's "affectionate study of eloquence."[71]

2

At the Crossroads: The Poetics of Reformation Iconoclasm

The conception of poetic language that I have been trying to sketch remains strong in England throughout the sixteenth and seventeenth centuries. Yet there, perhaps more urgently than in any other European literature, a thriving poetic founded on the iconic properties of the word would have to contend with the reformation of images. The history of overt image-breaking outlined at the start of the last chapter runs parallel to a history of polemical debate defending and attacking the practice. The debate directly addresses church ritual rather than literary composition, but its echoes in the halls of poetry are strong. The effects of this controversy on the plastic arts—in some respects very slight, in others profound— would include most obviously the shift from ecclesiastical to aristocratic and bourgeois patronage, and the changes in genre, style, and subject that might be adduced to distinguish the introspective, "Protestant" art of Rembrandt's Old Testament canvases from the flamboyant drama of Rubens's *The Raising of the Cross*. They would also include the various responses to the Reformers' campaign, such as the call, by Erasmus among others (notably Lodovico Dolce, in his post-Tridentine *Dialogo Della Pittura*) for stricter canons of moral decorum in sacred art, and the opposition within the Catholic church to pagan forms and styles, above all to nude figures, that came to focus on Michelangelo's *Last Judgment*. We would want to note, as Craig Harbison does, that in Protestant art the theme of the Last Judgment fell into disfavor because it was associated with a Catholic emphasis on the reward and punishment for works; and that, although Protestants did continue to represent the saints, they would do so out of an interest in the saint's career as a moral and

31

practical example of the Christian life rather than in the saint's portrait as an iconic object.[1] Early Protestant art in particular developed an armory of polemical themes that could be used in the struggle against the Roman whore: Lucas Cranach's woodcuts of the Apocalypse, featuring the Beast in a papal tiara, which were to appear in Luther's New Testament and in John Bale's *The Image of Both Churches*, the numerous illustrations of Solomon's idolatry, of the Brazen Serpent, or of the return of the Prodigal Son. These matters, to which a large art-historical bibliography is devoted, fall outside my immediate concern with poetry.[2] So, too, does the iconoclastic controversy in its wider ramifications in the history of the church. But here we can see at least how the issues of this controversy, touching on English poetry, restate those of the Renaissance *paragone*, with the difference that what had once been a kindly rivalry was now exacerbated often into hot dispute, the question of the relationship of the arts now amplified morally and exposed to a rigorous theological critique. No longer affectionate sisters given at times to gentle competition, the literary and verbal arts become, in some versions of reformed thought, mortal enemies on the battlefield of salvation.

Defenders of the sacred image would argue that pictures and statues in the church are warranted by Scripture and patristic commentary, and are helpful within limits as an aid to devotion. Had not Pope Gregory the Great (590–604) spoken sensibly of the role of images as the *biblia pauperum*, saying that "a picture is introduced into a church that those who are ignorant of letters may at least read by looking at the walls what they cannot read in books"?[3] Reaffirming the position taken by the Second Council of Nicaea in the eighth century against the iconoclasts in the Byzantine church, the Council of Trent decreed that "due honor and veneration is to be given" to "images of Christ, of the Virgin Mother of God, and of the other saints":

> not, however, that any divinity or virtue is believed to be in them by reason of which they are to be venerated, or that something is to be asked of them, or that trust is to be placed in images, as was done of old by the Gentiles who placed their hope in idols; but because the honor which is shown them is referred to the prototypes which they represent, so that by means of the images which we kiss and before which we uncover the head and prostrate ourselves, we adore Christ and venerate the saints whose likeness they bear.[4]

A moderate defense of images would stress that they are to be classed among the *adiaphora*, things not essential to salvation that are useful unless abused; it could come down to a matter of propriety, or seemliness, and Anglicanism would try to strike a balance between what Archbishop Laud called "overburdening the Service of God" and leaving it "naked."[5] Prudence dictated, not that images be abolished, but that Christians be instructed on the dangers of idolatry. This argument relies on language as a guide to images and a guard against their abuse. A more vigorous defense, founded partly on Aquinas, would insist on the autonomy of the image as a means of access to the divine—either on the Aristotelian ground that knowledge is acquired as an inward image through the senses, of which the eye is most noble, or on the Augustinian and Neo-platonic ground shared by Renaissance art theorists like Lomazzo that knowledge is implanted in the mind as an image of the divine intellect. Thanks to Haydocke's translation of Lomazzo, Englishmen knew that the artist conveys divine ideas into paint: the painter, as John Dee had already declared, "seemeth to have a certaine divine power."[6] Proponents of the image could combine the most fashionable tenets of Renaissance Platonism with that native strain of English mysticism exemplified by Walter Hilton, who had written in the fourteenth century that images "arouse [the mind] from vain and worldly thoughts to more intent and frequent meditation upon unseen things and the desire for them."[7] The artistic image must then be understood to consist not in its material accidents, in stone or pigment, but in the intelligible form impressed upon the material by the artist and abstracted from it by the viewer. Through the nexus of the mind, the image "refers" upward toward its source in God and is thus, ignorant superstition aside, a proper object of veneration.

The rejoinder—from the time of Karlstadt and Zwingli in the early reform through the two periods of active iconoclasm in England in the mid-sixteenth and mid-seventeenth centuries—is that the image is contaminated by the material, inseparable from the stocks and blocks condemned in the Bible's injunctions against idolatry. The image is dead. The word lives as the medium of revealed truth and the echo of the creating Logos resounding in the ear of the creation. The type of Christian faith is Abraham responding to the voice of the unseen God; the type of enslavement to the carnal, the worship of the golden calf, which would have its fulfillment in the visually splendid ceremonies of the Roman church. The Elizabethan homilist, paraphrasing Deuteronomy 4:12, declares that "The Lord spake unto you out of the middle of fire, you heard the voyce or sound of his wordes, but you did see no forme or shape at all, lest peradvanture you being deceiued, should make to your-selfe any grauen image or likenesse. . . . And therefore in the old Law, the middle of the propitiatorie, which presented GODS seate, was emptie, lest any should take occasion to make any similitude or likenesse of him."[8] For Donne and Milton as well as for Puritan op-ponents of the theater, the eye, traditionally the noblest of senses, is the "devils doore"—the portal of enticement and delusion.[9]

In the debate over sacred imagery in the early sixteenth century no one authoritative position emerges unqualified. Luther early de-clared that "images contrary to God's Word" should be "despised and destroyed," but then in occasional remarks came to a merely skeptical, even mildly affirmative, view of ecclesiastical art.[10] He specifically approved of history paintings on biblical subjects, and argued that the "reference to images in the first commandment is to a temporal ceremony"—applying, that is, only to the time of the Jews—"which has been abrogated by the New Testament."[11] In the *Small* and *Large Catechism* of 1529 Luther preserves the Roman Catholic order of the Decalogue in which the proscription of im-ages appears as part of the first commandment. Compared with later Calvinist practice, this classification had the effect of deem-phasizing the prohibition of images by denying it the status of a separate, second commandment. Concerned as always that the po-tentially explosive impulses of his followers be curbed and that even the removal of offensive images "take place without rioting" and be done "by the proper authorities," Luther would try to de-fuse the more radical iconoclasm of his Wittenberg colleague An-dreas Bodenstein von Karlstadt. He insisted that on the evidence of Scripture images were, doctrinally, a matter of indifference since God has given "neither commands nor prohibitions" binding on us.[12] With this view Luther defines a position that would later be available to moderate Anglicans, for whom Donne speaks when he argues "that where there is a frequent preaching, there is no *neces-sity* of pictures; but will not every man add this, That if the true use of Pictures bee preached unto them, there is *no danger* of an abuse."[13]

Indeed, following in the tradition of pre-Reformation illustrated Bibles, Luther's German New Testament of 1522 contained twenty-one woodcuts (the Cranach series on the Apocalypse), and many more were added in the subsequent Luther Bibles. By the mid-1530s a new school of Protestant Bible illustration had grown up in Wittenberg, Luther himself designating passages appropriate for artistic treatment.[14] He defended the illustrated portion of his personal prayer book by invoking the Gregorian justification of images as the layman's Bible. Pope Gregory had also maintained that "We do not bow down before [the image of our Savior] as a divinity, but we adore him whose Birth or Passion or Enthronement is brought to remembrance by the picture."[15] Although Luther would deny the distinctions drawn by Aquinas among the different degrees of reverence to be paid to various kinds of images, the venerable doctrine of the image as a commemoration would pass into Lutheran creed as part of the Augsburg Confession of 1530 and be repeated eventually by Andrewes and Donne. The Edwardian Injunctions of 1547 prohibit images "devysed by mennes phantasies" that would replace the word as the center of devotional life, but they permit images as objects of "remembraunce, whereby, men may be admonished, of the holy lifes and conversacion of theim, that the sayde Images do represent." Such images were in effect to act as a curb on the extravagance of the fallen imagination, recalling the mind from its idolatrous indulgence in phantasms to the historical reality of Scripture.[16] Luther himself approved of images for "memorial and witness," and he declared that he would be willing to see his own Bible illustrations "painted on walls for the sake of better remembrance and understanding, since they do no more harm on walls than in books":

> It is to be sure better to paint pictures on walls of how God created the world, how Noah built the ark, and whatever other good stories there may be, than to paint shamelessly worldly things. Yes, would to God that I could persuade the rich and mighty that they would permit the whole Bible to be painted on houses, on the outside and inside, so that all can see it. That would be a Christian work.[17]

For Luther, finally, pictures were no different from the preacher's word or from the sacraments themselves—all of them "outward" material signs, more or less efficacious, as God might will, toward the inner working of the Holy Spirit. In his commentary on Romans Luther understood the Pauline dualism of body and spirit to mean that for the "old man" all is flesh, "the whole man, with body and soul, mind and senses"; but for the new man, "who lives and works, inwardly and outwardly, in the service of the Spirit," images themselves, however "outward," will have their spiritual use.[18]

Yet if strictly speaking there can be no final distinction among "external" signs, Luther would still insist elsewhere that the spoken word is the chief external means of grace. Luther calls the Gospel a "*gut Geschrey*," and his German translation, itself a resanctification of the vernacular, spoken tongue, attempts to capture the colloquial force of that sacred yell. The significance of the Word does not lie, as it did for the medieval exegetes, in the visible *res* through which God speaks, and to which human language only points, but rather in the direct experience of words—in their sound and rhythm and impact on the hearer. For Luther, as Frederick Goldin notes, words "inverbate the Word as Christ incarnates it," bringing it to life for the Christian who hears it at the moment of its utterance. In Luther's *Lectures on the Psalms*, the Word "walks" through language, "into us and over us," so long as our obedience to Christ has made us his "footstool"—and that is why, says Luther, "syllables in poetry are called 'feet'."[19] Hence the famous Lutheran aphorisms: "Do not look for Christ with your eyes, but put your eyes in your ears"; for the "Kingdom of Christ is a hearing Kingdom, not a seeing Kingdom."

But since the spoken word loses much of its force in print ("printed words are dead, spoken words are living"), the pictorial image, itself the inferior sign, may nevertheless help to reanimate the words on the printed page.[20] However much at exuberant moments Luther might wish to have the "whole Bible . . . painted on houses," he typically thinks of the image as ancillary to a printed text and as a gloss upon the word. Such a view would account in part for the rapid development of the arts of the woodcut and engraving in the north. Produced by the same technology as the printed book and, in the case of text illustrations, contained within it, the Reformation image is absorbed into the verbal world and in a sense redeemed from the taint of idolatry by its verbal context. A sixteenth-century observer noted that the Lutherans in Padua refused to look "at images except those printed on paper."[21] When he speaks of panel painting rather than book illustration, Luther specifies that the image should be accompanied by an inscription—a recommendation taken to heart in some early Lutheran artworks in which large areas of the picture space are covered with painted text. It would be a short step in the history of Protestant church decoration to replace images entirely with passages of Scripture warning against the dangers of images, and over just this issue one of the battles of the English Reformation would be fought. Writing during the reign of Queen Mary, the Protestant martyr Nicholas Ridley laments:

> Of late that commandment of God, "Thou shalt not make to thyself any graven images" . . . was graven almost everywhere in churches . . . whereupon images that provoked the simple and idolatrous people into idolatry . . . were taken out of the churches . . . but now, alas! God's holy word is blotted and razed out of churches, and stocks and stones are set up in place thereof.[22]

From this competition of the image and the word for *lebensraum* on the walls of churches, it would require yet another short step to think of language as having vanquished the image entirely because the word alone can paint "the liveliest picture" of Christian truth while safeguarding the Christian from the dangers of idolatry.[23]

If Luther's scattered comments on the subject had stood unchallenged, the Reformation would have contributed its version of *ut pictura poesis* with the relative prestige of the two sisters shifted but slightly. In some respects the reformed image is more closely allied to the word than it had been in Italian humanist theory, the relationship of the arts now considered under a Christian epistemology more subtle than the *centi* of classical opinion that many Italian theorists had been content to gather. But despite Luther's determined moderation, a more radical debate was sparked by his fellow reformers. Karlstadt, in the first major Reformation statement on iconoclasm, argued for the complete abolition of statues and figure painting in churches. His pamphlet *On the Abolishing of Images* (1522) admits that the Bible contains images like that of the brazen serpent in Numbers 21:8–9, but points out that these are given by God as a special dispensation, not created by men.[24] As a scriptural crux in the debate, the meaning of the brazen serpent was one topic controverted at length in the public *disputatio* over images conducted in the Zurich town hall, before nearly nine hundred priests and laymen, in 1523. There Leo Jud argued that the raising of the Old Testament serpent must be understood in relation to its New Testament antitype, the lifting up of Christ on the cross: since "the living Serpent without poison has banished the deadly brass one, and is to be worshipped in the Spirit only," internal, invisible, and intangible revelation has replaced any external, visible and tangible representations, either in the Old Testament form of the brass serpent or in the New Testament form of the cross itself. Where Luther had argued that the commandment *against* images was limited in its application to the time of the Jews, the Zwinglians, who prevailed on this occasion, could reply that any seemingly positive sanction of a visual representation in the Old Testament was permitted under the Law *only* as pertaining to ceremonies that had since been annulled in the new covenant.[25]

The objection to visual ceremony came into special focus in the controversy over the Eucharist. From the thirteenth century Catholic practice had elaborated the visual aspect of the Mass, gradually adding crosses and candles, the representation of the cross on the priest's chasuble, the elevation of the Host, and the carrying of the Host through the streets during the Corpus Christi festival. Now, rejecting both the transubstantiation of the Roman church and the consubstantiation of Luther, Zwingli would conceive of Christ's presence in the Lord's Supper as spiritual only. Just as his divinity rather than his humanity had redeemed mankind, so Christ can be an object of faith only through that divinity. The Eucharist thus loses its status as a visual display enacting the corporeal presence of Christ in a hypostatic union and becomes instead, as a spoken memorial to its biblical prototype, a performance in and through language. "This is my body" means "This *means* my body," as the wafer is understood to be a sign of the body only. Neither the body of Christ nor the body of the wafer has any significance to the communicant apart from that mediated by the word. So in opposing all sacred imagery Zwingli departs from Luther in emphasizing the split between body and spirit even within the Christian life, and identifying them with the image and the word: the "story must be learned from the Word, and from the painting [of Christ] one learns nothing except the form of the body, the movements or constitution of the body or face."[26]

For Calvin, too, who in the *Institutes* would systematize the more radical side of this controversy, the sacraments are subsumed into the dominant idea of the book, since they are each joined to a "preceding promise" as "a sort of appendix, with the purpose of confirming or sealing the promise itself, and of making it more evident to us, and in a sense ratifying it" (4.14.3).[27] Calvin's lawyer's imagination leads him to compare these sacramental "seals" to those "attached to government documents and other public acts" merely to verify their authenticity (4.14.5). The word not only "makes us understand what the visible sign means," but empowers the elements of the sacrament themselves to become significant. Without the word, the images granted by God in the Bible would have left our senses "stunned in looking at the bare signs" (4.14.4). With no intrinsic meaning, the visible seals serve only as an accommodation: "Because we are of the flesh, they are shown to us under things of the flesh, to instruct us according to our dull capacity." Thus the sacramental sign may be understood in Augustine's phrase as *visibile verbum*, not because the visible carries any significant potency beyond that of the word, but because in recognition of our weakness God permits his word to become incarnate, "portrayed graphically," in an inferior material image (4.14.6).

Working from this view of the sacraments, Calvin is uncompromising when he comes specifically to treat the scriptural prohibition of images in *Institutes* 1.11. He marshals the testimony of the prophets against Gregory's opinion that "images may stand in place of books" for the unlettered. By encouraging the veneration of images, he argues, the church has abandoned to idols its role of educating the faithful "in the preaching of His word." In the "purer doctrine" of the early Christians, "churches were commonly empty of images." Calvin insists—in a tone that impugns the very motives for human craftsmanship—that even "direct signs" of the divine presence give no justification for imagery. The pillar of cloud and the burning bush "clearly told men of his incomprehensible essence." Such signs are intended to be "like a bridle placed on them, from attempting to penetrate too deeply." The Mercy Seat in Exodus 25 was designed so that "cherubim with wings outspread covered it" and "the veil shrouded it." Hence any who try to "defend images of God and the Saints with the examples of these cherubim are raving madmen."

The debate over images boils on in such terms, producing a remarkable flow of controversy within a very few years. I have preferred to summarize the issues as they were first defined by the major figures of the early Reformation rather than as they were tirelessly repeated and elaborated by those who came after. In England, after the death of Henry VIII, Nicholas Ridley was made bishop of Rochester and chosen by Cranmer to spearhead an attack on the Eucharist by preaching against images. Foxe, perhaps mistakenly, attributed to him an iconoclastic *Treatise of the Worship of Images*, since included among Ridley's published works.[28] This was followed by the long Elizabethan *Homilie against perill of Idolatrie* issued in the second book of homilies in 1563. Meanwhile, a rapid-fire pamphlet war, fought largely over images, had broken out be-

tween John Jewel, the bishop of Salisbury and a main spokesman
for the Elizabethan settlement, and his onetime pupil, the recusant
Thomas Harding. Jewel's *Apologia ecclesiae Anglicanae* of 1562 provoked a bitter *Answer* from Harding in 1564, which led to a *Reply*
from Jewel in 1565, a *Confutation* from Harding in 1566, and a *Defense* from Jewel in 1567. In 1567 Nicholas Sander threw himself
into the battle on the side of his fellow Catholic Harding with a
Treatise of the Images of Christ. The controversy would be temporarily
resolved at the end of the century in the magisterial compromise of
Hooker's *Laws of Ecclesiastical Polity* (Book 5, Section 17), only to
erupt again with new rancor in the pamphlet wars of the seventeenth century.

It would continue virtually without pause down to the Civil War.
Until the revolution of the 1640s, the Anglican establishment attempted to negotiate the middle way, arguing, under Laud, that
since popery had been abolished and the people were now properly admonished on the abuse of images, there could be no danger
of idolatry in Laud's program of refurbishing parish churches that
had been stripped of their adornment.[29] In this he had the support
of the king and the warm sympathy of the queen, in whose chapel
at Somerset House the Holy Sacrament was displayed in a forty-
foot high architectural setting decorated with hundreds of angels.
This compromise was challenged from the left by a growing, and
finally overwhelming, chorus of Puritan and Dissenting voices—
Ainsworth, Prynne, Cowper, Burges, Smart, Baxter, Milton—all
attacking the prelates for daring to "clothe the gospel" with idolatrous ceremonies. They were opposed in turn by recusant writers
holding fast to the Roman Catholic view that would, as Martz and
Tuve have shown, make itself felt in England in the continuities of
religious thought and practice bridging the Reformation.

For the literary imagination, what will in the end survive the particular points of dispute in these writings is suggested by the tone of
Calvin's remark about the Mercy Seat. For in its most telling moments the argument against sacred imagery drives below the realm
of "external" representation to relocate the iconoclastic struggle
within the individual Christian. The phenomenology set loose here
offers none of the comforts of Merleau-Ponty discovering that the
"visual and auditory experiences" within himself "are pregnant
with one another," or of Sidney's poet left wondrously free to roam
through the zodiac of his own wit in search of images on which to
tether his words.[30] The poet inebriated by the Ficinian belief that
the image-making power in man is the creative spark of the divine

intellect would have to confront himself as an idolator and use the power of the word to cleanse the temple of his own heart.

So Karlstadt confesses to having idolatrous images "firmly and deeply seated" in his heart; Luther, in an iconoclastic moment, would tear unsanctioned images "out of the heart of all," and Zwingli would discover the root of man's idolatry in those sinful temptations which actual statues and pictures only tempt into the open. The commandment against idols is aimed, therefore, not merely at the superstitions of the Jews or at the decorations of the church, but, as Zwingli argues, at any interior process turning the mind to anything but God. To dwell on the creature rather than on the Creator is to fashion it in that very instant into an *Abgott*—the "strange god" proscribed in the commandment against idolatry.[31] The world I find impossible not to picture in my mind, its color and shapeliness so alluring, springs up within me as the temple of Baal. Even the image of Christ the man that I envision, should I not "bridle" myself from thinking on it with reverence, becomes an idol for me that further estranges me from God.

"There is nobody," as Luther concedes, "or certainly very few, who do not understand that yonder crucifix is not my God, for my God is in Heaven, but that is simply a sign."[32] But given the power of what Zwingli calls the *inneren götzen der anfechtungen*—the inner idols that tempt us to love what we imagine—we cannot trust ourselves to act on that conviction.[33] Having fallen once, we can hardly avoid falling again and again when the devil represents himself at the doorway of our eyes—falling into a sin that the iconoclasts will come to regard as a kind of illicit visual intercourse. The homilist asks, "Doeth not the worde of GOD call Idolatrie spirituall fornication?"[34] On the authority of the Book of Wisdom, the invention of images marked the "beginning of spiritual fornication," and furthermore, "an image made by a father, as it appears in the same book, for the memorial of a son departed, was the first invention of images, and occasion of idolatry."[35] Henry Ainsworth cites a number of Biblical passages to demonstrate "that idolatrie is as sweet to the corrupted conscience and mind of man, as lust and fornication, is to any wanton body." When man "goeth a whoring with his own inventions,"

> Every man naturally pleaseth himselfe, and liketh wel of his own designes; loving the fruit of his wit as the child of his body: that when he hath conceived mischief, one brought forth (an idol, that is) iniquity; it groweth up with

him and he rejoyceth in his own invention. . . . Finally, the
Lord, to teach us, how fast this syn cleaveth unto us, sayth
by his Prophet of the idolatry of Iudah (his owne professt
people) that it was written with a pen of iron, and with the
point of a diamond graven upon the table of their hart;
shewing that the inmost affections are most deeply and
continually infected with this vice, and addicted unto it;
from which, no kind of perswasion, no earnest dehorta-
tion, nor dreadful threating will turn them.[36]

Ainsworth here echoes the carnal imagery of the homilist's Pauline
argument that even if we "know" images are not to be adored, their
very location in places of honor unwittingly "breedeth the most vile
affection of errour" in our minds.[37] Calvin's God stands imageless
and uncontaminated as the "sole and proper witness of himself,"
attested only in his word; but "man's nature, so to speak, is a perpetual factory of idols." His mind, "full as it is of pride and boldness,
tries to imagine a god according to its own capacity," whence a "new
wickedness joins itself, that man tries to express in his work the sort
of god he has inwardly conceived. Therefore the mind begets an
idol; the hand gives it birth" (1.11.8).

The dilemma here posed for the poet's hand is no less sharp than
for the painter's. For if the "factory of idols" is located not in the
choice of pigment over language but in the very mind behind the
work, and if no man can trust his own motives, then every poem
risks becoming a strange god even if the poet's declared intention is
to "plainly say, *My God, My King.*" Idolatry is a vice "written" as well
as "graven" upon the table of the heart. Taken to an extreme,
admittedly, such qualms would lead the Brownist defector John
Smyth to call for the abolition of all books as well as all images,
books being themselves only "signes or pictures."[38] But the poet's
self-consciousness about this peril will surely be the more acute insofar as he finds himself writing within, or even against, an aesthetic founded on the alliance of the word with the pictorial image.

The iconoclasts thus find their strongest arguments in these dark
corners of the idolatrous mind where poets conspire with painters
to produce strange gods. William Tyndale, who accused Thomas
More of being "fleshly-minded" for having maintained that images
can hold a reflection of spiritual truth, notes ironically of his famous opponent that the papists "did well to choose a poet to be
their defender," for the ceremonies of Rome are all blasphemous
confections of the human imagination, idols set up by worldly prel-

ates who have given "themselves only unto poetry, and shut up the Scripture."[39] Thomas Harding had asserted that the "use and profit of writing and pictures is one," and his argument had been grounded as firmly in the formulas of *ut pictura poesis* as in the fathers of the church: "[I]n old time the work of excellent poets was called a speaking picture, and the work of painters a still poetry." Bishop Jewel's *Reply* admits the analogy only to turn it into an unholy alliance that convicts poetry no less than the sister art:

> But the comparison that M. Harding useth between images and poetry seemeth nearest to express the truth. For painters and poets, for liberty of lying, have of long time been coupled both together. . . . And therefore, like as Plato commanded all poets for their lying to be banished out of his commonwealth, so likewise Almighty God, for like liberty, banished all painters out of Israel.[40]

To prove that "pictures have great force to move men's hearts," Harding had invoked the "stirring" ekphrastic moment in Book I of the *Aeneid*: "Virgil maketh Aeneas to weep, to hope for better fortune, to gather courage of mind, to take good advice and order for redress and help of his great calamities, by occasion of beholding a painter's work at Carthage, wherein the battle of Troy was expressed." Jewel brushes aside the opinion of the "heathenish poets" and their "idle fables" and insists instead on the cautionary word of Wisdom 15: "The sight of an image in the unwise stirreth up concupiscence."[41]

For those, like George Salteren, most deeply suspicious of the satanic power of the image, "the words of Gods Law" in the commandment against idols "are to be taken by a *senechdoche speciei, pro genere*, according to the doctrine of our Saviour, Mat. 5." And therefore, "the word graven Images must be extended to all Images, whether molten, carved, or painted; the word similitude to all kindes of similitude, though but in conceit."[42] On this principle, the "painter's work" described in the *Aeneid* must figure as an idol not only as it were on the walls of Carthage, but in the text that contains it, and not only in the "conceit" of the painter, but in that of the poet, of his hero, and of the reader exposed by the poem to the "sight of an image." Ainsworth drives the point home:

> For every man is forbidden to make unto himself, any *forme, shape* or *resemblance*, of things in the heavens earth or

waters; of any *similitude, shew,* or *likeness,* any *frame, figure, edifice,* or *structure,* of man or beast, fowl or fish or any creeping thing, any *image, type* or *shadowed representation;* any *imagined-picture, fabrick,* or *shape.* . . . So that it is not possible for the wit or hand of man to make any image or representation whatsoever, which cometh not within compasse of the words and things forewarned of God.[43]

Products of the "wit" rather than the "hands," idle fables harboring images are idol fables; "words and things" alike fall under the divine proscription.

A thorough reformation of images would thus have only begun if it succeeded in reversing Aquinas's traditional evaluation of sight as *sensus magis cognoscitivus* and in breaking the idols in the church.[44] It could not stop before it had broken language and thought themselves free of their attachment to the eye—and done so not just in the face of a vigorously pictorial literary aesthetic, but at the very moment in the history of literacy when, as Father Ong has argued, print technology heralded "a widespread reorganization of the sensorium favoring the visual in communication procedures."[45] Just when, in Ong's words, men "began to link visual perception to verbalization to a degree previously unknown," the iconoclastic impulse would in effect hold up before them, as the ideal of verbal purity, some impossibly chaste medium of unadulterated and unidolatrous signification. To achieve it, the mind would have to erase all the imaginative materials of what Rudolf Arnheim calls "visual thinking"—all the mental "imagery" which cannot be discarded as a "by-product of the 'real' thinking going on in some other region" of the mind, or as an "epiphenomenon" upon thought, but which is for many thinkers at least "the very arena in which the action takes place."[46]

Such a project had its practical application through the influence of Ramist thought on the traditional art of memory. As Frances Yates has explained, in the classical memory systems inherited by the Renaissance, knowledge is stored in a lexicon of allegorical figures of the sort that appear in Ripa's *Iconologia,* figures like that of Mercury with his wand, winged feet, and so on, that incorporate a complex of related ideas in a kind of visual shorthand. An argument would be committed to memory by the memorizer imagining a series of "places" (like the rooms in a building) filled with such figures, through which the eye of the mind would then walk as the argument was retrieved. Yates shows that, although "many surviving influences of the old art of memory may be detected in the Ramist 'method' of memorising through dialectical order,'' Ramus "deliberately gets rid of its most characteristic feature, the use of the imagination. No more will 'places' in churches or other buildings filled with statuary be vividly impressed on the imagination. And, above all, gone in the Ramist system are the images, the emotionally striking and stimulating images the use of which had come down through the centuries from the art of the classical rhetor." With Ramus we are very far from the rival Neoplatonic conception of thought reflected in Giordano Bruno's declaration that "to think is to speculate with images." Yates goes on to suggest that "The extraordinary success of Ramism . . . in Protestant countries like England may perhaps be partly accounted for by the fact that it provided a kind of inner iconoclasm," a smashing of the pictures and statues of the mind, "corresponding to the outer iconoclasm" devoted to smashing the images of the church.[47]

My survey of the battlefield in the preceding pages will have perhaps suggested, I hope not inadvertently, how confused the issues of the dispute over "images" could be. In the heat of polemical cut and thrust, arguments were seldom rigorously pursued or even basic terms scrupulously defined. The word could be declared free of idolatry by its very nature because it was not pictorial, or else superior to the image because it could more vividly engage the imagination than any picture, and do so without the treacherous mediation of the eye. An "image" itself could be the external object of perception (the painting) or the inward, mental unit of the imaginative faculty. If the latter, it was either a good or a bad thing: bad (for the iconoclasts) as it was thought to be the mental copy, or the mental prototype, of the idolatrous artwork, good (for their opponents) as it was understood to be a copy of, or a participant in, the true divine "image." For many reformers, the use of the imaging faculty in meditative exercises is preferred to the Catholic veneration of images because the mind's constructions are inward and immaterial. Even so, anyone who carnally conceives in himself a false image is no less guilty of idolatry than if he had bowed down before a block of wood. As the debate turns from the ontology of artifacts to the psychology of the imagination, it begins to raise questions and anxieties that it cannot resolve: how is a Christian to know whether the pictures in his mind are the marks of his spiritual illumination or the residue of his depravity? The same Puritans who reviled the sensual attractions of images could embrace the educa-

45

tional reforms of Comenius, whose *Orbis Sensualium Pictus* (1657) was an illustrated primer headed by the Aristotelian motto: *Nihil est in intellectu, quod non prius fuit in sensu.* Richard Sibbes could believe that, since "God hath condescended to represent Heavenly things to us under earthly terms, we should follow Gods dealing herein. . . . Here is a large field for our imagination to walk in" (p. 178), but at the same time that "Imagination is the womb, and Satan the father of all monstrous conceptions and disordered lusts" (p. 184). Chief among Satan's progeny, popery is "but an artificial frame of mans brain to please mens imaginations by outward state and pomp of ceremonies" (p. 161), ceremonies in which "men worship the image of their own fancie" (p. 185). The title of Sibbes' treatise is *The Soules Conflict with it selfe* (London, 1651); Sibbes' own conflict with himself is nowhere sharper than over the contradictory nature of the "image."[48]

My point in what follows will be that for the major writers of the period, this confusion is a creative confusion, and that the conflicts raised by the image debate are not simply reflected in their work but help to shape it in interesting and powerfully generative ways. What is mere befuddlement in a Sibbes becomes art in Spenser, Donne, and Milton. In them the simultaneously glorious and dangerous potential of the poem to become a speaking picture becomes part of the poem's meaning, and it is to them that we turn for the most ambitious imaginative strategies for producing and exploring that meaning. Three preliminary examples, from Foxe, Jonson, and Herbert, will set the scene.

John Foxe's *Acts and Monuments of the Church* (1563) is both a literary act and a literary monument—and, as such, stands as a central document and a telling paradox in the history of English iconoclasm. Dedicated to recording the "acts of God's holy martyrs" from the time of the early church through that of the Marian persecutions in the 1550s, its two million words represent the product of an equally heroic and grueling act of authorship, "my seven years' labour about this Ecclesiastical history" (1).[49] What fires Foxe's imagination throughout this long ordeal is fire. Hundreds upon hundreds of martyrs are burned at the stake, and Foxe often lingers over the details of their death. The longer his text grows through its successive editions, the greater the number of the faithful who are heaped on the fagots—as if, with his materials being constantly consumed, Foxe had constantly to add new fuel to his narrative fire. The reader opens the book almost at random and finds that Thomas Bilney tested his resolve the night before his execution in

1531 by "putting his hand to the flame of the candle." The next morning,

> the officers put reeds and fagots about his body, and set fire to them, which made a very great flame, and deformed his face, he holding up his hands and knocking upon his breast, crying sometimes, "Jesus," sometimes "I believe." The flame was blown away from him by the violence of the wind . . . and so for a little pause he stood without flame, but soon the wood again took the flame, and then he gave up the ghost, and his body being withered, bowed downward upon the chain. Then one of the officers with his halbert smote out the staple in the stake behind him, and suffered his body to fall into the bottom of the fire, laying wood on it, and so he was consumed. (513)

Perhaps Foxe's most gruesome account is that of the immolation of Nicholas Ridley in 1555. Ridley's agony was prolonged "by reason of the badness of the fire, which only burned beneath, being kept down by the wood":

> so that it burned all his lower parts, before it once touched the upper, and that made him leap up and down under the fagots, and often desire them to let the fire come to him, saying, "I cannot burn." Which was apparent: for after his legs were consumed, he shewed his other side toward us, shirt and all untouched with flame! (854)

Ridley's suffering ended only "when the flame touched the gunpowder" in the little sack hung, as a gesture of mercy, around the neck of the condemned. So strong indeed is the fascination with flame that it burns its way into the texture of Foxe's language. The heathen emperors of Rome "did all the world could do to extinguish the name and church of Christ" (3). The eyes of the infuriated judge "glowed like fire" as he ordered the grilling of St. Lawrence: "Roast him, broil him, toss him, turn him" (52). But God "so miraculously tempered his element, the fire," that not Lawrence "but the emperor, might seem to be tormented: the one broiling in the flesh, the other burning in the heart." To the reader who understands how the ardent faith of the saint can transform a "fiery bed of iron" into a "soft bed of down," Foxe extends a curiously quaint and appalling invitation: "Let us draw near to the fire of martyred Lawrence, that our cold hearts may be warmed thereby."

Like Ridley, a number of Foxe's martyrs won the crown in the pe-
rennial battle against idolatry—among them, the three men condemned in 1532 for burning the Rood of Dover-court: "Then they
struck fire with a flint-stone, and suddenly set him on fire, and he
burned so brightly that he lighted them homeward" (524). Foxe ap-
plauds the resourcefulness of the reformers in Basel, who in 1529
saw to it that "all the wooden images were distributed among the
poor of the city, to serve them for firewood" (442). When, however,
arguments broke out about the division of the wood, it was decided
that "the images should be burned all together . . . in nine great
heaps" before the church door. This "joyful day, for turning their
images to ashes" fell, appropriately, on Ash Wednesday. In 1553
when John Maundrel was asked by his interrogators "whether images were necessary to be in the churches, as laymen's books," his
reply—"That wooden images were good to roast a shoulder of
mutton, but were bad in the church; whereby idolatry was committed"—was heated enough to send him to the stake (909).

Itself a contribution to that battle, Foxe's book is an incendiary
act, politically as well as imaginatively. Its intention is not merely to
correct or supplant a corrupt tradition of ecclesiastical histories,
but, figuratively at least, to smash them to kindling. Having created
in their words a blatantly idolatrous image of the Roman church,
such books leave the "simple folk of Christ, especially the un-
learned sort . . . miserably deluded" (1). As the plain truth, his
book relies on the reader's judgment and holds no such glittering
attraction: "I allure neither one or other to read my book; let every
man do as he pleases" (1). Their books "play with us"

> as the painter Apelles did, who, painting the one half of
> Venus coming out of the sea, left the other half imperfect.
> So these writers, while they show us one half of the bishop
> of Rome, leave the other half of him imperfect, and utterly
> untold. For as they paint him on the one part glittering in
> wealth and glory . . . [they say nothing of] what vices these
> popes brought with them to their seat, what abominations
> they practised, what superstition they maintained, what
> idolatry they procured, what wicked doctrine they de-
> fended contrary to the express word of God. . . . (2)

Where they display "the church of Rome so visible and glorious in
the eyes of all the world" (2), Foxe records the acts of the true but
persecuted church that until now has endured "neglected in the

world, not regarded in histories, and scarce visible or known to worldly eyes" (2). Abjuring the deceitful history-painting of the earlier chroniclers, Foxe would speak with a tongue of flame to roast the false image of the Roman Venus like a shoulder of mutton.

The difference between historical depiction and historical speech is reinforced by the woodcut on Foxe's title page, which follows Bale in setting "The Image of the persecuted Church" (as the motto added in the 1570 edition declares) against "The Image of the persecuting Church." On one side, a minister preaches the Gospel to an audience of Christians holding their Bibles. On the other, a Corpus Christi procession draws a crowd of infatuated spectators. But the allusion to Bale's illustrated *Image of Both Churches*, the woodcut itself, and the quasi-ceremonial role of Foxe's Protestant martyrology, especially as it was officially installed in English churches, all contribute to a sense of the book as a visible "monument." Foxe echoes Bale again in his preface when he proposes to show "the image of both churches" (2). Indeed, since the church of the devil has always attempted to "deface and malign" the true church, it is all the more urgent that the image of the true church be restored and that "the difference between them should be seen." Latimer's scriptural quip at the stake is exactly appropriate to this aspect of Foxe's design: "Well, there is nothing hid but it shall be made manifest" (354). Just as salvation history manifests the truth, Foxe, as its agent, will bring to light those obscure acts of faith long "trodden under foot" by oppressors (2). And by bringing to light the abominations of the oppressor at the same time, Foxe in effect completes that half-finished portrait by Apelles: in the act of "drawing out the descent of the [true] church" (4), of showing us how the fire burned Ridley's "lower parts," he succeeds in drawing in the hideous lower parts of the persecuting church. This restorative and representational impulse leads Foxe to compare his writing to the construction of Solomon's temple (1); its opposite, an equally strong corrosive and iconoclastic impulse, leads him to declare on the next page, "[T]hey who require that God's holy church should be evident and visible to the whole world, seem to define the great synagogue of the world, rather than the true spiritual church of God" (2). To hold these two violently paradoxical sides of his project together over the many years of its composition, Foxe must surely have needed that "unaccustomed patience" and "faith invincible" that sustained his own St. Lawrence in the fire—a faith "that by means unspeakable dost recreate, refresh, establish, and strengthen those that are burned, afflicted, and troubled" (52).

As we have seen in the case of Chapman, the tensions between the word and the image straining through Foxe's *Acts and Monuments* make themselves felt in the very different contexts of English Renaissance poetry. They are perceptible in Ben Jonson's ambivalent discussion of *ut pictura poesis* in the *Discoveries*:

> *Poetry*, and *Picture*, are Arts of a like nature; and both are busie about imitation. It was excellently said of *Plutarch*, *Poetry* was a speaking Picture, and *Picture* a mute Poesie. For they both invent, faine, and devise many things, and accommodate all they invent to the use, and service of nature. Yet of the two, the Pen is more noble, then the Pencill. For that can speake to the Understanding; the other, but to the Sense. They both behold pleasure, and profit, as their common Object. . . .
> *Whosoever* loves not *Picture*, is injurious to Truth: and all the wisdome of *Poetry*. Picture is the invention of Heaven: the most ancient, and most a kinne to Nature. It is itselfe a silent worke: and alwayes of one and the same habit: Yet it doth so enter, and penetrate the inmost affection (being done by an excellent Artificer) as sometimes it orecomes the power of speech, and oratory.[50]

In just as mechanical a way as Sidney had done, Jonson rolls out the commonplaces that declare the affiliation of "*Poetry*, and *Picture*"; but then, pausing between the shade of Sidney ("they both invent, faine, and devise") and the shade of Horace ("pleasure, and profit"), he registers the conviction that will inform his verse: "Yet of the two, the Pen is more noble, then the Pencill." Yet having just asserted the advantage of poetry by limiting the impact of painting to the outward "Sense," Jonson is led to acknowledge—by the authority of Quintilian (*Inst. Orat.* 11.3.67), if not by the wonders of an "excellent Artificer" at Whitehall—that painting "sometimes . . . orecomes the power" of language. Introduced by another "yet," what had been a topic of praise in Quintilian becomes almost a warning as Jonson transcribes it. These bits of ancient wisdom are patched into a mosaic that reveals the crack between the arts. "Picture" may be "a mute Poesie" and the "invention of Heaven," but its very silence here must seem vaguely threatening, like the stealth of an invader bent on penetrating the "inmost" domain of the word. Thus the Prologue to *The Staple of News* (1626) wishes that the audience "were come to heare, not see a Play," for the author would "haue you wise, / much rather by your eares, then by your eyes." For

a court performance of the same play, Jonson added a second prologue directed at what he hoped would be a more discerning audience of "schollers" who can "iudge, and faire report / The sense
they heare, aboue the vulgar sort / Of Nut-crackers, that onely
come for sight."[51]

Jonson could scarcely have expected to encourage such an audience among the courtly spectators of his masques. In performance,
his masque-texts must as often as not have been experienced as
pale commentaries on the astonishing scenic "wonders" conjured
up by his collaborator, Inigo Jones. Jonson, as is well known, grew
increasingly embittered by the successes of the brilliant designer.[52]
He launched guerrilla attacks in his anti-masques against the "superfluous excesses" of courtly entertainments. He did a send-up of
Jones as "Lanthorn Leatherhead, a hobbyhorse seller" in *Bartholomew Fair*. In 1631 he finally provoked a break by insisting that
his own name appear over Jones's on the title page of *Love's Triumph
Through Callipolis*—a masque that, unfortunately for the justice of
Jonson's claim to top billing, is almost all spectacle. Jonson under-
standably took great care to preserve his masques as well as his
plays in the more hospitable form of the published book. In the
1616 folio of his *Works* (and in the material he prepared for the second, posthumous, folio of 1640), the stage directions Jonson supplies tend to be skimpy and confusing, but the texts of the masques
themselves are scrupulously edited and shored up with massive
buttresses of scholarly annotation, as if Jonson were determined to
secure for his language an authority in print that it had been denied on the masquing platform.[53]

Arguably Jonson's nastiest poem, "An Expostulation with Inigo
Jones," hammers away at the deceptiveness of Jones's "shows":

> O Showes! Showes! Mighty Showes!
> The Eloquence of Masques! What need of prose
> Or Verse, or Sense t'express Immortall you?
> You are ye Spectacles of State! Tis true
> Court Hieroglyphicks! & all Artes affoord
> In ye mere perspectiue of an Inch board!
>
> (ll. 39–44)[54]

As the antagonist of "prose / Or Verse," the visual image draws
much of its power, both for Jonson and for the spectators whose
perceptions he here tries to reform, from a capacity for dazzling
perspectival illusions realized in masque design. I have argued else-

where that the literary imagination in England assimilates the idea of linear perspective in a deeply problematic way.[55] It regards the technique of generating a mathematically rationalized and optically convincing projection of three-dimensional space, as Alberti had, as the *theoria* that raised painting to the level of an intellectual discipline and justified its membership in the liberal arts. "*Picture* tooke . . . from *Geometry* her rule, compasse, lines, proportion, and the whole *Symmetry*," Jonson continues in the *Discoveries*, and from "the *Opticks* it drew reasons; by which it considered, how things plac'd at distance, and a farre off, should appeare less: how above, or beneath the head, should deceive the eye, &c."[56] Perspective offers a model of the eye gaining a commanding and clarified "prospect" over the *superficies* of the world it surveys, but also, through the eye, of the mind piercing to the "reasons" of things—to the rational substratum of surface appearance. Yet as Jonson's final emphasis on deceiving the eye suggests, the inmost reach of perspective is as delusory as the inch-deep vistas of an Inigo Jones masquing set. Like so many optical tricks that exploit its duplicity, the perspective image may shift irreconcilably from spatial depth to mere surface pattern. As a literary analogy drawn from the sister art of painting, and more crucially as a metaphor for cognition, perspective offers the poet a set of terms for distortion, confusion, and enchantment as well as for insight.

As a sometime Catholic and, perhaps more important, a full-time dependent on the good will of his royal patrons, Jonson did not for all his satire on court life explicitly draw the conclusion that less constrained and more zealous critics of Stuart theatrics like William Prynne shouted aloud at the risk of their ears and their lives. The court had imported the most fashionable Italianate artistic techniques to create an idolatrous spectacle for the worship of the king. The annual rites at Whitehall, on which vast fortunes were lavished for costumes, scene-painting, and ingenious "machines," were gaudier but no less pernicious than the images that enticed the simple people in parish churches—the same images that the king's prelates refused to remove.

In his nondramatic poetry, however, Jonson presides forcefully over a reformed domain free of images and governed solely by the power of his word. He spurns the muse that has made him "commit most fierce idolatrie / To a great image" by praising the worthless at court. Drawn as he is to the world of "shows" in his masques and plays, in his verse he praises Sir Robert Wroth for avoiding the temptation "(when masquing is) to haue a sight / Of the short brauerie of the night," and for preferring the "painted meades" of nature's better art. Jonson insists at the beginning of "To Penshvrst" that the Sidney estate was not "built to envious show," and the poem as a whole represents a kind of 'blind' revision of the classical country-house poem in that Jonson offers none of the conventional description of the great house. Instead, he emphasizes the inner moral architecture of the Sidney family and declares that the Sidney children may "Reade, in their vertuous parents noble parts, / The mysteries of manners, armes, and arts." Just as the Sidneys have been transformed into texts, Jonson's first son is commemorated as "his best piece of poetrie," and Jonson's Scottish lady is criticized for having mistaken the poet's picture for the poet. Unfortunately given to reading images rather than verse, she is "deafe" to the graces of Jonson's language, having

> Read so much wast, as she cannot imbrace
> My mountaine belly and my rockie face,
> As all these through her eyes, have stopt her eares.

When Jonson elsewhere honors Camden for the "weight" and "authority" of his speech; when he challenges a "fine" court lady to "write" an epitaph "on thy wombe" for the child she refuses to bear; when, in an epistle "Inviting a Friend to Svpper," a "piece" of Virgil, Tacitus, and Livy appears on the same prospective menu with the partridge, pheasant, and woodcock; and when, in another epistle, he urges an aspirant to the Tribe of Ben to "read my Character," and offers to "take you so, / As you have writ your selfe," we realize that the world presents itself to Jonson in these poems as a body of texts, its collected works subsumed for him, and consumed by him, under metaphors of reading, writing, and speaking. For Jonson, the character of the virtuous is stamped in their names, and his own poetic authority issues from the power to evoke those names: "I Doe but name thee PEMBROKE, and I find / It is an *Epigramme*, on all man-kind." When he "wish'd to see" his subject, his "*Muse* bad, *Bedford* write, and that was shee." The resonantly Latinate vocative of "CAMDEN, most reuerend head" is deepened by our understanding that Jonson's teacher is himself a namer—it is to his *Britannia* that "my country owes / The greate renowne, and name wherewith shee goes." Jonson here takes his place at the head of a moral and intellectual lineage confirmed by acts of nomina-

tion, each name re-sounding the chords of filial obligation ultimately binding the poet's "pietie" to the *pietas* of Virgilian Rome.
"*Language* most shewes a man: speake that I may see thee." An imperialism of the word in one region of Jonson's writing compensates
for the word's captivation by the image in another.[57]

Foxe and Jonson, the militant iconoclast and the master craftsman
of words fit to images, have arrived at a common crossroads from
opposite directions. George Herbert occupies the same ground.
Preeminent among seventeenth-century devotional poets as an advocate of humility and simplicity of expression, Herbert is faithfully
attentive to the comforting whispers of the divine voice and faithfully resolved to submit his language for pruning and paring at the
hands of a higher artist. At the same time he is the author of a biblical love song to his own verse who, despite the consolations of a residual simplicity, mourns the imagined loss of his "Lovely enchant-
ing language, sugar-cane" (176).[58] The poet who wishes "In all
things thee to see" (184), Herbert is also the emblematist and verbal
architect, the designer of poetic wings and altars. Herbert's poems,
however, have been carried across the Jordan, washed with his tears
and "Brought . . . to Church well drest and clad" (176). Borrowed
from the profane devices of the *Greek Anthology* and its Elizabethan
imitators, the visual artifacts in Herbert's *The Temple* are rededi-
cated to sacred uses. In the echo poem "Heaven," the question,
"what is that supreme delight?" is immediately answered: "Light."
But the next line just as quickly reinterprets the reply: "Light to the
minde" (188); and our understanding of the shift is deepened by
an awareness that in this poem as elsewhere in Herbert, heaven's
delights are not revealed in splendid illuminations but rehearsed in
a dialogue of interior voices. When we cross the threshold of *The
Temple*, we are allowed literally to see "The Altar" (26), but only as a
second threshold to another, iconoclastic meaning spoken in the
first line. This object has been "broken" and reared again "of a
heart"; its architecture, like that of "The Windows" and "The
Church-floore," is inward an unseen.

In "Church-monuments," while Herbert's soul "repairs to her devotion," the poet entrusts his body (rather like a child put in day-
care) "to this school" of the monuments themselves,

> that it may learn
> To spell his elements, and finde his birth
> Written in dusty heraldrie and lines;

> Which dissolution sure doth best discern,
> Comparing dust with dust, and earth with earth.

The body can "spell" out the "elements" of the language inscribed on the tombstones, but the truer knowledge concealed by the stones—the knowledge of the body's own "elements"—is to be gained by "Comparing" the dust that fills our bodies with the same dust of those already interred. Visible monuments "put up for signes" in fact stand in the way of that education about the true nature of the body because their image of the occupant's "heraldrie" and their record of his family "lines" (as well as their own apparent stability) interpose an illusion of permanence between the body and its own self-knowledge as "flesh" which "also shall / Be crumbled unto dust." As signs, monuments reveal their significance—the transience of even the most durable earthly things—most clearly by their own inevitable "dissolution." In a sardonic question that glances at the idolatry of those who would confuse the soul's proper "devotion" with a carnal respect for monuments, Herbert asks of these stony signs: "What shall point out them, / When they shall bow, and kneel, and fall down flat / To kisse those heaps, which now they have in trust?" (64–65).

Dramatizing the fulfillment of Old Testament types in the spirit of the Gospel, these poems record the dimensions of the interior Christian life. Yet their wit often depends on the revelation of this inner architecture by a quick shift in perception that undermines but never completely effaces the outward sign: it is not until the final line of "The Church-floore" that we discover that the "floor" so meticulously inspected by the poem is located "in a weak heart" (67). Absorbed as they are in the Parson's inner devotions, the poems nonetheless reflect Herbert's conviction that the "Parson hath a speciall care of his Church, that all things there be decent." He must take pains to see that "all things be in good repair; as walls plaistered, windows glazed, floore paved," and that "there be fit, and proper texts of Scripture every where painted" on the walls— for it is the Parson's responsibility to "keep the middle way between superstition, and slovenlinesse," even in "externall and indifferent things" (246). In this context, Herbert's desire to rear a "broken ALTAR," its "stones" resanctified in the new temple of the heart, may be felt as a response to the radical iconoclasm of a Separatist like Henry Barrow, who would have all churches destroyed for carrying in their "every stone" the contamination of the workman's tool: "The Idolatrous shape so cleaveth to every stone, as it by no

means can be severed from them whiles there is a stone left standing upon a stone."[59]

Nevertheless, Herbert—who also believed that if the Parson "be
marryed, the choyce of his wife was made rather by his eare, then
by his eye" (238)—could not accept Valdesso's opinion that

> The unlearned man, that hath the spirit, serveth him-
> selfe of *Images* as of an Alphabet of Christian Pietie; for-
> asmuch as hee so much serves himselfe of the *Picture* of
> Christ Crucified, as much as serves to imprint in his mind
> that which Christ suffered. . . . In like manner a learned
> man, that hath the spirit, serveth himselfe of *holy Scriptures*,
> as of an Alphabet of Christian pietie, . . . untill such time,
> as it penetrate into his minde." (309)

Against this version of the Gregorian defense of images, Herbert
argues that he much mislikes

> the Comparison of Images, and H. Scripture, as if they were
> both Alphabets and after a time to be left. The H. Scrip-
> tures . . . have not only an Elementary use, but a use of per-
> fection, neither can they ever be exhausted, (as Pictures
> may be by a plenarie circumspection) but still even to the
> most learned and perfect in them, there is somewhat to be
> learned more. (309)

God, Herbert insists, "workes" in us "by his Word, and ever in the
reading of it" (310). A central dilemma of Herbert's poetry stems
from his fear that to rewrite the word is to violate the biblical prohibition of craftsmanship in Deuteronomy 25:2–8, the verses alluded to in "The Altar's" denial that any "workmans tool" has
touched this carefully tooled artifact. To further transform the
word into an image is to channel the flow of God's inexhaustible
work into the stagnant pool of our own limited imagination. In the
commentary on Valdesso's *Considerations*, the middle way leads
Herbert to grant the image at least as "Elementary use." But it
is Calvin's sterner critique of what "man tries to express in his
work"—a "new wickedness joins itself. . . . the mind begets an idol;
the hand gives it birth"—that haunts Herbert's meditation on his
own artistry in the poem "Sinnes round":

> Sorrie I am, my God, sorrie I am,
> That my offences course it in a ring.

My thoughts are working like a busie flame,
Untill their cockatrice they hatch and bring:
And when they once have perfected their draughts,
My words take fire from my inflamed thoughts.

My words take fire from my inflamed thoughts,
Which spit it forth like the Sicilian hill.
They vent the wares, and passe them with their faults,
And by their breathing ventilate the ill.
But words suffice not, where are lewd intentions:
My hands do joyn to finish the inventions.

My hands do joyn to finish the inventions:
And so my sinnes ascend three stories high,
As Babel grew, before there were dissentions.
Yet ill deeds loyter not: for they supplie
New thoughts of sinning: wherefore, to my shame,
Sorrie I am, my God, sorrie I am.

(122)

The poet's "sorrie I am"—for such is the nature of rounds—
must repeat itself endlessly. There is no "finish" to his "inventions"
because they must circle round again to reinflame his "lewd intentions"—the two locked together in the mind as they are made to
chime in the text. The intertwining stanzas, bending back to their
beginning, describe the vicious circle in which thoughts, words, and
hands "joyn" in a venture at once, and unceasingly, constructive
and incendiary. Shamefully aware of its own combustion in the
poet's mind, the poem's "busie flame" generates puns on language
and visual design that glance at the making of the work. Its "perfected . . . draughts" are not in the end completed drawings for a
stable structure but, in a parody of poetic inspiration, the hot winds
that will fan the fire of his words. The attempt to compose the
poem's three "stories" (thoughts, words, and deeds) produces, in
the three stanzas of the poem, the three architectural "stories" of
Babel fashioned in the poet's factory of idols (and finished, as buildings are, by the craft of the joiner). But no sooner does the poem
"ascend" to its full height than it must be abandoned like the biblical tower of which it is the replica, and for the same reason:

And the Lord came down to see the city and the tower,
which the children of men builded. And the Lord said, Behold, the people is one, and they have all one language; and

this they begin to do: and now nothing will be restrained from them, which they have imagined to do. Go to, let us go down, and there confound their language, that they may not understand one another's speech. (Gen. 11:5–7)

Like the architects of Babel, the poet must be struck down for what he has "imagined to do." And as in Genesis, the penalty exacted on the poem is the confounding of language, for the words of sorrow which the poem achieves must run their course back to the new offenses that spark them again into futile repetition.

The double force of "draughts" and "stories," their verbal and pictorial implications pulling against each other, finally comes to bear on the meaning of the "round" itself as both song and emblem. As the new Psalmist trying to compose a worthy song of prayer and praise to lay on the altar of the new *Temple* of the heart, Herbert is both singer and builder. Here—with an ingenuity that the poem itself does not leave unindicted—the "round" as song hardens into the stony emblem of the "ring," the posy in which the speaker is joined to his sin to form the appropriate figure of his continuing shame. The very success of an iconic poem erected on the foundations of literary architecture and literary emblematics, and apparently complete in visual terms, only betrays its failure to "perfect" the word. Bricked up in its stories and tied to the circular frame of its own devising, the poet's language can spurn its idols momentarily in stanza three: "wherefore, to my shame. . . ." But as long as the new motions of remorse are twined with the restlessness of "new thoughts of sinning," the resolve to "loyter not" frees the poet's voice at the end only to enclose it again in an old beginning.

The battered sculpture in West Cheap Cross stood at the head of the last chapter as an emblem of the agon between image-making and iconoclasm. Herbert's poem is its literary counterpart. Inflamed by great brilliance and great anguish, "Sinnes round" records a moment in the history of the period's "inventions" far more intense than anything we have seen in Foxe or Jonson. Those writers negotiate the same crossroads more easily by maintaining a distance in their work between the two antagonists—Jonson by virtually banning the world of "shows" from the guarded province of his lyric poetry, Foxe by managing to sustain his history at once as a destructive act and a reconstructive monument. Foxe solves the problem in a sense by splitting the authority of his text between two opposed intentions without acknowledging that their collaboration conceals an unresolved conflict. In Herbert's poem the confrontation is met head-on, the battle between *pictura* and *poesis* is joined. The double sense of companionship and antipathy compressed in Herbert's "joyn" is writ large in the poetry of the English Reformation.

3

Spenser's
"Painted Forgery"

Set next to the poetry of Jonson or Herbert, *The Faerie Queene* may
seem to envision a far more clearly composed and fully rendered
pictorial world. Apparently free of Jonson's disdain for "show"
and unhampered by Herbert's suspicion of the "workmans tool,"
Spenser eagerly mines all the painterly resources available to the
Renaissance poet through the sisterhood of the arts. Like the
chamber of the imagination in Alma's house, the ampler frame of
Spenser's lavish poem is itself "dispainted all within, / With sundry
colours" (2.9.50)—with landscape, portraiture, description, emblem, pageantry, ekphrasis, and the many other riches of the *picta
poesis*.[1] To say as much, however, is to stop at a broad but superficial
view of Spenser's "pictorialism," one that (as the wordplay between
"painted" and "dis-painted" in Spenser's term suggests) we will
do well to revise by considering the deeper debate between pictorialism and iconoclasm in *The Faerie Queene*.[2] Spenser's melancholy Phantastes, though he inhabits the well-regulated Castle of
Alma, and is a "man of yeares yet fresh," has "sharpe foresight, and
working wit," nevertheless is also plagued by "idle thoughts and
fantasies." His chamber swarms with insects ambiguously both
"flyes" and "Bees" returning to "their hiues with honny." His productions spill out in a jumble of the "daily seene" and the bizarre
(2.9.49–52). A part-time resident in this chamber, the Spenserean
poet also inhabits the chamber of memory, where he sits, like the
ancient but vigorous Eumnestes, "halfe blind" to the world: there
his authority rests not on the buzz of fresh perception, but no less
precariously on "old records" and "scrolles" that are "all worme-
eaten, and full of canker holes" (2.9.55–58). His problematic dual
citizenship in the realms of texts and images must lead us to recon-
sider the views of readers who have long approached Spenser's at-

tempt "to portray . . . the image of a braue knight"[3] with an eye for the visual dimension of his work.

It was Warton who praised Spenser for rivaling Rubens; Hazlitt, for his "high picturesque character"; and Yeats, for his seeming "always to feel through the eyes, imaging everything in pictures."[4] Fifty years ago Greenlaw noted Spenser's debts to court pageantry and masquing; while forty years ago Josephine Waters Bennett characterized the poet as a "creator of mosaics" whose "imagination was pictorial, not dramatic." Miss Bennett declared that Spenser "saw the world as a series of vignettes" and that he therefore worked by "juxtaposition," "putting together small pieces, with an eye for harmony and symmetry, making a large composition out of many small ones."[5] The structure of *The Faerie Queene*, from its tightly framed individual stanzas, to the mirroring organization of the books, to the shape of the whole, may well have "worked" for Spenser as it does for many readers—as an interlocking visual system, the sum of our journeys in the poem mapped as a geography of the poem. On this model, as James Nohrnberg has demonstrated so exhaustively, reading is the process of completing analogies implied between the parts of the poem.[6] In more than a manner of speaking, Spenser's prudent reader is compelled to "look" both before and behind, tracing the lines connecting one motif with another (often to be found at a "distance"), as if on some vast spatial plan, or on a work of visual art like the Sistine ceiling. Among a number of recent formal and iconographical studies confirming this perception in various ways, Alastair Fowler charts the astonishing complication of the poem's numerological patterning, Angus Fletcher finds the structure of *The Faerie Queene* crystallized in the archetypes of the "temple" and the "labyrinth," and Jane Aptekar argues that Book 5 depends on an arrangement of the "icons of justice," images familiar from paintings and emblem books.[7]

Graham Hough gives the argument the grander sweep of the Romantic critics. In Ariosto and Tasso, he says, "we are continually haunted by reminiscences and suggestions of Renaissance painting, but these elusive parallels are far stronger in Spenser." Even though, as he notes, Spenser's acquaintance with Renaissance art beyond pageant scenery, tapestries, and emblem books was necessarily slight, Hough is taken by what seem to him striking "parallels" between Calidore's vision of the Graces in Book 6 and the *Primavera* of Botticelli, or between Spenser's forest landscape in Book 2 and Giorgione's *Tempesta*.[8] So other of Spenser's commentators have been struck by the similarity between Book 1 and the surprisingly large body of fifteenth- and sixteenth-century murals, panel paintings, tapestries, pageant decorations, and other images in England on the theme of St. George and the Dragon.[9] Indeed it is likely—and symptomatic of Spenser's practice elsewhere—that Book 1 is "based primarily upon the pictorial tradition [associated with St. George] rather than upon the literary tradition established by the *Legenda Aurea*," since Spenser's text "has little but a general similarity to the literary versions which depend on the *Legenda Aurea*, and he made use only of the combat episode in his story— precisely the episode which was most popular in art." On these grounds Kellogg and Steele, from whose school edition of Spenser I have just been quoting, are able to explicate much of Book 1 through a discussion of Carpaccio's *St. George Slaying the Dragon* in the Scuola San Giorgio Degli Schiavone, Venice—an image "very much in the spirit of Spenser's story," but one which Spenser of course never saw.[10] What precision lacks in such comparisons ingenuity supplies. Yet they all hint at one fundamental conclusion about Spenser's sensibility, most crisply put by Northrop Frye: "Spenser, unlike Milton, is a poet of very limited conceptual powers, and is helpless without some kind of visualization to start him thinking."[11]

Perhaps intended, in some oddly charitable way, to relieve the poet of the burden of his own allegory, such responses assert the "freshness" and "immediacy" of Spenser's vision. This pictorial Spenser seems especially congenial to the modern reader, for the core of the poem no longer lies in the complexities of its "dark conceit" or even in the "good discipline" which might otherwise justify the enormous enterprise. *The Faerie Queene* may be, as Spenser goes on to concede in the prefatory "Letter" to Raleigh, a work "cloudily enwrapped in allegorical devices." But behind the conceptual difficulty of the poem, and shining through it, is a bright world of form and color registered by the eye before it is "enwrapped" by the mind.

For this Spenser, the tutelage of the eye began with his earliest published verses, the translations from Petrarch, Du Bellay, and Van der Noot that appeared in the English version of *A Theatre for Voluptuous Worldlings* (London, 1569). In what is arguably the first English emblem book, the poems selected for the volume are matched with appropriate woodcuts and followed by a long antipapal polemic offered as a commentary on these preceding "visions." The young translator would profit from Van der Noot's method:

And to settle the vanitie and inconstancie of worldly and
transitorie thyngs, the liuelier before your eyes, I have
broughte in here twentie sights or vysions, & caused them
to be grauen, to the ende al men may see that with their
eyes, which I go aboute to expresse by writing, to the delight and plesure of the eye and eares. . . .[12]

In at least one instance—the Coliseum in the illustration to Sonet 7
from Du Bellay—a motif evidently remembered from the *Theatre*
will surface ten years later in the woodcuts for *The Shepheardes Calendar*, appearing at the end of a decade during which Spenser also
produced *The Visions of Petrarch*, *The Visions of Bellay*, and, probably,
the *Visions of the Worlds Vanitie*.[13] Working now, in 1579, in the tradition of the illustrated almanac, Spenser is concerned equally with
the overall visual format of the *Calendar*, with its suggestively spatial structure of circular return, and with the sequence of woodcuts
as they unfold in relation to the text.[14] Here are "Pictures," Spenser
remarks only half jokingly to Gabriel Harvey, "so singularly set
forth, and purtrayed, as if Michael Angelo were there, he could (I
think) not amende the best, nor reprehende the worste."[15]

Even so quick a glance back over Spenser's career reveals how
strongly visual his developing poetic is, and how much of Van der
Noot's "plesure of the eye" flows into *The Faerie Queene*. For, even
more than the iconography of St. George, the Reformation's highly
visual sense of the Book of Revelation lies at the wellhead of the
poem in Book 1. This tradition runs from the wealth of early Protestant illustrations of the Apocalypse—best known in England
through the set of Cranach woodcuts, first used to illustrate Luther's
German New Testament of 1522, and reproduced in John Bale's *The
Image of Both Churches* (c. 1548)—to the speculation, after Spenser,
that the wondrous volume with seven seals, in which the last awesome vision of salvation history is revealed, might have been a kind
of emblem book.[16] But Spenser would have needed to look no further than the concluding four "visions" in Van der Noot, whose illustrations of the beast from the sea "still freshly bleeding of a
grieuous wounde" (Rev. 13), the scarlet woman (Rev. 17), the "faithfull man" upon a white horse (Rev. 19), and the heavenly city (Rev.
21) are richly suggestive as a pictorial context for the Legend of
Holiness.[17] The echo of the *Aeneid* in the opening lines of *The Faerie
Queene* recasts Spenser's career as an emulation of the Virgilian *cur-
sus* and hints that we are not to enter upon a work like Virgil's epic,
prized in the Renaissance especially for its depiction of Dido's

frescoes at the beginning and Aeneas's shield in Book 8.[18] In the muse's charge to Spenser to "blazon broad" his "song"—as if to give voice to "praises" that have "slept in silence long" by awakening them through the heraldry of a new poetic shield—the Proem also announces the ambition to enliven the image in the word for which Spenser's earlier performances "in lowly shepherd's weeds" had been the rehearsal.

This, however, is Spenser's "sacred muse." In her service the knight must carry, not the speaking picture of Aeneas's shield prophesying the spectacle of worldly dominion, but (as Spenser tells Raleigh) "the armour of a Christian man specified by Saint Paul" in Ephesians 6:10–22.[19] Which is to say the "shield of faith" (Eph. 6:16) and the "sword of the Spirit, which is the word of God" (Eph. 6:17). Hefting the shield that Virgil had, so to speak, laid down at the end of his poem, Spenser introduces the "siluer shielde" of the Red Crosse Knight at the very beginning of his own (1.1.1–2)—but in such a way, given the merest glimpse of "siluer" and the momentary but disappointed expectation that this shield will imitate the classical ekphrasis, as to suggest a deliberate refusal to describe the object. We hear only that "old dints of deepe wounds did remaine" in it, and that it was "scor'd" with a cross. Here Spenser clearly sets himself apart from those who would object to any representation of the cross as idolatrous. As a commemoration rather than an image of Christ, this cross, like the one displayed on the knight's breast as the "deare remembrance of his dying Lord," points back to the enduring word of salvation symbolized on the cross by the piercing of its visible incarnation. The Christ remembered here is both image and word, as Van der Noot makes clear in his gloss on Revelation 19:13:

> *And his name was called the word of God.* Christ Jesu the sonne of god, is that eternall and euerlasting word of God, which was from the beginning by God, by whom also heauen and earth are made, and all that in them is, the verye Image of his substance in whom the father is represented, wherby also we vnderstand and know the wil of the father, for the word of God is a true guid of conscience. The word was made flesh: that is, became mā for our sakes, sauing, justifying, and glorifying all those that beleeue on him.[20]

But a Reformation understanding of the Logos would emphasize, as Van der Noot does here by the order of his exposition, that for Christians the "Image" proceeds contingently out of the "eter-nall and euerlasting word" as an accommodation only, "for our sakes." The word "is"; the image is "made" as its representation. Visible "flesh" is a fiction and can serve only to adumbrate the maker whom—such is the nature of accommodations in Protestant thought—it conceals more than reveals. The meaning of the cross for us is not the portrait of Christ but his passion; the word of the Gospel and not any visible image of it is, in Calvin's phrase, "the mirror in which faith beholds God." [21]

In this context, that Spenser's shield of faith is "scor'd" means not simply that it is painted (with an image of the cross), as the word is commonly glossed, but, more suggestively, incised with a sharp in-strument as in a woodcut or metal engraving, crisscrossed by sword cuts, scratched out, or even scourged, marked by the cuts of a lash (OED). In its "scor'd" design no less than in its "dints" and "wounds" the shield becomes significant only in the damage it has sustained. Thus "scor'd," it is purified in a process similar to Blake's "infernal method" of etching, where meaning is achieved "by corrosives"— by a harsh subtraction of material which is nevertheless "salutary and medicinal, melting apparent surfaces away, and displaying the infinite which was hid." [22] This sense of the shield as an antiartifact is heightened by the comparison with Arthur's shield, despite the difference between Red Crosse's battered armor and the "Diamond perfect pure and cleene" (1.7.33) that blazes in Arthur's hand. For the sight of Arthur's shield, itself faceless, not only causes "all that was not such, as seemd in sight" to "fade, and suddeine fall." It is also capable of wreaking a kind of grinding destruction *ad nihilum*, felt in the rhythm of Spenser's verse, of "Men into stones . . . / And stones to dust, and dust to nought at all" (1.7.35). In this it goes beyond its literary predecessors in Ovid's Perseus and in Ariosto to become the instrument of the image-breaker, and so it will later serve Arthur to dismay the beast guarding the "idole" in Geryoneo's church (5.11.19–26). These deeper implications wipe away any sense of a pleasingly decorated surface that might otherwise have been contained in the prospect of a painted shield, and they recast the shield as a symbol of spiritual militancy rather than an objet d'art. Spenser's defacement of the Virgilian shield teaches in brief the lesson of iconoclasm—that the only way to represent our dying Lord is by the imageless reminder of his inward suffering as a true guide of conscience.

This tiny confrontation with the classical ekphrasis at the opening of Spenser's poem restates the typical dilemma of the Reformation poet, a dilemma all the more urgent, for Spenser, as the pleasures of the eye are the more seductive. It compresses a pattern that is played out at greater length, and perhaps without the author's being fully aware of it, in Van der Noot's *Theatre*: the book moves from the introductory "grauen" visions, through a commentary drawn out of these visions which pauses again and again to attack the idolatrous "grauen Images" of the Roman church in terms strong enough to implicate all devotional imagery, to a conclusion which calls upon us to don the Pauline armor of God's word as the only protection against an inconstant and transitory world. The effect of this final emphasis, as of Spenser's treatment of the shield, is to redefine the text's own initial appeal to the eye (given there, on the authority of Horace, as a means of teaching "pleasantly and well")[23] as a species of vanity, its images now understood as part of a lively but deceptive world that must be rejected on the word of a higher authority than Horace: "Earthy & transitorie things are like vnto a cloude painted on a wall, whiche seemeth to be some thing, where as it is nothyng."[24]

Van der Noot's four woodcuts from Revelation could, it is true, claim their own special sanction. Barring representations of the Trinity, the Virgin, the saints, and other sacred subjects "devysed," as it is stipulated in the Edwardian Injunctions of 1547, "by mannes phantasies," most reformers would not on principle prohibit illustrations that were faithful, so to speak, to the word of Scripture. What more fitting subject for the artist, therefore, than the one book of the Bible in which the word is itself openly presented as a vision? Yet it is symptomatic of Van der Noot's logocentrism that he "interprets St. John's esoteric, visionary experience as an allegory of the simple act of reading (or hearing) Scripture."[25] With the exception of the final, transcendent vision of the heavenly city, the woodcuts show scenes of horror—the "sauage beast" from the sea, the scarlet woman "fierce and fell" delighting in the "bloud of martyrs," the impious kings of the earth "Ioinyng their force to slea the faithfull man." From these images we should in good faith recoil, since to be "drawn into" them is—as the kneeling figures in the plates themselves do, gazing reverently at the beast and the woman (fig. 6)—to "adore / The beast in setting of hir image up."[26] The imagery from Revelation only emphasizes the vigilance required of the Christian in recognizing, as the strategy of Bale's commentary teaches, the image of the false church by the word of the true.

D.iiij.

Figure 6. *A Theatre for Voluptuous Worldlings* (1569), sig. D4

The apocalyptic violence of these last four plates heightens the same motifs of crumbling, fire, desiccation, and general ruin that appear in the illustrations to the preceding poems by Petrarch and Du Bellay. There we see the "fresh and lusty Laurell tree" struck down "When sodaine flash of heauens fire outbrast," a Roman temple thrown "downe . . . to the lowest stone" by a "sodein earthquake," a triumphal arch "With sodaine falling broken all to dust" (fig. 7). It is as if such images are admissible because they envision their own collapse. In these visions of vanity brought low, not even a fanciful obelisk decorated with hieroglyphs in the style of the *Hypnerotomachia*—to the devotees of pagan mysteries the very image of ancient wisdom preserved in an enduring pictorial form— can survive intact: "A sodaine tempest from the heauen, I saw, / With flushe stroke downe this noble monument" (fig. 8).[27]

68

Figure 7. *A Theatre for Voluptuous Worldlings* (1569), sig. C3

Spenser will summon these sudden forces again, and with even greater speed and violence, when the "Pittifull spectacle" of Amavia's suffering at the beginning of Book 2 (2.1.40) is avenged by Guyon's "rigour pittilesse" at the end, in the destruction of the spectacular Bower of Bliss. The richly duplicitous image of Acrasia's realm, built up over an entire canto and, like Acrasia's bare breast at its center, the "readie spoyle / Of hungry eies" (2.12.78), will shatter in nine lines under the hammer blows of Spenser's verbs:

> But all those pleasant bowres and Pallace braue,
> *Guyon* broke downe, with rigour pittiless;
> Ne ought their goodly workmanship might saue
> Them from the tempest of his wrathfulnesse,
> But that their blisse he turn'd to balefulnesse:
> Their groues he feld, their gardins did deface,

69

Figure 8. *A Theatre for Voluptuous Worldlings* (1569), sig. C2

Their arbers spoyle, their Cabinets suppresse,
Their banket houses burne, their buildings race,
And of the fairest late, now made the fowlest place.

(2.12.83)

Just as Hezekiah "brake the images and cut down the groves" of the
idolators in Judah (2 Kings 18:4), Guyon "broke downe . . . feld . . .
did deface . . . spoyle . . . suppresse . . . burne . . . race": the zeal,
indeed, the near exhilaration and sense of explosive release in this
famous passage replaces the leisurely pleasures of the eye with the
more furious pleasures of iconoclasm. Harry Berger calls it a "Puritan frenzy."[28]

The phrase is apt despite the fact that Spenser's theme is the classical virtue of temperance, and that even this very intemperate
Bower does not at first seem to display the overt enticements of an

idolatrous artwork. For so cunning is its lure to "sense" and "fantasie" (2.12.42) that "One would haue thought . . . nature had for wantonesse ensude / Art" (2.12.59). The presiding spirit, Genius, is like Archimago a "foe of life" who "secretly doth vs procure to fall, / Through guilefull semblaunts, which he makes vs see" (2.12.48). In this realm the flowers are "painted" (2.12.58) and the fountain that seems to merge in Spenser's description of it with its 'natural' setting is "ouerwrought" with "curious imageree" (2.12.60). Behind all this lies the fashionable guile "which all faire workes doth most aggrace," of art concealing art: "The art, which all that wrought, appeared in no place" (2.12.58). To the "sober eye" (2.12.18) inspecting such a scene, the delightful deceptions recommended in Italian theory as the means to "grace" the work of art might well seem as duplicitous as the concealed wires inside the abominable Rood of Grace.[29] Indeed, as Stephen Greenblatt notes, the Bower has about it "the taint of a graven image": Spenser's own response "in the face of a deep anxiety about the impure claims of art" is to purify his writing by making the "createdness" of *The Faerie Queene* explicit.[30] The archaic language, the sound effects, the obvious intrusions and digressions—all this conspicuous machinery of authorship in effect defaces the text to expose the wires. Like the rude mechanical playing the lion in Peter Quince's production of "Pyramus and Thisby," Spenser himself "must speak through, saying thus, or to the same defect," "No! I am no such thing; I am a man as other men are" (*MND* 3.1.38–44).

It is just this salutary "defect" of art that the Bower conceals in an aura of quasi-Catholic ritual until those it attracts are themselves unmanned. At its entrance, Genius holds a staff in his hand "for more formalitee" (2.12.48), and he offers Guyon wine from a bowl set by his side "as if it had to him bene sacrifide" (2.12.49). At its heart, Verdant lies with his head in Acrasia's lap—a detail that has struck more than one reader as an "uncanny parody of the Pietà."[31] The point of these associations is not that the Bower is an allegory of the perils of idolatry, but that the roots of idolatrous veneration are sunk deep in the Bower's appeal to venereal man. On the authority of this very "similitude" drawn in the Elizabethan *Homilies* of 1563, Christians had long been instructed from the pulpit that the "spirituall wickednesses of an Idols inticing" are "like the flatteries of a wanton harlot"—for "Doeth not the worde of GOD . . . call a gylte or painted Idole or Image, a strumpet with a painted face?" Against the force of such enticement, the homilist insists, "ye shall in vaine preach and teach"—as the Palmer does when he rebukes Guyon's "wandring eyes" (2.12.69)—for many will nonetheless fall headlong into idolatry by the "inclinations of their owne corrupt nature."[32] At the sight of the "wanton Maidens" bathing in the fountain, Guyon's "sparkling face" had betrayed the "secret signes of kindled lust" (2.12.68). Ironically, as they point toward the oblivion and Circean bestiality that awaits Acrasia's victims—even when they are restored by Guyon they retain their "vnmanly looke" (2.12.86)—these "signes" in the face presage the effacement of all human significance. At the center of Acrasia's "painted" world, Guyon must not simply face the temptation of the Bower but "deface" it (2.12.83).

The implications of the scene for Spenser's pictorialism are deepened insofar as this confrontation between Guyon and the enchantress is also a confrontation between Spenser and his sources. Moving again in Virgil's shadow, Spenser had begun the description of the Bower (2.12.44) with the "piteous spectacle" of Jason and Medea decorating its ivory gate. Carved in the material of false dreams, this had been the image of woman's "mighty charms" which Guyon, like Aeneas, would have to break, and, as an "admirable" piece of ekphrasis at the threshold of the action, a reminiscence of Dido's frescoes. Now at the end of the canto, and just before Guyon's explosion, there is the suggestion of yet another revision of Aeneas's shield. For, as if to hint that in a realm where *pictura* is the medium of treachery the framed picture of the classical shield must fail as a defense, Guyon uses no shield at all. Indeed, we are shown the "braue shield" of Acrasia's captive, Verdant, hanging useless in a tree. It is a shield "full of old moniments" but "fowly ra'st, that none the signes might see" (2.12.80). In the face of Acrasia's more powerfully malignant art its potency to signify is wiped away, just as the "nobilitie" of the narcotized Verdant—the emblem of Guyon as he might have been had he yielded to the concupiscence of the eye—is "deface[d]" (2.12.79). In a sense Guyon's choice is to become an inert (and, like some eroded figure in an antique frieze, an ironically insignificant) motif in Acrasia's composition, or to unlease a "tempest" that will crack the frame and spill its contents back into the flow of time. Against such a threat, the hero must forgo the nobility of epic combat—just as the poet at the end must refuse the challenge of emulating the pictorial triumphs of his predecessors—for a style at once more crude and more effective: he must become a defacer of images.

The psychology of iconoclasm implied here gives full play to the mixed feelings of joy and rage as they "well/Out" like the streams of the fountain Guyon destroys. A. C. Hamilton has noted how Guyon's successful passage requires him to withstand the "guilefull semblaunts" (2.12.48) tempting him at every turn to caress the delights of the Bower with his gaze.[33] The erotic "courage" aroused in Guyon at the fountain by the sight of the naked damsels (2.12.68) but rebuked by the Palmer returns in the masculine "rigour" of the knight's final assault on the Bower. One might see the damsels' wrestling (2.12.63) as itself the counterpart of the knight's inner *agon* between the image of desire and the words of temperate counsel—an analogy strengthened by the interpretation of the name "gyon" in the *Legenda Aurea* life of St. George, "that [it] is an holy wrasteler." Hamilton, invoking *The Birth of Tragedy*, goes on to underscore the "Dionysian happiness" of the moment, which "reaches its zenith" in "the annihilation of the most beautiful phenomena in the world of appearances."[34]

Because Acrasia's torpid realm is envisioned as a kind of sleep—its languorous scenes a kind of dreamscape through which Guyon glides, and from which he wakes the poem—the concept of repression particularly deepens our sense of the obscure connections between the manifest content of Guyon's adventure and its latent, inner meaning. The violent tempest of Guyon's wrath, collapsing the suspended *otium* of the Bower, churns somehow out of the measured temperance he represents. Although for the temperate man there is a time for anger as well as for restraint, the disturbing gap between the virtue and its expression makes itself felt, not least in the lingering regret that marks the closing stanzas of the canto as the conquered Acrasia and her liberated captive are led away, "both sorrowfull and sad" (2.12.84). For Guyon's destructiveness appears as the displacement of an inadmissable wish to violate the Bower in another sense, his power tapped indirectly from that of the vision he obliterates.

On this point Greenblatt's analysis is acute in that it attends both to the threat to "self-fashioning" represented by Acrasia's power and to the political as well as the psychological dimensions of that power. Whether in the psyche, in Ireland, or in the New World, civility is achieved—as, in this canto, Spenser shows us long before Freud—"only through sexual renunciation and the constant exercise of power." The self establishes its "difference," the firm boundary of its own identity, by imposing and indeed celebrating its control over that which attracts it and (as in the case of the Anglo-Irish) threatens it with absorption. For Greenblatt the underlying paradox is that while power controls excess, power is itself "invented by excess": were Acrasia not to exist as a constant threat, "the power Guyon embodies would also cease to exist."[35] In one sense, this is a truism. The exercise of pitiless rigor by English colonialists in Ireland requires a supply of Irish to be colonized, just as the iconoclast needs images to break. Yet as Spenser's episode drives below the surface of the image debate it discloses a tangle of desire and repudiation barely visible in the polemical literature. It is no longer possible to rest on the reassuring distinction between the vulgar many prone to idolatry and the instructed few immune to its lure, or on the belief that the surge of desire directed to the image can be safely channeled through it to its spiritual archetype. The most rigorous opponent of the image would have to admit its power not only over those for whose sake he would abolish it, but over himself; and he would have to acknowledge that the force wielded to "suppresse" it cannot be detached from the wanton force generated by the image in him.

Indeed in its violence Guyon's attack verges upon all the monstrous predations in the poem, from the fury of Error in Book 1 to the assaults of the Blatant Beast in Book 6. The affiliation is discomforting, but it enables us to see in our hero the tie between "destructive energy" and "reformation" that Giamatti finds in Spenser's manifold fascination for the bestial: "In a sinister way, the poem is sustained by the destructive energy contained and released through all these monsters. The poet's power of formation and reformation, in an aesthetic and moral sense, seems to draw strength from what the poem abhors, the images and sources of deformation."[36] The paradox is echoed in a darkly Georgic episode of comparable mayhem in Book 5 where Talus, wielding an iron flail that is ambiguously a weapon and an agricultural implement, "battred" his enemies "without remorse": the dead "lay scattred ouer all the land," but somehow miraculously rejuvenated by the force of Spenser's simile, "As thicke as doth the seede after the sowers hand" (5.12.7) The local politics behind the allegory—that the Irish must be killed for Ireland to live—may be repellent, but it is akin to a more fundamental iconoclastic poetics that sees the possibility of renewal through destruction while it recognizes the price of the harvest by portraying Talus as even fiercer than his victims. Guyon's temperate iconoclasm is thus bound, like Acrasia in her "chaines of adamant" (2.12.82), to the most intemperate impulse to penetrate a world of pure indulgence—a yoking of opposites not to be explained away by saying that Guyon merely resists temptation or observes a golden mean. The episode points rather to a dark labyrinth at the heart of a conventional idea like temperance, a labyrinth into which the reader is often led in *The Faerie Queene* as Spenser drives toward meaning hidden from the eye.

This radical inwardness of Spenser's poem, countering its tendency to display, has often been remarked. It involves a "penetrating ever more deeply until we achieve some vision of perfection at the centre," and an increasing awareness—as the successive books of the poem grow shorter and the final rampage of the Blatant Beast (both out of, and in a sense against, the poem) draws nearer—that not even the "goodly workmanship" of images like that of the Bower of Bliss can protect Spenser from the charge of having produced a vast pageant of "painted forgery" (2.Proem.1).[37] With something of the force of a retraction, the last book tells us that "vertues seat is deepe within the mynd, / And not in outward shows, but inward thoughts defynd" (6.Proem.5). The problematic thought beneath Guyon's outward show, defined in part by his subterranean kinship with the poem's scattered family of beasts, suggests how *The Faerie Queene* grows centripetally, twining its various shows into a root sunk too deep for *pictura* to represent in its superficial analogy with *poesis*. Indeed, with Una as its inaugural symbol and its goal, the poem's redeeming search for its own integrity would issue, at some theoretical limit or vanishing point, in the collapse of all its intricate and proliferating workmanship into one dense word under the veil of its multiform plastic imagination.

The implication of a paradoxical alliance between the poet and his beasts is writ large in the relationship between the narrator of the poem and Archimago. Spenser's satanic illusionist, the forger of "true-seeming lyes" (1.1.38), is the internal competitor with the voice of the poet for authorial control of *The Faerie Queene*. This "cunning Architect of cancred guile" (2.1.1) not only schemes to seize the action for himself by snaring Spenser's heroes, he does so through the creation of a false "Una" and a false "Red Crosse," by an art that exactly replicates Spenser's own. It is as if a false "*Faerie Queene*" were being written inside the "true" one—a contained counterpoem on which Spenser must depend to establish the truth of the container. But Archimago cannot be easily contained, for as we learn when we are told of his escape from prison at the beginning of Book 2, "out of caytiues hands / Himselfe he frees by secret meanes vnseene" (2.1.1). The authority of the poem thus hangs on a precarious ability to assert its difference from the antagonist it projects but cannot subdue, the opponent whose arts seem at moments to be indistinguishable from Spenser's. It amounts to an artful strategy of taking and yet disclaiming responsibility for a large share of the poet's art—everything in the poem generated by the "pictorial" Spenser of tradition—by ascribing it to the machinations of an other, a false "Spenser" who must be constantly held at bay.

In the poem's fictive account of its own production, *The Faerie Queene* unfolds (like the Reformation program from the primitive church) from the "antique rolles" of Faerie land laid open for the poet in the first Proem (1.Proem.2). His is the medium of "words and sound" (2.10.1), not of the "painted forgery" rejected in the Proem to Book 2 (2.Proem.1)—the forging and framing that mark the devices of the "Arch-imager" and the hypocrisy of Catholic misdevotion he embodies. But the sharp distinction cannot be maintained, and the poem in fact seems compelled to notice the connections between the two. If the poet prays to his epic muse to "sharpen my dull tong" as the fit instrument of his holy writing (1.Proem.2), Archimago can also "file his tongue as smooth as glas" to tell of "Saintes and Popes" (1.1.35). If the poet hopes that the "happy land of Faery," suspected of being a mere "forgery," might actually be found somewhere in the "great Regions" of the New World (2.Proem.1, 2), a moment later Archimago is reported to have discovered Duessa, the material of his own forgery, "Where she did wander in waste wildernesse" (2.1.22). Archimago's confederate Despayre tries to drive Red Crosse to suicide by showing him the torments of the damned "painted in a table plain" (1.9.49). Una breaks the grip of the image by reminding the knight that "Where iustice growes, there growes eke greater grace" which "that accursed hand-writing doth deface" (1.19.53), but Spenser's attempt to deface the handwriting "painted" in his text is no less an act of self-mutilation. Archimago, we learn, had been imprisoned for "falsed letters" (2.1.1). His escape is announced at the beginning of Book 2, as if his release were necessary for the book itself to open: it symbolizes both the poet's vindication of the charge of literary falsehood (Archimago was imprisoned for the crime, and it is he who now fares forth to "Worken mischiefe") and the continuing power of a falsehood from which the poem cannot be set free.

With Book 2, Archimago begins to fade from sight as a character in the poem. There are good reasons for his disappearance—his specific role as the hypocrite loses much of its force outside the Legende of Holinesse—but one surely is that Spenser has already begun to work out subtler strategies for mastering his own Archimagean designs. The Proem to Book 3, although it acknowledges that the poet can "marre" his subject just as the painter can "taint" it "with his error," still insists that the wit of the poet "passeth Painter farre" (3.Proem.2). However conventional the declaration, it seems to reflect directly on the competition in the earlier books. To have passed Archimago does not mean that he has been vanquished, despite the ruining of his most lavish creation, the Bower of Bliss, at the end of Book 2, but it does mean that by this point in the poem, Spenser has found ways of using his own arts against him:

> It was a chosen plot of fertile land
> Emongst wide waues set, like a litle nest,
> As if it had by Natures cunning hand
> Bene choisely picked out from all the rest,
> And laid forth for ensample of the best:
> No daintie flowre or herbe, that growes on ground,
> No arboret with painted blossomes drest,
> And smelling sweet, but there it might be found
> To bud out faire, and her sweet smels throw all around.
>
> No tree, whose braunches did not brauely spring;
> No braunch, whereon a fine bird did not sit:
> No bird, but did her shrill notes sweetly sing;
> No song but did containe a louely dit:
> Trees, braunches, birds, and songs were framed fit,
> For to allure fraile mind to carelesse ease.
> Carelesse the man soone woxe, and his weake wit
> Was ouercome of thing, that did him please;
> So pleased, did his wrathfull purpose faire appease.

In this description of Phaedria's island (2.6.12–13), flowers, trees, branches, and birds have all been carefully "framed" by a cunning hand to "allure" the "fraile mind" to idleness. In two ways made clear by the larger context of the poem, this seductive island in the "*Idle lake*" (2.6.10) floats in the lake of idolatry. Like the satyrs in Book 1 who are "content to please their feeble eyes" on Una's outward beauty and so, refusing to hear her efforts to "teach them truth," make even her "th'Image of Idolatryes" (1.6.19), Cymochles is lured by the apparent charms of what he is given to see. And the threat is no less grave for him than it will be in Book 6 for Serena, whose "liking led / Her wauering lust after her wandring sight" (6.3.23) into the jaws of the Blatant Beast. For Spenser, furthermore, the connection between "Idle" and Idol is no mere coincidence. The idolater captivated by the image "sits down" with the wanton harlot. He is deluded into exchanging a perilous "ease" for the no less perilous but more fruitful effort required of the true Christian. Spenser's world, as we have recently been reminded by Jonathan Goldberg, is a world of "endlesse worke"—demanding of the reader as well as of the characters in the poem the kind of sustained and vigilant commitment to active interpretation that Cymochles is pleased to put out of mind.[38]

As these stanzas present them, the attractions of the island are all twined together by repeated verbal strands and by alliteration ("sweetly sing; / No song"), artfully woven like the "litle nest" of the island itself that contains them all. What is offered to Cymochles, the man "soone . . . ouercome," is a deceptive image of plenitude, a full "nest" in which he is invited to take his "carelesse ease": no tree without its flourishing branch, no branch without its bird, no bird but full of song, no song "but did contain a louely dit." As Spenser had earlier said, however, "Trust me": "Who euer doth to temperaunce apply / His stedfast life, and all his actions frame" (2.5.1)— including the action of reading—will not have been so careless as to forget what the poet had announced before the description began, that this was "an Island, waste and voyd" (2.6.11). Nor will the reader have forgotten the perceptual error in Book 1 that left the Red Crosse Knight "More busying his quicke eyes" on Fidessa's face "Then his dull eares" on the words that would have given her away as Duessa (1.2.26). The "framed" description is itself contained within a rhetorical and visual frame constructed on the word "No." Indeed a negative charge runs so powerfully through these stanzas ("No braunch . . . No bird . . . No song") that Spenser's language virtually denies the existence of anything at all on this "chosen plot" except the delusions of the plot chosen by Phaedria. With the same stroke by which the island's landscape is "painted" on the page as a snare to the "weake wit," it is struck down by the stronger wit of the poet. The Archimagean impulse is momentarily indulged, only to be (momentarily) restrained, imprisoned behind a barricade of No's. The cunning reader who shuts his eyes to what Phaedria "shew'd" Cymochles will understand that here, as in the chamber of the heart in Alma's house, there is "nothing pourtrahed, nor wrought / Not wrought, not pourtrahed, but easie to be thought" (2.9.33).

These observations permit us to return to the issue of Spenser's "pictorialism" with a fuller appreciation of the difficulties it poses.

Paul Alpers, for example, finds that passages frequently cited *in bono* or *in malo* for their "pictorial effects"—the presentation of Busyrane's tapestries (3.11.28), or of Calidore's vision of the Graces (6.10.11–12)—are not really descriptive at all in the sense of rendering visual experience. Rather they employ what Alpers terms the "rhetorical use of pictorial diction" to convey the moral and "psychological impact" of what is seen. Words, therefore, do not strive for the optical illusionism of the sister art. Instead they enlist (and sometimes subvert) the expectation of a descriptive technique toward the end of persuasion: the "gold and silke" in Busyrane's "goodly arras" do not figure as a poetic replication of the tapestry, but, in their being "Woven . . . so close and nere / That the rich metal lurked prively," as a rhetorical strategy designed to evoke the "sinister moral atmosphere of Busyrane's palace."[39] The tapestry is no sooner held up to our inspection than it is pierced by an inward thought that rends the visual object.

Similarly, John Bender insists upon the distinction between descriptive "pictures" offered for their own sake and, as it were, without tampering, and Spenser's actual practice of thrusting "the specifically visual impact of his materials upon us."[40] By the techniques that Bender calls "focusing," "framing," and "scanning," Spenser imitates the "process of visualization" and not the thing visualized or the "registration of visible things on the retina."[41] So much might be said on Lessing's authority of any literary text insofar as the most determined attempt to describe a visual object must yield, at the same time and perhaps even more clearly, a record of how the object is seen. But the implications of Bender's work point to a greater unease in Spenser with the poet's "tendency to linger over the embroidery of senuous experience."[42] Bender proposes that as an artist more "Gothic" than "Renaissance" (as these styles are distinguished by Dagobert Frey), Spenser leads us to perceive space "not as a continuum but as a series of individual subjective experiences," so that even if he is capable of suggesting a unified perspectival vista, his poem is rather characterized by its "discontinuous and fragmented anatomizing" of the visual field.[43] An engagement with the world as vivid panorama is countered by the survival, or the revival, of an older "pictorial" style, now made to reflect the uncertain glance of the spectator. It is a style that not only seems to distance that world from us in time and space, but to splinter it.

This estrangement holds in a special sense from the vantage of Spenser's heroes, who "live in a world," as C. S. Lewis remarks, "compact of wonders, beauties, and terrors which are mostly quite unintelligible to them."[44] Calidore stands "astonished" by his vision, caught between his marvel at the dancing maidens and the suspicion that his "eyes mote haue deluded beene," until at his approach the whole scene vanishes like a mystery before the gaze of the uninitiated (6.10.17). Perhaps just as disturbing to the reader, the center of the vision is itself unseeable: the damsel placed "in the middest" of the "Three other Ladies" dancing around her cannot at the same time be "seen" in the terms of Spenser's simile "as a precious gemme, / Amidst a ring" (6.10.12).[45] The more notorious instance is the opening of Book 1, where the knight "pricking on the plaine" (1.1), Una riding "beside" him on an ass (1.4), and her dwarf lagging far behind (1.6) are all said to "passe" together (1.8) over a period of time in some manner apparently impossible to visualize. Spenser may just be careless of spatial consistency, even willing to violate it because he works on an entirely allegorical "plain" on which Zeal spurs ahead of Truth even though the two are companionable ideas.[46] Or he may offer us here, as Joseph Dallet believes, yet another intentionally archaic, Gothic composition splicing together in tapestry fashion a sequence of impressions no less pictorial for failing to be spatially homogeneous.[47] In either case meaning is secured through a disruption of the poem's visual domain, as the "scoring" force of an otherwise heightened pictorial style mars its own surface.

Such differences in approach between Spenser's iconographical critics and the defenders, like Alpers and Gottfried, of a poetry that subdues the eye to the ear would seem to reflect not simply the capaciousness of The Faerie Queene, but more precisely the agonistic mode of its pictorialism: the urge to depict and the complementary urge to deface are both necessary for the game to go on, just as the personified struggle between split impulses in the mind of the hero is necessary to the game of Spenser's allegory. Depending on the passage that falls open, one can find in Spenser a militant reformer on the question of images or a lover of decoration and display willing to employ more traditional discriminations between their use and abuse.[48] Arthur's devastation of Geryoneo's "Church" (5.11.19–33), with its golden "Idol" framed of the Giant's "owne vaine fancies," its "Beast" under the "Altar," and its hideous sacrifices and tortures, is set against a disturbingly similar act of destruction in Book 6. There the Blatant Beast, "regarding nought religion," despoils a monastery, casting "th' Images, for all their goodly hew, / . . . to ground" (6.12.24–25). The laudable iconoclasm in Book 5—authored presumably by a Puritan Spenser—is cast in doubt retrospectively in

Book 6 by the Beast's rampage through what is now acknowledged, despite the exposure of its "filth and ordure," to be a "sacred Church." At the end of Book 6 the Beast, once more rending "without regard of person or of time," poses an identical threat to what Angus Fletcher would see, through the archetype of the Temple, as the sacred precinct of the poem itself: "Ne may this homely verse, or many meanest, / Hope to escape his venomous despite" (6.12.40–41). The idolatrous "vain fancies" of Geryoneo's creation were purged from the poem by the iconoclasm of its hero; now the poem envisions itself, with more urgency than in the usual *envoi*, as not free from "blameful blot," and foresees its own destruction in kind. It is as if the work has not merely chronicled but set free some force ultimately beyond its control—a beast whose iconoclastic "despite" against the text that gave him birth destroys any sense of closure, any final framing of a "homely" structure, intended by its (and his) author.

Carol Kaske cites the juxtaposition of these two episodes— Geryoneo's church in Book 5 set against the monastery in Book 6— as a large-scale example of the rhetorical device called *epanothorsis* or *correctio*. Appearing frequently in Spenser's style, this trope mimics the "jerkiness and self-correction of thought," as when the poet observes that Acrasia "was arrayd, or rather disarayd, / All in a vele of silke" (2.12.77). Kaske's argument that, in *The Faerie Queene*, *correctio* "becomes a structuring principle, with canto correcting canto and book correcting book" offers a term that aptly glosses the agonism of the pictorial poet writing in the climate of the Reformation—a term with a special imaginative force in a poem so full of the energy of marring, effacing, and scoring.[49] The Bower of Bliss in Book 2 is corrected by the Garden of Adonis in Book 3, with its "pleasant arbour" made "not by art" like Phaedria's little nest but by the "knitting" of nature herself (3.6.44). The house of Pride in Book 1—its foundation crumbling and its brightness merely "golden foile"—is a speaking picture "painted cunningly" over two stanzas, but "nothing strong, nor thick" (1.4.4–5). It is corrected at the end of the same book by the house of Holiness, which is not described at all. Here Speranza's "stedfast eyes" are bent "euer vp to heauen" (1.10.14), the "earthly eyen" of Contemplation are "blunt and bad" (1.10.47), and guided by him, the Red Crosse Knight is granted a transcendent vision of the New Jerusalem "that earthly tong / Cannot describe" (1.10.55). In one sense, a larger irony attaches to these mutually correcting pairs: the strategy deployed (among other purposes) for balancing pictorial excess against pictorial effacement itself depends, as Patrick Grant has shown, on the "tableaux-like structures" of *effectus passionis* iconography, in which the image of a world in thrall to sin on one side of the composition is contrasted with an image showing the "effects of the passion" on the other.[50]

This is the poem engaged in a process of continual self-correction, presenting itself as arrayed, or rather disarrayed, in visual finery. An artistic self divided, Spenser may thus be said to internalize and, if uneasily, to accommodate the adversary postures of the age. A Christian seeking the right path up the cragged hill of truth (as Donne imagines him in "Satyre III") "about must, and about must goe." He is met at every turn by the rival claims of "true" churches; by Luther's *Bondage of the Will* to its own idolatry and Erasmus's *Freedom of the Will* as an image, and an imager, of the divine; or, in the controversy most pressing for Spenser's technique, by the most radical whitewashing and image-breaking at the one extreme and the Tridentine reaffirmation of a sacred pictorialism on the other. At one moment in the "Fowre Hymnes" the poet so confronted gathers the "plumes of perfect speculation" and urges his "high flying mynd" to "Mount vp aloft through heauenly contemplation." At the next—just as Sidney does when he swerves from glorying in the poet's visionary power to reminding us of our "degenerate soules, made worse by theyr clayey lodgings"—Spenser corrects himself in the sternest Calvinist tone:

> Humbled with feare and awfull reuerence,
> Before the footestoole of his Maiestie,
> Throw thy selfe downe with trembling innocence,
> Ne dare look vp with corruptible eye
> On the dred face of that great Deity. . . .[52]

So too in *The Faerie Queene*, as in Donne's Holy Sonnet, "contraryes meet in one."

In their widest reach the antagonists joined by the *correctio* of Spenser's pictorialism can be variously described. Fletcher, we have noted, poses the poem as "temple" against the poem as "labyrinth"—the former an image of architectural solidity where the "rooms" of the individual stanzas are the "templar monuments of which the whole templar vision is made," the latter an image of "terror and panic" where the vision of the poem and its enclosures as a sacred space is countered (indeed, profanely violated) by the archetype of darkened wandering.[52] We have also noted the Dionysiac frenzy of Guyon's iconoclasm, imageless and insistently rhythmic, set loose against the Apollonian plastic form of the Bower. At their collision an art of the "flood tide," in Nietzsche's phrase, runs up against rival art committed to inscribing "boundary lines." In the distinction Nietzsche draws out of Schopenhauer, we attend the contest between the "pure contemplation of images" and the blind but more purposefully assertive urges of the "will."[53] Participants, as Nietzsche sees them, in the "discordant concord" of creativity, these two arts also correspond in Spenser's poetic to the joint rule of Pan and Proteus—in Nohrnberg's criticism, the two presiding deities of *The Faerie Queene*. Pan stands behind the "formal coherence" of the poem, its "consecution of episodes" and its comprehensiveness, while Proteus sponsors its "generativity," its vast "elemental" shapelessness.[54] In all of these formulations the flow of the creative imagination plays against the architectonic structures that, moment by moment, it both engenders and threatens—building up an image only to submerge it again into process by the very momentum that brought it into being. At the most general level such terms define a basic condition of any narrative art. In Spenser, however, there is a greater potential for discord between two aspects of the poet's art more concordantly joined in other writers—in Virgil, for example, or in Ariosto—and a correspondingly greater and more self-conscious need to hold the two together. In this *The Faerie Queene* minutely inspects its own procedures. The poetic dilemmas so conspicuous in the work are formed around the theological dilemma of the poet as a speaker of the word confronting and (in both the moral and the authorial sense) correcting the iconic power of his own language.

4

Quarles's Emblematic Agon: "Break That Fond Glasse"

Given its current reputation, we might be surprised to learn that Francis Quarles's *Emblemes* (London, 1635) came out in three editions during the author's life and, in nearly fifty subsequent editions, long remained among the staple works of piety on English bookshelves from London and Little Gidding to the sugar plantations in Jamaica. According to Horace Walpole, even Milton "had to wait until the world had done admiring Quarles." Although some, like Anthony Wood, dismissed Quarles as an "old puritanical poet," and although that poet was given his place of dishonor in the *Dunciad*, Coleridge believed that "Quarles, Withers, and others have been unkindly under-rated," and that "their want of Taste was from fullness of appetite, their sound Hunger and Thirst after religion."[1] Yet modern critics, reflecting Edward Phillips's view of him as the "darling of our plebeian judgments," have been willing to grant Quarles and his fellow emblem-writers only the distinction of the second-rate. Rosemary Freeman argues that in the mechanical "imposition of meaning upon a predetermined image lies the essential weakness of the emblem writer's method," while Mario Praz concludes that "Quarles's *Emblemes* supplied the wider public with a cheap substitute for that metaphysical wit which authors like George Chapman and John Donne provided for a more refined audience."[2] Not even the recent appearance of the first full-scale treatment of the life and works has sparked anything like a Quarles revival.[3]

As Praz's comments suggest, in the study of seventeenth-century literature we are likely to read Henry Hawkins or George Wither or Quarles, if at all, as a professional duty. We come to them for the raw material of the emblematic imagination so conspicuous in their work, but only to equip ourselves (with the help of the indexes and bibliographies now available to facilitate research in emblematics) to recognize that material in a more finished or subtle form in the major dramatists and lyric poets.[4] Indeed, George Herbert's achievement is measured by his ability to go beyond the merely emblematic, while the stuff of emblems may even be seen to clog the work of other writers. Alan B. Howard has claimed, for example, that the work of the American poet Edward Taylor is unfortunately trapped inside the emblem tradition:

> The emblem tradition—both as a body of conventional analogies and as a habit of mind—allowed [Taylor] to use metaphors drawn from the book of the scriptures and the book of nature without, he thought, leading the reader to delight sinfully in the beauties of his language or in the world of "mere appearances" which it reflected. It allowed him to use those metaphors as transparent counters, valueless in themselves, through which he might see the wonders of God's truth as revealed in Puritan doctrine.

Such "counters" permitted Taylor to pile his verse richly with emblematic images and to manipulate them with the most fervent ingenuity, all the while blinding himself, Howard argues, to the fresh vision of William Bradford or Anne Bradstreet, whose "contemplation of the natural world, perceived in its complexity, richness, and beauty, leads gracefully and inevitably to a consideration of God; then, just as naturally, it leads back into this world and a heightened appreciation of its significance."[5] Taylor attempted instead to strain the sinfulness of the visible world through a filter of emblematic imagery; the result was a failure of vision. Taylor's bookish verse confirms Walter Benjamin's remark that "the Renaissance explores the universe; the Baroque explores libraries." Benjamin's meditation on the ruined, grieving world of the seventeenth-century German *Trauerspiel* reveals its similarity to the mood of Taylor's verse: in each the clutter of emblematic fragments becomes the appropriate furniture of the artist's imagination.[6]

I would like to propose here that we reexamine that perception of failure—the dissatisfaction with the emblem, finally, as mechanical, inadequate, brittle—not in order to argue that we have made a mistake all along in regarding Milton as a better poet than Quarles, but to look closely at our assumptions about success. How well, and under what circumstances, does the emblem "work"? The interest of Quarles's *Emblemes*, as I will argue, lies, at crucial moments, precisely in a certain kind of failure—their failure to accommodate the illustrations to the texts. The energy of the book flows less from the plates or the poems taken separately, or from the harmony of their cooperation, than from the discord of the confrontation between them. That confrontation displays their ultimate success in reconceiving the emblem to enact a new relationship between the word and the image.

We have already seen that for the Renaissance, the emblem is the exemplary genre declaring the close alliance of *pictura* and *poesis*.[7] Juxtaposed on the page as the "body" and "soul" of the emblem, picture and poem were regarded as not merely complementary but indivisible. Its visual potential illuminated by the woodcut or engraving, the text of the sacred emblem especially might be "opened," allowing the reader a Neoplatonic glimpse through the door of language "to the realities themselves, from the temporal realities to the eternal realities, from talk to silence, from discourse to vision."[8] In less ethereal terms, the emblem, as opposed to the more esoteric or "symbolic" *impresa*, was intended to teach and persuade. Emblem design was thus typically regarded as a branch of rhetoric— the *Typus Mundi*, one of Quarles's two main sources, was produced by the College of Rhetoric of the Society of Jesus—and the emblematic device as a metaphor or conceit in visual form. As a rhetorical image that needed to be interpreted, spoken out with the help of the poem and not simply inspected, the picture might be understood to embody a language *in rebus* continuous with the language *in verbis* of the accompanying text.[9]

Quarles himself shrouds his *Emblemes* in the fashionable mysteries of Egyptian picture-writing, instructing the reader beforehand that

> An *Embleme* is but a silent Parable. Let not the tender Eye
> check, to see the allusion of our blessed Saviour figured in
> these Types. In holy Scripture, he is sometimes called a
> Sower; sometimes, a Fisher; sometimes a Physician: And
> why not presented so as well to the eye as to the eare? Be-
> fore the knowledge of letters God was known by *Hiero-
> glyphicks*: And indeed, what are the Heavens, the Earth,
> nay every Creature, but *Hieroglyphicks* and *Emblemes* of his
> Glory?[10]

As a "hieroglyphic" and a "silent parable," the pictorial device served the emblem writer as a *Praetextum*, a "text-before" the adjoining text of the motto or epigram, so that the whole series was intertranslatable. Many emblems, the Jesuit publications especially, appeared in polyglot editions: the *Typus Mundi* appends Latin, French, and German versions of the epigram to each plate. In such a sequence, the engraving stands as yet another version of the conceit, only in a pictorial tongue. Furthermore, as Höltgen notes, Quarles "establishes in Protestant England the leading form of the Baroque devotional emblem" that fuses "the meditative and emblematic traditions":

> Here the icon represents the Ignatian *Compositio loci*, while the explanatory poem stands for the *Analysis*, and the final epigram for the *Colloquium*. All three parts of the emblem have a share in its dual function of representation and interpretation.[11]

On such a model, the three formal parts of the emblem flow together in a single spiritual exercise drawing equally upon the imaginative and vocal powers of the soul.

The close bond between the word and image was forged principally in Italy and, in the case of the devotional emblem, reinforced by the spiritual programs of the Counter-Reformation. Quarles's work, however, acutely reveals the strain placed on that emblem in an English Protestant culture founded on the primacy of the word. That culture was not only peripheral to the great achievements in painting and sculpture on the Continent, but as we have seen, in its recent history actively iconoclastic. The confrontation between the visual and verbal elements in the *Emblemes* was in effect a far more militant, far less playful, version of the *paragone* between the arts that had always been a feature of the *ut pictura* tradition. Whereas a Leonardo might base a defense of painting on the Platonic and Christian ground, endorsed by Augustine, that the sense of sight is the highest of the faculties, a Protestant reader of Augustine would also find ample reason for distrusting the visual arts: the divine medium is the creating Word, and the Christian must beware of the enticements of the eye and the delusions of the visual imagination. That suspicion is all the more deeply rooted in the great devotional poetry of the seventeenth century, with its preference for notations of the dramatic voice and the mind in motion over composed pictorial structures.

This logocentric bias is strong in the religious verses of the English poets. Vasari's idea of God as the primordial painter and architect is alien to Herbert's conception of writing as the challenge to copy the "fair, though bloudie hand" of a divine author ("The Thanksgiving"). Like Donne in the "Anniversary" poems ("I am The Trumpet, at whose voice the people came"), Herbert associates himself as a poet with music and preaching. Where the analogy is with painting ("Jordan II") or with architecture ("Sinnes Round"), Herbert's point is always that his art has been tainted by "lewd intentions." When reassurance comes, it makes itself heard, not seen, in whispers and echoes. Henry Vaughan's obsession with recovering special moments of visual illumination propels him inward on a pilgrimage down the road of memory. The brilliant flashes of regeneration all too seldom granted his "restless Eye" are etched against a foggy, shrouded external world eclipsed in sin. The surprisingly pervasive influence of Ignatian and Salesian meditative procedures in English sacred poetry, first investigated by Martz, may be understood in this context: as the starting point for meditation, the Catholic manuals encouraged the "composition" of an inward "place"—a mental picture which Protestants could safely substitute for the painted devotional images condemned by Calvin and Luther.[12] And yet the more radical side of the iconoclastic controversy makes it plain to the meditator that not even the image inwardly conceived, much less the one engraved externally on the page of an emblem as an aid to the step of *compositio*, can be completely exempted from the charge of idolatry.

In this context, too, a volume like Jonson's *Epigrammes* (1616)—a genre whose origin in incised inscriptions led to its close association with the emblem in Renaissance theorizing—might well be regarded as a kind of "blind" emblem book. Here was a collection of poems of praise and blame that a Whitney or a Peacham would likely have been tempted to illustrate with *imprese*, heraldic designs, or other allegorical devices. As we have seen, although Jonson translated Horace's *Ars Poetica* and transcribed for his own use all the commonplaces of *ut pictura poesis*, he added the note that "of the two, the Pen is more noble than the Pencill"; and he placed his faith as a poet in the moral "weight" of language, in the unique "authority" of the word to speak the inner truth of things to the understanding, not just to display surfaces to the sense.[13] Jonson exercises this power magisterially in the *Epigrammes*, where the highest praise for the virtuous is to honor their names ("On Lvcy Covntesse of Bedford"), while the severest punishment for the vicious is either to rechristen them with their true names ("On Sir Volvptvous Beast"), or else to withhold the dignity of a name altogether ("On some-thing, that walkes some-where"). In Jonson's verbal common-wealth, people who are idolized by the world for cutting an imposing figure to the eye—like the nameless and inwardly "dead" lord who "made me a great face"—are too morally insubstantial to deserve the attention of language. As it reflects a distinction, not only between independence of mind and servility, but between the inner fortitude of language and the ephemeral luster of visual representation, Jonson's declaration "To all, to whom I write" might serve as the motto for much of the best English poetry written during Quarles's lifetime: "I a *Poet* here, no *Herald* am."

Quarles's own volume appears near the end of a line of Reformation sacred emblem books (as distinguished from the more general category of "moralized" emblem books that would include Whitney's) beginning with the *Emblemes, ou Deuises Chrestiennes* (Lyon, 1571) composed by the French Protestant Georgette de Montenay and available in English in a later polyglot edition under the title, *A book of armes, or remembrance* (Frankfurt, 1619). It includes, as we have seen, Van der Noot's *A Theatre for Worldlings*, translated by Spenser (1569), as well as two other explicitly anti-Catholic English texts, Andrew Willet's *Sacrorum emblematum centuria una* (c. 1592–96) and Thomas Jenner's *The Soules Solace, or Thirtie and one Spirituall Emblemes* (1626, 1631). Barbara Lewalski has summarized what stands out as specifically "Protestant" about such collections.[14] They tend to "move resolutely away from Neoplatonic esotericism," drawing their mottoes and inscriptions from the Bible rather than from the pagan mysteries, and "thereby relating the wit of the emblems not to human ingenuity" but—as Quarles does in equating emblems with scriptural parables—to the "true wit of God's Word" (185). They exemplify Calvin's "emblematic" description of the "interplay of word and sign in the sacraments," where the visible sign is as it were the "seal" of the divine promise, and the word of the promise the explanatory motto—but with the crucial proviso, as Calvin says, that "the sign serves the word," and that only the word can reveal to us "what the visible sign means" (186–87). Of Quarles in particular, Lewalski notes that he rearranges the plates of his sources to "create a new Protestant narrative sequence on the spiritual life which deliberately undermines the orderly progressions of the Jesuit devotional books"; that he "adds plates presenting more serious aspects of worldly wickedness in heavier and more somber pictures than those of *Typus Mundi*"; and that "several [Jesuit] figures rendering contemplative and mystical ecstasy . . . are reinterpreted as the enjoyment of meditative solitude and the desire for Christ's presence, rather than achieved union" (192–93). These changes contribute to what she rightly regards as Quarles's "thoroughgoing Protestant reworking" of his Catholic sources (192). To this account, I would add that in his reformation of the sacred emblem, Quarles responds to an even deeper iconoclastic strain in the earlier collections. Much of the "uneven, uneasy" sense of Protestant life that Lewalski finds evoked in these emblems—an "episodic sequence of trials, temptations, failures, successes" (192)— arises in Quarles from a tension between the poet's attraction to the images he borrows and his suspicion of their idolatrous appeal.

The *Emblemes* of Georgette de Montenay, like those of her successors, elaborate upon two main polemical themes. One is the corruption of the Catholic church, a theme typically emphasized by devices exposing the delusions of the eye upon which papal authority depends: the seemingly virtuous man shows his spotless heart to the world, but God knows he is inwardly impure (Emblem 34, p. 166); a hypocritical monk displays his tongue in his hand, but drags his heart concealed behind him (Emblem 25, p. 130).[15] Beneath the image of a Levitical sacrifice, Jenner drives home the point that the Mass is no less a "needlesse Ceremonie" now that Christ's offering of himself has brought all other corporal sacrifice to an end (Emblem 11). The corresponding emphasis on the living power of the word is felt in Willet's conventional identification of the whore of Revelation 17:3 with the Antichrist pope "whom Gospell doth confound," and in his assurance that when God's truth is revealed the pope will be "vtterly deface[d]" (Emblem 23, sigs. D3-D3v). Jenner explains the "Foolishnesse of Transubstantiation" in the emblem of a tavern sign. The illustration of a man climbing up to taste the painted grapes is accompanied by the motto: "The *Bush* that hangs at Tavern dore doth show / That there is *Wine within*." Anyone not so foolish as to linger outside the door in the hope of being satisfied by the bush—or, in effect, by the engraving of the bush—must know that "In *Christ* alone stands that *spirituall food*; / Which must not of these *signes* be understood" (Emblem 28). Like the archer whose aim is true only when he shuts the eye not focused on the target, the Christian who aims his devotions at God must shut the eye "that vseth to survey / Honours, or prayse of men, or worldly pelfe" (Emblem 14). In Georgette de Montenay the eye is caught by the engraving of a *putto* urinating into the fountain of Christ (Emblem 93, p. 402), but then warned off by a motto that echoes through these collections: "*converte ocvlos*," "avert your eyes."

The related theme struck again and again in these volumes is the danger of idolatry and the faithful zeal of those whom the word has inspired to break the image. Georgette de Montenay juxtaposes a plate showing the worship of the Golden Calf (*Servitum idolorum*, Emblem 71, p. 314) with one showing the book of Scriptures (Emblem 72, p. 318), and she cautions the reader that "Gods desire is, that we shall look / Alwayes, in his Beebel-booke" (p. 320). Willet commemorates both the destruction of the Brazen Serpent by King Hezekiah in 2 Kings 18:4 (Emblem 51, sigs. G1v–G2) and the maiming of Dagon in the presence of the Ark in 1 Samuel 5:4 (Emblem 61, sig. H1). Dagon serves Thomas Jenner as the type of the "mortall Enmitie twixt *sinne* and *grace*" because "The one the other striveth to deface"; but "Soone as *Gods Arke* to *Dagons temple* came, / The *Idoll* falls, and brake, to *Ashdods* shame" (Emblem 23). The destructive mood of these openly iconoclastic emblems is intensified by the emphasis in many others on a world of visible objects fallen, cracked, and smashed. Worldly princes are ruinous pillars (de Montenay, Emblem 10, p. 170). The arrows of the enemies of Christ are broken against God's anvil (de Montenay, Emblem 14, p. 86). Like a raven dropping nuts, God cracks sinners who are mounted high in pride (de Montenay, Emblem 16, p. 94), or else He demolishes the wheel of fortune (de Montenay, Emblem 31, p. 154), or blows down the proud oak (de Montenay, Emblem 58, p. 262), or breaks the obdurate heart with his hammer (Jenner, Emblem 4), or shatters the sinner as the potter shatters his defective pots (de Montenay, Emblem 74, p. 326; Willet, Emblem 66, sig. H2v).

These Protestant sacred emblem books would seem to "undermine" not merely the doctrines of the Catholic devotional books with which they were engaged in spiritual combat, but the very justification for an illustrated devotional book. Thomas Jenner extends to the reader the traditional invitation of the emblem book, observing that "because men are more led by the eye, then eare, it may be, thou looking vpon these little Prints, maist conceiue of that which many words would not make so plaine vnto thee" (sigs. A2–A2v). As in the Catholic books, the "little Prints" are designed as guideposts to the spiritual life, but now the Protestant wayfarer is put on warning by the composers of the emblems themselves that his soul is at risk if he allows himself to be "led by the eye." Might that reader not regard the prints he confronts on the way as so many tavern-bushes distracting him from, as much as pointing him toward, the "wine within"? Here if anywhere in Renaissance literature one might hope to discover a self-consuming artifact, one inviting inspection and demolition at the same time.

Perhaps the most interesting of Quarles's predecessors in this respect is Andrew Willet, whose *Sacrorum emblematum* is in fact not illustrated at all. In this blind emblem book, the poems are allowed to speak, or to depict, for themselves. In Willet's section on "Types or Allegories," the mere citation of a biblical passage stands in place of the graphic image, as if the invocation of the Scripture's invisible emblems were sufficient illustration for the adjoined poems. Willet comments on this editorial decision in only one place in a long dedicatory epistle addressed to Essex. What he has to say reflects the inevitable pragmatic concerns of bookmaking. The right plates weren't available. It would have meant too much work. Putting out an illustrated edition would have "overburdened the press with expense"—a telling objection then as now, and all the more so in that a number of Protestant emblems condemn extravagance. But he also writes that such engravings would be "*alienor*" to his book— "alien," "foreign," "unsuitable" (sig. A3).[16] The remark seems to imply a contemporary application of the lesson Willet later draws from Hezekiah's destruction of the Brazen Serpent, "*Scandala remouenda sunt*": "What things were approued / In times that are past / Abused at the last / Must cease" (Emblem 51, sigs. G1v–G2).

Quarles is the indirect heir to this tradition. His motives as an emblematist (surely including the need to support eighteen children largely by his writing) are more complex, his solutions not so easily available as Willet's. Although his *Emblemes* was a best seller among Puritans and Dissenters—the audience for Prynne's *Histriomastix* and for Milton's antiprelatical tracts—Quarles himself was a staunch supporter of the established church and its Laudian tolerance for images. He was, as the title of a posthumous collection of his political writings declares, "The Profest Royalist," and his biographer argues that the title can "stand as the motto for the last phase of the poet's life," when he became more and more the "literary apologist of the King."[17] Somewhere at the crossroads between the militantly Protestant emblematists he follows and the Jesuit adversaries he imitates, Quarles evidently approached his project in a spirit of emulation and respect for the Catholic sources he was nevertheless about to reform, if not subvert. On the question of images he would need the Anglican finesse of a George Jenny, who could maintain at once that the unholy Church of Rome harbors "superstition, and idolatry" because the true Church of Christ is

lodged invisibly in His "spirituall and mysticall body," and that the
Church of England is the true "holy and faithful Visible Church."[18]
Quarles's task was to domesticate the imported Jesuit engravings of
his sources to a potentially inhospitable English Protestant poetic
sensibility that lacked the Jesuits' confidence, sanctioned by the
edicts of Trent, in the efficacy of the visual image to embody and
teach sacred truths. In some respects the Jesuit emblems were pliable enough to withstand the change of context. One aspect of
their wide appeal had always been the latitude of interpretation
that they would permit. Many of their motifs had already been
adapted by the Jesuits from Dutch secular love emblems, and the
Alexandria Eros was transformed into Divine Love by the substitution of biblical for Ovidian and Petrarchan texts.[19] Still, the peril
involved in Quarles's further adapting these sacred figures to a
Protestant setting is reflected in Luther's *Theses*: "The one who beholds what is invisible of God, through the perception of what is
made, is not rightly called a theologian."[20]

In his other writings, Quarles suggests the difficulty of this task.
He distinguishes between the "soul's two Eyes," the eye of faith
being more clear-sighted than the eye of reason, and so objects to
the attempt of Raymond Sebond to understand divine mysteries
"By Nature's feeble light."[21] But both these inner sources of vision
are surer guides than the eye of sense fixed on the objects on which
it feeds: "Gaze not on Beauty too much, lest it blast thee; nor too
long lest it blind thee. . . . If thou like it, it deceives thee."[22] God's
image in us before the Fall was the one perfect picture, "a dainty
Piece! In every part, Drawne to the Life, and full of curious Art."
Its restoration must await not the smudged hand of the human artist but Christ, the

> . . . great Apelles that can lim
> With thy owne Pencill; we have sought to Him:
> His skilfull hand will wash off all the Soyle
> And clense thy picture with his sacred Oyle.[23]

We cannot emulate the "skilfull hand" that painted our redemption
by the sufferings of the cross. When he asks, "Why not the Picture
of our dying Lord, As of a Friend," Quarles takes up the issue of
sacred imagery explicitly: "does not th' eternall Law command, that
thou Shalt ev'n as well forbeare to make, as bow?" And he concludes: "No, no; the beauty of his Picture lies Within; 'Tis th' object

of our Faith, not Eyes."[24] With this attitude Quarles precariously inserted the alien engravings into his *Emblemes*.

Quarles takes all but ten of his plates from two Jesuit emblem books published in Antwerp in the 1620s, the *Pia Desideria* (1624), by Herman Hugo, and the *Typus Mundi* (1628), put out by the College of Rhetoric of the Society of Jesus and dedicated to Saint Ignatius. With only a few departures, Quarles's engravers, William Marshall and William Simpson, have carefully reproduced the Jesuit plates (designed, in Hugo's case, by the great baroque engraver, Boethius a Bolswert), although the debt is not acknowledged.[25] But like Christopher Harvey and John Hall, who later also produced Protestant emblem books around the illustrations in Catholic sources, Quarles largely ignores the texts in the *Typus Mundi* and the *Pia Desideria* except for an occasional paraphrase or for a general similarity in theme dictated by the content of the device. His poems simplify the sensual texture and mythological decoration, which in the Jesuit verses had echoed the rapturous feeling of the plates, and concentrate instead on a more austere psychological and moral drama of the soul.[26] In the process of adaptation, furthermore, Quarles subtly modifies his sources to give the larger design of the work a distinctively Protestant cast.

The *Emblemes* is divided into five books of fifteen emblems each.[27] The last three books reproduce in order the forty-five engravings of the *Pia Desideria*, itself falling into three books. But Quarles omits the subtitles of the Jesuit work. These subtitles correspond to the three-part movement—much in the fashion of a sequential meditation—from the soul's grief-stricken search for penitence (*Gemitus Animae Poenitentis*), through the expression of its desire (*Desideria Animae Sanctae*), to the more fervent sighs of the soul yearning for and at moments touching the sweetness of divine love (*Suspiria Animae Amantis*). The pattern implicit here is repeated in other Catholic emblem books such as Henry Hawkins's *Partheneia Sacra* (1633), in which the twenty-four plants in the garden of the sacred Parthenes correspond to twenty-four acts of devotion and provide the mnemonic framework for a whole meditative scheme. With no such framework, each of Quarles's poems stands independent, as an individual moment in a Christian life rather than as a step in a sequence which presupposes the smooth cooperation of text and image to guide the reader along a steady course.

In books 1 and 2 (evidently written last) Quarles follows the *Typus*

Mundi's presentation of the rivalry between human and divine love against the background of a fallen world. But taking even more liberty with this source than he had with Hugo, Quarles changes the original order of the emblems he selects (twenty-two of the thirty-two in the *Typus Mundi*) and adds others not found in the *Typus* at all. Those he adds—for example, the concluding five emblems in book 1—portray the delusions of a world suffering under the reign of the Devil, who rides off with the world despite the efforts of *Amor Divinis* to restrain his chariot with a rope (1:11) or who presides over the scene of Fraud scourging Justice and Sense clipping the wings of Faith (1:15). The last five emblems in book 2 restructure the conclusion of *Typus Mundi* into a darker, more precariously Protestant ending. The Jesuit work ends by revealing the monstrous nature of the earthly Cupid (plate 27), contrasting the blind Cupid to Divine Love reveling in a vision of heaven (plate 28), and finally banishing him altogether as Divine Love emerges triumphant with his foot on the world (plate 30). When in the final emblem (plate 32) Cupid reappears holding the orb of the world, he is countered by Divine Love displaying the purified heart which streams upward toward heaven. Quarles retains that emblem of the heart "restor'd and purg'd" from the "drossie nature" of the world (2:15) but makes it the last element in an antithetical series:

2:11 (emblem 23 in *Typus*): Divine Love, playing billiards with Cupid, admonishes his earthly opponent that the heavenly shot is the more difficult: "My way is hard and strait."

2:12 (emblem 22 in the *Typus*): Divine Love stands secure on the cross above the world, unmoved by adverse winds or fortune's wheel.

2:13 (newly added): Cupid is wounded into repentance by a shaft from the bow of Divine Love, but the Devil pours his own poison into the wound, and the soul's desire for this "most delicious world" revives. The motto, from Proverbs 26:11, warns: "As a dog returneth to his vomit, so a fool returneth to his folly."

2:14 (newly added): Although in a wrestling match with Cupid Divine Love is thrown down, the victory is only temporary because "A just man falleth seven times and riseth up again" (Prov. 24:16).

This ending reflects what an emblem later in the volume (4:1), its motto drawn from Saint Paul, will call the "unresolv'd resolves" of the will: "O how my will is hurried to and fro, / And how my un-

Figure 9. Francis Quarles, *Emblemes* (1635),
Book 4, Emblem 2

resolv'd resolves do vary!" The poet's "rambling thought" (4:12)
carries him along a pilgrimage of self-scrutiny whose emblem (4:2)
is the labyrinth: "The world's a lab'rinth whose anfractuous ways /
Are all compos'd of rubs and crook'd meanders: / No resting here."
At the center of the plate (fig. 9) the soul takes a direct sighting of
Divine Love on a distant watchtower, but the poem is spoken by a
smaller figure haltingly negotiating the maze with his dog and staff.
In an Augustinian mood of spiritual restlessness, the epigram offers
the pilgrim only the encouragement of an unresolved resolve:

> Pilgrime, trudge on; What makes thy soul complain
> Crownes thy complaint. The way to rest is pain:
> The road to resolution lies by doubt.

Far less sure than the meditative steps of the Jesuits, these "trem-
bling paces" between pain and comfort, doubt and resolution,

mark the larger rhythm of Quarles's book. Like Donne's Holy Sonnets ("Oh, to vex me, contraryes are met in one"), this poem is an inner spiritual autobiography rather than a public manual of pious instruction.

The rhythm of self-scrutiny apparent in the overall movement of the *Emblemes* is central in every respect to Quarles's project—to the materials of his art, and to the bond between the pictorial device and the adjoining text. Just as the pilgrim's staff probes his path, the poet probes the crooked meanders of composing sacred emblems. At poignant moments the probing extends to the authority of language (4:1):

> The curious Penman, having trimm'd his page
>   With the dead language of his dabbled quill;
> Lets fall a heedlesse drop, then in a rage
> Cashiers the fruits of his unlucky skill;
>   Ev'n so my pregnant soul in th' infant bud
>   Of her best thoughts, showrs down a cole-black flood
> Of unadvised ills, and cancels all her good.

The plate shows the soul trying to fend off the enticements of Amor while fixing her gaze on the tablets of the law held by Divine Love; the implicit contrast between that indelible writing and the poet's "dead language" sharpens the rueful tone. As the spiritual and verbal fertility of a "pregnant soul" is canceled by its own heedlessness and rage, the Pauline drama of the motto to this emblem—"I see another Law in my members warring against the Law of my mind"—plays itself out in the very process of writing. In another emblem (5:9), the soul, her flight prevented because her foot is chained to the ball of the globe, complains, "I cannot speak a word which earth profanes not." In yet another (4:12), her "unregarded language" only vents the "sad tautologies of lavish passion," "feeding Upon the rad'cal humour of her thought," until comfort appears suddenly to resolve the labyrinthine circling of language: "Ev'n whilst mine eyes were blind, and heart was bleeding, / He that was sought, unfound, was found unsought." The verbal play here deepens the irony of a language that achieves its end despite itself through its own failure and exhaustion. "Unregarded" language is heedless language, like the penman's spilled ink. Its plea is apparently not heeded, yet love comes unexpectedly, and unseen—that is, "unregarded"—before the blinded eye of the poet. Divine Love reverses the order and logic of the poet's language ("sought, unfound . . . found, unsought"), saves it from the sad tautologies of unresolved repetition, and so subtly cancels the penman's original error: his words are "regarded" after all. A similar treatment of sinful language resolved despite the poet is reflected in Marvell's "The Coronet" and Herbert's "The Collar."

In this passage about language, the latent visual meaning of "unregarded" as *unseen* is one instance of Quarles's nearly obsessive concern with the act of seeing. If for Quarles language is at times ink-spotted, it is nonetheless the more stable medium, while sight and its objects are presented again and again as infected, dark, and treacherous. In the "Invocation" to the *Emblemes*, the poet rouses his soul so that the "sacred influences" of heaven may "hallow" his "high-bred strains" and the music of his words may "reach th'Olympick ear." As the "consort" grows more perfect, however, the eye is dimmed: it too rises above the "dark fog / Of dungeon-earth," but to a vantage point from which "this base world" will "appear / A thin blew Lanskip." The eye is to be enlightened by withdrawing its gaze from a world now seen in its correct anagogical perspective—a mere painted image, diminished and hazy despite the artist's skill, offering only the false "lanskip joyes" (4:12) of human love, and smudged by a "poore mortall blaze . . . whose flames are dark / And dangerous, a dull blew-burning light" (1:14). This long perspective secures a view removed from the world's contamination but nearer the clarity of true vision.

The embodiment of this mode of perception appears in engraving 3:14 (fig. 10). There Spirit looks through an "Optick glass" at the distant prospect of death and the fires of the last judgment—the "latter end" that the motto from Deuteronomy 32:29 exhorts us to consider. In the Jesuit version of this plate (*Pia Desideria*, 1:14), Spirit stands alone, her telescopic view sufficient and unchallenged (fig. 11). She is accompanied only by a marigold, leaning, as she leans, toward the distant object of her sight to suggest both how faithful and how effortless the act of vision is: eyes and plants alike are drawn heliotropically toward the light. But Quarles replaces the marigold with the naked figure of Flesh, who now attempts to distract her companion with a triangular prism displaying a distorted "world in colours" to "ravish eyes." Spirit, echoed by the appended quotation from Bonaventura's *De Contemptu Seculi* ("O that men would be wise, understand, and foresee"), replies that "Foresight of future torments is the way. . . . / Break that fond glasse, and let's be wise together." Quarles thus crystallizes the problem of vision: in order to focus therapeutically on "future tor-

Figure 10. Francis Quarles, *Emblemes* (1635), Book 3, Emblem 14.

Oh that they were wise, then they would
vnderstand this; they would consider
their latter end. Deeteron: 32 · I Payne scul

Figure 11. Herman Hugo, *Pia Desideria* (1624), Book 1, Emblem 14

Vtinam saperent, & intelligerent, ac noviſsima
providerent! Deut. 32.

XIV.

ments," the eye must resist the present torment of taking pleasure
in what it sees close at hand. Here, as in other emblems where the
state of the soul is at issue between two contestants (Eve and the
serpent, Divine Love and Justice), Quarles recasts the poetic commentary of his sources into dramatic dialogue which charges the
moment more fully with the energy of competition. The condition
of sight has become a kind of agon between Flesh and Spirit for the
eye of the viewer, who is made to feel the pull on him from two
directions.

As we are thus led self-consciously to reflect on our own perception, we appreciate how precariously the engravings that meet the
eye in the *Emblemes* must balance between these two poles of Flesh
and Spirit, prismatic sight and telescopic foresight. More radically
than other visual allegories, these bizarre, colorless configurations are drained of the usual contents of our visual experience
and jumbled with devils, souls, cupids, globes, wheels of fortune,
candles, and bowling balls. From a spiritual point of view, that they
so defamiliarize the visible is their great advantage: by engaging
what the *Everyman* poet had called our "ghostly sight," they intend
to refocus our sight telescopically from the image before us—now
become "thin" and "indistinct" and not to be mistaken for a representation of Flesh's world—to the "latter end" of spiritual insight,
the object of thought and meditation beyond the pictorial surface.
Their vanishing point is not in the depths of the image but in the
soul of the viewer. Emblematic images might thus be regarded as
partially immune to strictures against sacred imagery, since they do
not claim to be objects of devotion in themselves but, as for Edward
Taylor, signs pointing away from the image, declaring their own in-
sufficiency, and so, in the tradition of the *via negativa*, extinguish-
ing themselves. As "types," engravings are to be seen not in the
literal sense as palpable incarnations signifying "through the perception of what is made" but rather understood in the allegorical
sense as figures of "the sufferings of the cross": here we may find,
as Quarles himself instructs us, "the allusion to our blessed Savior
figured in these Types" ("To the Reader"). Seen—or rather, exe-
getically read—in a way that virtually deprives them of their pictorial content, emblematic images are thus textualized. They may
be regarded, as Joseph Hall regards all "material objects," as "altogether transparent" and opening onto the invisible world of "spiritual objects," or else as configurations of linguistic signs in which
that same invisible world is to be deciphered by the keys of allusion

and allegory. Either way, as the mere indices of interior and superior truths, they may be safe from any suspicions of idolatry.[28]

Yet by their very nature as pictorial images—the "body" of the emblem—they can hardly escape some implication in the world of flesh. We see and dwell on their intricacies in a way strikingly similar to that of Flesh taking pleasure in her prism: "here mayst thou tire thy fancy, and advise / With shows more apt to please more curious eyes." Indeed the insistent reminders of our "benighted eyes" (1:14), our "faithless Opticks" (1:7), our "Owl-eyed lust" (2:9), our "deluded eye (3:2), our "Leprous eyes" (3:13)—all cast doubt on the very faculty we must exercise in a collection of emblems. In 2:6 we look at Cupid looking at his own image mirrored in the globe of the world. The text's warning on the theme of vanity reflects outward to our own act of perceiving the emblem as well as inward to Cupid admiring himself:

> Believe her not: Her glasse diffuses
> False portraitures: thou canst espie
> No true reflection: She abuses
> Her mis-inform'd beholder's eye.

No longer a glass channeling the eye to a world beyond the flesh, the engraving as a mirror of the flesh distorts the gaze and returns it upon the viewer as an indictment of his cupidity: he is "mis-inform'd" because of his own deformity. The tension between the need to see and the perils of sight complicates our passage through the labyrinth at every step and asserts itself as the true subject of Quarles's book.

I would like to explore this tension in detail in four particular emblems, 1:1–2, 1:14, 1:15, and 3:2 and 10, and then consider the broader significance of Quarles's work. The examples I have chosen are of special interest because they confront the problematic nature of the image directly, unlike others which find strategies for avoiding it. Elsewhere Quarles may either draw out the allegorical interpretation of a complicated image point for point (e.g., 1:10 or 3:9) or, at the other extreme, use some feature of the image as the inspiration for a poem that develops along a tangent tenuously connected to the given engraving (e.g., 3:8). The first method relegates the text to a gloss on the picture and so collapses the bond between the two; the second ignores the engraving to establish the independence of the text and so severs the bond entirely. In 1:1 and 1:2, however, the strength of that bond is put to the test.

The first emblem (1:1) shows the temptation in the garden, the serpent coiled around the trunk of the tree and Eve listening to his blandishments (fig. 12). In the second (1:2), Adam, holding the fruit, stands before a background depicting the four elements whose fury (in contrast to the harmony of the animals in the background of the first plate) is now unleashed by the act of disobedience: "Fire, Water, Earth and Aire, that first were made / To be subdu'd, see how they now invade" (fig. 13). At Adam's feet is the image of the world—literally the *Typus Mundi* of Quarles's source. As the principal motif of books 1 and 2, this globe will reappear some twenty times ingeniously transformed into a wasp's nest (1:3), a top (1:5), a breast (1:12), or a mirror (2:6). Here, like some enormous, wormy fruit (the plate suggests the visual parallel between the globe and the fruit in Adam's hand), the world spawns the seven heads of the deadly sins. Quarles emphasizes the theme of malignant fertility, both by the motto from James 1:15 ("when lust hath conceived it bringeth forth sinne") and by the main text:

> See how the world (whose chast and pregnant womb
>   Of late conceiv'd, and brought forth nothing ill)
> Is not degenerated, and become
>   A base Adultresse, whose false births do fill
>   The earth with Monsters.

These passages also draw out the visual implication that the globe we see before us in 1:2 is the monstrous version of Eve's naked and globular womb pictured in 1:1, deceptively planted by "lust" with the seeds of sin and death, and now grown "thriving, rank and proud" into the horrid fruit. This fruit will recur later in the volume as "earth's false pleasure. . . . / Whose fruit is fair and pleasing to the sight, / But soure in tast, false at the putrid core" (1:7). It appears again near the end, fulfilled typologically in 4:14, where the soul raises its "humble eye" to gaze at Divine Love hanging in the branches of a tree; the motto reminds us not only of the crucifixion but of the final harvest of Eve's seed at the heavenly banquet: "I sat under his shadow with great delight, and his fruit was sweet to my tast."

The energy of each of these moments—Eve entranced by the serpent, Adam regarding the globe, the soul enjoying the sight of

Figure 12. Francis Quarles, *Emblemes* (1635), Book 1, Emblem 1

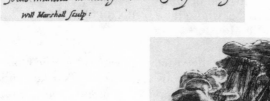

Figure 13. Francis Quarles, *Emblemes* (1635), Book 1, Emblem 2

Love—flows through an act of vision. At the same time the texts engage the reader in the drama by channeling his sight to the scene. In 4:14 the reader is implored to "permit [his] eyes to climbe this fruitfull tree," in 1:2 he is forced repeatedly to rivet his gaze on the consequences of the Fall from which he would rather turn away: "Poor man! Are not thy joynts grown sore with shaking, / To view th'effect of thy bold undertaking?" The poet's command, "Lament, lament; look, look what thou hast done," indicts us as fully as it does Adam. It would appear to assume that regarding an image of the fallen world will humiliate the eye and so raise it for its climb to Divine Love. As a form of lamentation, vision prepares for penitence, and penitence for spiritual sight. The scene of emblem 1:2, "degenerated" as it is to the sight, is still invested with an exemplary moral value by the text.

But for the reader who has passed to that scene from 1:1, the poet's emphatic pleas to "look," to "see," to "behold" curiously echo the voice of the serpent:

> Not eat? Not tast? Not touch? Not *cast an eye*
> Upon the fruit of this fair Tree? and why?
> *See* how the laden boughs make silent suit
> To be enjoy'd; *Look* how their bending fruit
> Meet thee half-way; *Observe* but how they crouch
> To kisse thy hand; Coy woman, Do but touch:
> *Mark* what a pure Vermillion blush has dy'd
> Their swelling cheeks, and how for shame they hide
> Their palsie heads, to *see* themselves stand by
> Neglected: Women, Do but *cast an eye*.
>
> (Emphases added)

The ironic parallel between the two emblems could not be clearer, or more troubling. The serpent's insidious and successful method had been less to befuddle Eve's reason or stimulate her taste than to awaken her visual lust—to tempt her as Flesh tempts Spirit in 3:14. He had done so by presenting the image of the fruit emblematically as a blushing lover making "silent suit" to her eye. Eve had in effect become a "base Adultresse" by being tempted to engage in illicit visual intercourse with an image already forming itself, as the serpent offers it to her, into the cupid figure of Amor. We are perhaps reminded that according to one of the several competing contemporary theories of vision, the eye sees by projecting its "visual spirits" outward in a kind of coupling with the object of sight—a theory reflected as well in the lovers' "eye-beames twisted" in

Donne's "The Extasie": "And pictures in our eyes to get / Was all our propagation."

Worse yet, the serpent's visual art challenges the verbal art of God's "strict commands" to Eve to avoid the fruit. This enticement to lust forms a contrast to, but also a reflection of, the poet's enticement to remorse in 1:2. The poet establishes the authority of the engraving by using its harsh theme to cleanse the viewer's eye with tears; the serpent in effect undermines the authority of *all* engravings by making us realize both their covertly lustful appearance and our complicity in that lust. Adam's ability before the Fall to name the animals with what Milton calls "sudden apprehension"— to see through their "body" to their linguistic "soul" and thereby to perceive the essential connection between *res* and *verbum*—made him the ideal viewer of the emblem. But ever since Eve set the pattern for art appreciation, our motives for viewing are compromised whenever we open our eyes. Thus the irony of the poet's remark to Adam, and to us, "thou lamentst too late," is directed at more than our tardy regret over an unforeseen catastrophe in Eden; it tells us at the beginning of the *Emblemes* that the innocent vision that alone would purify lamentation is debased by the very sin we would lament. Our "freedome gone"—and this will be Milton's point as well—we are no longer free as we once were not to sin with the eye. Which is to say that the perfect penitential emblem could have existed only in Eden, where it would not have been needed.

The need to grapple with this paradox in perception runs throughout the rest of Quarles's book, beneath the various moral lessons developed in the individual emblems. Quarles's solutions reflect more sharply than do purely literary forms a Protestant strategy for accommodating—or rather, for enacting the failure to accommodate—the visual image: destruction of the image (1:14), mortification of the viewer (1:15), and lifting the burden of sight (3:2 and 10).

Plate 1:14 presents the soul praying for morning while seated before a looming black globe (fig. 14). The scene is lit by a single candle—"this poore mortall blaze, a dying spark." The soul's anguish increases as she realizes that even though the candle may burn with the intensity of "all the Sunnes that glister in the Sphere / Of earth" its power is insufficient to bring into view the "promised light" for which she longs. Indeed its dull flame conceals that greater light and must be dispelled before "the day" can be revealed: "Haste, haste away / Heav'n's loytring lamp." For the viewer this implies that the image before him is not a transparent sign

Figure 14. Francis Quarles, *Emblemes* (1635), Book 1,
Emblem 14

pointing toward a spiritual meaning but an impediment to what he
would truly wish to see. Like the faithful soul in the illustration, he
must correct his vision by refusing to look—by turning his back on
the image of the globe and repudiating spectatorship for prayerful
expectation. As it thus defeats our penetration, the image is recon-
ceived as an emblem of its own opacity. The natural—that is, sinful—desire to see better by having the image more brilliantly lit
only further darkens the vision. The soul therefore calls upon Ignorance to complete the image by destroying it: "Blow Ignorance . . . blow, blow thy spite; / Since thou has pufft our greater
Tapour, do / Puffe on, and out the lesser too." The epigram finishes
the thought:

> My soul, if Ignorance puffe out this light,
> Shee'll do a favour that intends a spight:
> 'T seems dark abroad; but take this light away,
> Thy windows will discover break a day.

Debilitata fides : Terbras Astrœa reliquit.

w : M : fcul :

Figure 15. Francis Quarles, *Emblemes* (1635), Book 1, Emblem 15

By such creative iconoclasm, the image is made significant by being obliterated.

Ignorance is here the victim of the traditional irony associated with the fortunate fall. As Herbert's "The Sacrifice" shows in its dramatization of the liturgy of the Reproaches for Good Friday, even those who spitefully crucified "our greater Tapour" furthered the divine plan despite themselves. The soul's ignorance allies it with the prismatic Israelites who were dark to the light of Christ shining behind his incarnate flesh. The crucifixion was the result of their failure to perceive Christ truly as a kind of divine emblem, and yet their violence wondrously "opened" him, as the hidden meaning of an enigmatic device is laid bare. As an alternative to our prismatic delight in the image itself, this passage justifies "spight" as a mode of pictorial exegesis and carries the reassurance that the spiteful act will be a "favour" in effect. This response to the image proposes an uneasy compromise between the corrosive and the therapeutic nature of vision. It acknowledges the sinfulness of the viewer and the inadequacy of the image but redeems both through their very susceptibility to violence.

This emblem directs the destructive force of perception against the image. The one following (1:15) directs this force inward against the viewer (fig. 15). The engraving shows Astraea driven off with a scourge by Fraud, and Faith, holding the cross, threatened by Sense wielding a pair of shears: "Her wings are clipt, and eyes put out by sense." Again, as in 1:2, the text repeatedly enjoins us to look at the scene ("See how the bold Usurper . . . ; See how she flutters . . . ; Behold how double Fraud . . . ; See how she stands"), and again, as in 1:14, it implies that our vision is impaired, for "Quick-seeing Faith" is "now blind" and imprisoned and the slow eye of Sense usurps her place. This brutal scene is conceived as a revenge tragedy in which the soul and God are both apparently helpless spectators. Although with the foresight of Revelation 12:12 the motto assures us that the Devil "hath but a short time" to rule, the poet addresses the rightful king impatiently:

> Lord! canst thou see and suffer? is thy hand
>   Still bound to th' peace? Shall earth's black Monarch take
> A full possession of thy wasted land?
>   O, will thy slumb'ring vengeance never wake?
>   . . . revenge, revenge thy own.

But at the end the poet turns the rebuke upon himself:

> My soul, sit thou a patient looker on;
> Judge not the Play before the Play is done:
> Her Plot has many changes: Every day
> Speaks a new Scene; the last act crowns the Play.

The role of the spectator here grows out of an awareness, implied in the full meaning of "patience," that vision is a form of suffering. Like Christ, the viewer will "see and suffer" not only because he can foresee the "last act" and so suffer patiently the presence of evil but also because—as for Christ—the sight of that evil is itself a suffering to be endured. In this sense, "see" and "suffer" are synonymous. The viewer's patient inspection of every detail of the image reveals nothing that he does not already know about its contents. Vision is not a form of knowledge but a form of pain, and thus every "see" and "behold" in the text inflicts another lash in a process of visual scourging. In moving from the impatient opening of the poem to the wish for patience at the close, the reader moves toward a bitterly unresolved resolve, for these opposite terms both mean suffering.

In each of these two modes of perception—destruction and mortification—the verbal "soul" of the emblem locks us into a struggle with the pictorial "body" which reenacts the Pauline struggle within the self. Between the viewer and the image flows a charge of lust, compulsion, and violence which cannot find release so long as the eye in its "blind dungeon" (1:15) is sealed off from the satisfaction of an unmediated, untainted vision. The relation between the eye and the image darkly parodies our perfect vision at the "last act," when we have Saint Paul's assurance of seeing God "face to face" in a reflection bound by love.

Until then the only relief from the burden of sight can come from shifting it onto the one viewer willing to bear its weight; for what matters ultimately in the *Emblemes* is not how we see but how we are seen. When Divine Love conceals himself behind a "fleshly curtain" (5:12), the soul's desire to see "the full beams of thy Meridien eye" remains unfulfilled; and when Divine Love holds an "eclipsing hand" before his eye, the soul cannot remove it (3:7). But when Justice brings the "prisner" soul before Jesus (3:10), the soul makes the proper defense even though she stands condemned of sin by her own confession (fig. 16):

> Vile as I am, and of myself abhorr'd
> I am thy handy-work, thy creature, Lord,
> Stampt with thy glorious Image, and at first
> Most like to thee, though now a poore accurst
> Convicted catiff, and degen'rous creature,
> Here trembling at thy bar.

And Jesus must reply:

> Stay, Justice, hold;
> My bowels yearn, my fainting bloud growes cold,
> To view the trembling wretch; me thinks I spy
> My Father's image in the prisner's eye.

In the context of an emblem book, the words "handy-work" and "stampt" take on a special suggestiveness that suddenly revises the dilemma of sight. The crucial emblem is not the one the viewer sees but the one stamped in his eyes, the crucial perception is of the di-

Figure 16. Francis Quarles, *Emblemes* (1635),
Book 3, Emblem 10

vine emblematist's visual repossession of his handiwork—and his
yearning to absorb the pain of looking.

Thus in plate 3:2 the soul appears in a fool's cap and bells as the
emblem of its own love for "antick pleasure," and the text places us
into the image (fig. 17): "Such very fools are thou and I." Divine
Love holds his hand before his face to shield his eye from this vision
of human folly but sees it nonetheless—through the *stigmatum* in
his palm. The dot signifying the hole in Christ's hand is the tiniest
and yet the most telling of Quarles's emendations. Without it, the
identical image in the *Pia Desideria* conveys a very different feeling.
In Hugo's work, Love indulgently plays a childlike game of for-
giveness with his childish companion; peeking between his fingers,
he sees but pretends not to, hiding his eye from our sins by regarding them as follies:

O Lord Thou knowest my Foolishnesse,
& my Sins are not hid fro Thee Ps:
W. Simson Sc: 69.5.

Figure 17. Francis Quarles, *Emblemes* (1635),
Book 3, Emblem 2

But by Heav'n's piercing Eye we are descry'd,
Which does our Sins with Follies Mantle hide.
He's pleased to wink at Errors too in me,
And seeing seems as tho' he did not see.[29]

In the *Emblemes*, divine sight passes through an "open wound," the
very medium of its vision inseparable from pain:

O canst thou choose but see,
That mad'st the eye? can ought be hid from thee?
Thou seest our persons, Lord, and not our guilt;
Thou seest not what thou maist but what thou wilt:
The Hand that form'd us, is enforced to be
A Screen set up betwixt thy work and thee:

> Look, look upon that Hand, and thou shalt spy
> An open wound, a through-fare for thine eye.

"Open" in pain, Christ's wound opens a clear channel for the healing power of his "gracious eyes" to see through the flesh—through a hand raised to "screen" the guilt of his handiwork rather than to "confound" it. Having once willingly joined himself to a body of flesh, he cannot now avoid the compulsion and suffering of mortal sight—he cannot "choose but see" his creation. But for that very reason, divine sight is free to transform the object of its vision from our "guilt" to our "persons" within or beyond the obstruction of sin: "Thou seest not what thou maist but what thou wilt." The "through-fare" of the wound uniquely joins the two perspectives of Flesh and Spirit in a way that resolves the tension between the two and measures the distance between our sight and God's.

Playing on the "empty fulnesse" of our "vain desire," the text guides our vision of this image of our folly: the soul is full of "empty dreams," yet feeding on emptiness this "fulsome Ideot" must be "insatiate" in its desires. Driven by the insatiate need to "please / The fond aspect" of our "deluded eye," we could find no deliverance from the labyrinth of perception were it not possible to transfer the unresolved paradox of full yet empty vision to Christ as he regards his "handy-work." We empty the images that fill our eyes by feeding on them, and so diminish ourselves by the emptiness of our diet; but Christ's eye sees by replenishing the object of his sight in us. He is willing to suffer an emptiness in his own flesh to fill the emptiness of ours. Thus the drama of perception includes, at moments, the "new Scene" of regeneration: the mutual destructiveness of the viewer's engagement with the emblem is repaired by the flow of grace from the divine eye to *its* emblem within the viewer. The image given body by the engraver's hand fills the page of an emblem book. It releases, but cannot satisfy, our desire to see: we cannot see through the guilt, as Christ can, because our eye is itself guilty, and so our act of perception empties the image. In this sense, the images before us may be regarded as open wounds in the text—the visual "body" of the emblem pierced by our attempt to see through it. These empty spaces can be filled only at points where the labyrinth of our perception intersects the "through-fare" of grace. Our unaided vision either defaces the image or suffers the pain the image inflicts on us. In Quarles's *Emblemes*, only by our faith in Christ-as-viewer looking at us through the body of the book can the integrity and significance of the image be sustained.

The *Emblemes* enacts the difficult attempt to insert a pictorial element into what I have called a potentially inhospitable literary culture. In the Catholic emblems from which Quarles departs, the connection between the visual and the verbal remains untroubled; for Quarles, as we have seen, it is intensely problematic. Catholic emblematists assume that what we see is congruent with the inner life, with what we feel and think. There is no better contemporary example of this in the visual arts than the relationship between the sculpture of Saint Teresa in ecstasy in Bernini's Cornaro Chapel and the figure of Federigo Cornaro in the right perspective frame of that same chapel. The ecstasy we see presented in the figure of the saint is represented, we sense, inside the vast, bulbous head of Federigo—who is, in fact, looking away from Teresa, intently focused on his own thought. Teresa is for him, as she is to become for us, an object of meditation, just as immediate to his mind and spirit as the sculpture of the saint and the seraph is to our eye. Indeed the chapel itself is the direct translation of a private experience into a public spectacle—just as it is a translation of a written text, Saint Teresa's *Vida*, into a visual form. But when the pictorial presses too closely on the prior claims of language in a Protestant setting, when the visual intrudes upon a culture that values introspection over spectatorship, the strain on Quarles's *Emblemes* reveals the failure of accommodation between the two.

But the strain also reveals an extraordinarily intense way of being in the world—or of being split off from it. Insofar as the experience of reading answers to the experience of everyday life—and the book's popularity argues an intimate response for seventeenth-century readers—the *Emblemes* dramatizes a radical estrangement of the authentic *linguistic* self from its visual bond to the world. We can no longer verbalize the world by a process of direct translation. We no longer walk through a world whose divine hieroglyphic imprint speaks to us at every turn—such a fully signifying world appears in Vaughan's poetry only as a memory. Instead we stumble among blinding images that continually tempt us to repeat the fall in the garden. Spiritual advisors like Richard Sibbes warn us at great length how "*imagination* hurteth us" by "false representations."[30] The visual world falls silent and recedes from our immediate comprehension, yet beckons dangerously. It becomes less a "readable text" and more an "unreadable rebus"—like a dream, dissociated, compressed, and deceptive in ways that jeopardize discursive interpretation. The implicit analogy—that dreams are to their interpretations as emblematic images are to their texts—suggests that the visible world, as it is pictured in Quarles, becomes a realm of concealment that both resists and fascinates us.[31] No longer a mirror of the divine, it reflects the anxieties of our own attempts to decipher it.

The power of Quarles's *Emblemes* stems from that dynamic. In the Catholic sacred emblem, language and image are duplicative: their redundant relationship assumes a world in which words are essentially connected to the objects they name. This relationship gives way in Quarles to a new form of the emblem whose inner tension is its coherence. Despite his invocation of a hieroglyphic cosmos, his work assumes and enacts a drama of perception in which names have become conventional, detached from their objects. Like Hobbes and Descartes, Quarles is wary of the ephemeral nature of sense experience: the mind must reconstitute itself in the isolation of its own language; it can no longer take for granted a network of correspondences between its speech and the language of imagery. The task for philosophy will henceforth be to construct new languages, like the language of mathematics, independent of the evidence of the eye.

In Quarles's world the emblem as traditionally conceived must strain across a widening gap between the verbal and the visual. Rosemary Freeman's criticism of Quarles, that in a mechanical "imposition of meaning" the text of the emblem applies an interpretation to, rather than discovers a significance within, the image, is more apt than Freeman perhaps realized. With the semantic congruence between word and image no longer guaranteed, artists attempting to yoke the two would have to reconceive the relationship between them. Seen as a response to this need, Blake's illuminated books complicate the emblem tradition in an art of dazzling improvisatory juxtapositions. Indeed, his revaluation of the ties between "body" and "soul" may be taken in one sense as a revision of the emblematist's traditional distinction. Words, once the soul of the emblem, now become truly animate for Blake—flowing, sprouting, multicolored—while their quirky energy, no longer restrained by standardized print, is embodied in sensual, quasi-pictorial shapes; images speak in a new and private vocabulary of emblematic birds, curling tendrils, and other forms that gesture allusively from plate to plate. These frame, underscore, celebrate, intrude upon, parody, or oppose themselves by "contraries" to the meaning of the adjoining text. Thus if Quarles's work signals the failure of the emblem in England, its success in probing the problems of combining language and imagery points toward the renewal of the form in Blake.

5

Donne's
"Pictures Made and Mard"

In the third "Satyre" Donne imagines that "On a huge hill, /
Cragged, and steep, Truth stands . . ." (ll. 79–80).[1] Proclaimed so
firmly as the goal of our ascent toward true religion, "she" may
seem about to take shape as the kind of personified *Veritas* described in Ripa's *Iconologia*. Such a figure—an indomitable nude,
her sun and palm leaf and open book in hand, her foot planted on
the globe—would convincingly replace the procession of ragged
and sullen mistresses who had earlier in the poem embodied the
choice of available religions. Or again she might be drawn in the
style of the many Renaissance versions of *Cebes' Tablet* (fig. 19);
where, in the text and often in accompanying illustrations, philosophical mountaineers are shown clambering past Fortune, Opinion, and other distracting women toward the chaste figures of
Truth and Felicity on the summit.[2] But the iconographic potential
of Donne's "Truth" fades as he urges us on to the rigors of the climb
itself:

> . . . and hee that will
> Reach her, about must, and about must goe;
> And what the hills suddennes resists, winne so.
>
> (ll. 80–82)

In a time when the resolve to "Seeke true religion" must immediately stumble, as it does in Donne's poem, on the question, "O
where?" (l. 43), our assurance can be only that truth lies in the striv-
ing toward her, in the tortuous activity of "inquiring right" (l. 78)
rather than in the leisurely contemplation of an achieved vision.
For Donne as for Petrarch and Augustine before him, the pursuit
of truth is not a "matter of romping around on level ground," but

of "puffing and panting up a steep mountain-face."[3] We reach toward the "hard knowledge" of "mysteries" that "Are like the Sunne, dazling, yet plaine to all eyes" (ll. 86–88). Here the chief attribute of Ripa's *Veritas* finally shines forth. Yet the female Truth has now, at the end of the quest, become vaguely masculine by virtue of the pun on "Sunne" and the association of this hill with the Psalmist's "holy hill of Zion" on which, he says, "have I set my King" (2:6). She has also dissolved into paradoxical "mysteries" at once evident ("plaine" oddly recalls the "plaine" and "unhansome" Genevan mistress rejected before) and yet impossible to behold. It is as if the blinding illumination to be gained on the summit should serve, like the satire as a whole, to question the conventional representations of truth we may have (untruthfully) pictured when we stood with the poet at the foot of the hill, before answering the poem's call to exercise the "mindes indeavours" (l. 87).

This subtle play on the image of truth may seem incidental to the passage, but it is surely intriguing that as Donne broods on the hard and lonely climb around the obstacles of competing churches, a part of his imagination should fasten on the controversy over images. A little after the passage on the "huge hill" he charges those who would humble themselves to the tyrannous power of popes and reformers alike with "idolatrie" (ll. 95–102). A little before it he invokes this very controversy as the touchstone of his skepticism: "To adore, or scorne an image, or protest, / May all be bad; doubt wisely" (ll. 76–77). If the search for truth raises the problem of giving her a form "plaine to all eyes," Donne's evoking and then retracting "her" image seems to move doubtfully between adoration and scorn. Indeed, the Second Psalm, on which Donne would later preach, seems to hover over these lines, not only in their echo of the "holy hill of Zion" but in the psalm's emphasis on breaking the bonds of the "kings of the earth" (2:2–3), in its appeal to wisdom (10), and in its derision and anger that match the "brave scorn" (l. 1) of Donne's tone. In this context the satire's final meditation on authority—with its broad contempt for the Gregories and the Martins of the world who have fashioned themselves into idols by "unjust / Power from God claym'd"—taps the psalm's own destructive force: "Why do the heathen rage, and the people imagine a vain thing? . . . Thou shalt break them with a rod of iron; thou shalt dash them in pieces like a potter's vessel" (2:1, 9).

Some twenty years later, when Donne comes to preach on the "outward helps" to devotion afforded by ritual and ceremony, the doubt seems to be resolved and the anger cooled in the conciliatory rhetoric molded for the Anglican church by Hooker and Andrewes as well as by Donne himself: "If our Adversaries would be bought in [*sic*] . . . we should not be difficult in meeting them halfe way, in things, in their nature, *indifferent*" (7:433).[4] Donne argues that the Elizabethan *Injunctions* of 1559 were properly directed against the abuse of sacred imagery, especially against "*monuments of feigned miracles*" which could be made to "*speak*, and *move*, and *weep*, and *bleed*," and against "Images of *God* who was never seen" (7:432). Such "pernicious Errors" apart, the impartial Christian will understand that images have "sometimes a good, sometimes a bad sense in the Scriptures" (7:431), and that, as Jerome and Calvin would agree, so far as pictures in the church "may conduce to a reverend *adorning* of the place, so farre as they may conduce to a familiar *instructing* of unlettered people, it may be a losse to lack them" (7:432). It is true, Donne concedes, "that where there is a frequent preaching, there is *no necessity* of pictures; but will not every man adde this, That if the true use of Pictures bee preached unto them, there is *no danger* of an abuse; and so, *as Remembrancers* of that which hath been taught in the Pulpit, they may be retained" (7:432). The careful navigation between "sometimes a good" sense and "sometimes a bad," and between "no necessity" and "no danger," is typical of Donne's strategy in the sermon. Having asked us to imagine his biblical text (Hosea 3:4) as "*our Mappe*" (7:415), as "a *whole Globe*" and "an *intire Spheare*" (7:416), he charts our course between Rome and Geneva, "as farre from their blasphemous overboldnesse" who profane the spiritual significance of Christ's sacrifice in the idolatry of the Mass, "as from their over-tendernesse, who startle at the name of *Sacrifice*" (7:429). "*Vae Idololatris*," Donne concludes, "woe to such advancers of Images, as would throw down Christ rather then his Image: But *Vae Iconoclastis* too, woe to such peremptory abhorrers of Pictures . . . as had rather throw down a Church, then let a Picture stand" (7:433).

There is one revealing tack in the course of this argument. The Elizabethan injunctions Donne alludes to had sought to ban offensive images secreted for private use as well as those on public display. The construction Donne puts on this point of the law, however, virtually reverses its original thrust. He tells us that it "reaches as well to pictures in private houses, as in Churches, and forbids nothing in the Church, that might be retained in the house" (7:432). The strained emphasis on what the law permits, despite its obvious overall intention to discourage the keeping of religious pictures, hints as little else does in this disinterested performance at Donne's personal stake in the topic. For its effect is to disarm the busy old fools who, in the *Songs and Sonets*, always threaten to intrude on Donne's perfect but fragile private retreats, to violate the "pretty roomes" of the poet's intimate life.

Of Donne's own rooms in the Deanery at St. Paul's, we have an intriguing if partial record in the bequests specified in his will.[5] His closest friends were to be given pictures as mementos. Henry King, his executor, was to have the two portraits of Paolo Sarpi and his biographer, Fulgenzio, which hung in the parlor. Robert Ker would have Donne's own portrait "Taken in Shaddowes . . . many yeares before," presumably the Lothian portrait of the young Donne as a melancholy lover, with its inscription parodied from the Third Collect for Evensong: *Illvmina tenebras nostras Domina*. The four "large Pictures of the fower greate Prophettes" were, however, to remain in the hall, just as "that large Picture of auncient Churchework" was to be left in the lobby leading to Donne's chamber, and still other unspecified pictures were to stay in the garden as part of the Deanery furniture Donne would reserve for his successors. Several of Donne's friends were to have their choice from among still other unnamed paintings "that hange on the same syde of the Parlour" or in the "little Dynynge Rowme" or elsewhere in Donne's house. The will lists fifteen paintings by subject matter and suggests through such other provisions that there may have been twenty-five or thirty pictures in all, not counting the hanging maps one would like to suppose were also in Donne's possession—for maps are prominent in the inventories of other private holdings and, as a source of imagery, nearly inevitable in Donne's writing.[6]

The only identifiable picture mentioned in the will is the Lothian portrait, one of the seven surviving images of Donne that begin with an unassuming miniature of him at age eighteen, in 1591, and end with the macabre drawing, immortalized by Walton's *Life*, of Donne in his shroud; this final sketch, itself lost, served as the model for both the Droeshout engraving published in 1632 as the frontispiece to *Deaths Duell* and the carved effigy of Donne in St. Paul's Cathedral. His own image, as we might guess from Walton's report of the meticulous ritual that surrounded the making of the deathbed sketch, fascinated Donne. The surviving portraits offer a series of shifting, carefully contrived poses that vividly reflect the several different selves Donne would fashion for himself—the fastidious "Jack," the sober courtier, the august divine. It would be no less revealing to have a clearer sense of Donne's other pictures.

His was not a large collection by the standard of the long galleries then coming into fashion in great houses, but it was surely large enough to have filled nearly every corner of Donne's little world with imagery.

What we can tell about the display of these paintings, however, betrays the concern of the preacher who had so carefully balanced the scruples of the iconoclastic controversy. The public rooms contained paintings, like the portrait of King James also among Donne's bequests, on which no suspicion could fall: the large architectural study in the lobby, the "Sceleton" in the hall, the portraits of Sarpi and Fulgenzio in the parlor. These last quite possibly came to Donne from Italy by way of Henry Wotton, who is known to have sent portraits of Sarpi to several of his friends as well as to the king.[7] Just as Herbert was pleased to find in the writings of the Spaniard Valdesso "that God in the midst of Popery should open the eyes of one to understand and expresse so clearly and excellently the intent of the Gospell," Donne admired Sarpi for the Venetian's opposition to the papacy and for the reformist cast of his *History of the Council of Trent*.[8] Sarpi's portrait on Donne's wall would have symbolized Donne's hope for an eventual reunion of the churches in a moderate consensus of the sort implied by his willingness to meet "our Adversaries . . . halfe way." Otherwise the four prophets in the hall and the "Picture of Adam and Eve which hanges in the greate Chamber" suggest that the public areas of the Deanery were decorated with Old Testament histories securely within the unobjectionable category of commemorative images. The furnishing of Donne's smaller, private rooms, though, reveals an eye still drawn far more than half way toward the devotional imagery of his mother church. A "Picture of the blessed Virgin Marye" hung in the "little Dynyng Chamber" and a "Picture of Marie Magdalene in my Chamber" (as opposed to the "greate Chamber"). Two paintings are noted as hanging in Donne's "Studdy"—the room he would turn, on his deathbed, into an artist's studio for the sake of the final portrait that would become, says Walton, "his hourly object till his death." Here were a "B: Virgin and Joseph" and a "Picture of layinge Christe in his Toombe," the latter an appropriate backdrop for the "entombment of Donne" sketched out under its gaze.

Such quarters would have preserved more than a whiff of Roman piety. They would, indeed, have struck an observer familiar with Donne's poetry as not only deeply reminiscent of the adoration for the Virgin that suffuses Donne's earlier "La Corona" and "A

Litanie," but also the perfect imaginative setting for those poems. Shut in the "little roome" of the Virgin's womb, the God of "La Corona" who is "all" and "every where" "Yeelds himselfe to lye / In prison," his "Immensity cloysterd" in a tiny space both "*deare*" and claustrophobic (Sonnet 2, p. 319).[9] Later in this sequence of sonnets modeled on the rosary, Christ's confinement becomes the type of his sacrifice, when his "infinity" is measured "to'a span, / Nay to an inch," almost as a prisoner paces off the dimensions of his cell (Sonnet 5, p. 320). The very coincidence of a "Mary and Joseph" and an "Entombment" on the study's wall may have seemed to Donne an emblem of the mystery implied in this echo of womb and tomb. When, in another poem, the feasts of the Annunciation and of the Passion should chance to fall on the same day, Donne's soul can see "Christ hither and away," and his virgin mother "at once . . . stay / Reclus'd at home, Publique at Golgotha" (pp. 334–36, ll. 2, 11–12). In "A Litanie" the Virgin is "That she-Cherubin, / Which unlock'd Paradise" by unlocking her womb, thereby opening a chamber that her illustrious tenant could use as a kind of dressing room in which to button up his flesh before leaving the house on his public ministry, "for there / God cloath'd himselfe" (p. 339). Christ, here in Mary's womb, is "light in darke," a chiaroscuro detail that may remind us of the way Donne himself, save for the dramatic illumination of his face and hand, seems muffled within the somber "Shaddowes" of the Lothian portrait. In these lines the room-as-womb becomes a hidden, sacred enclosure, nurturing and stifling at the same time.

In the sermons as well as the poems Donne seems preoccupied with such ambivalent distinctions between private and public spaces. On Candlemas Day Donne's text is Matthew 5:16, "Let your light so shine before men, that they may see your good works." Preaching once more on the uses and abuses of ceremonies, Donne again takes the middle road by defending the proper and modest function of lights in the church—to "awaken devotion"—from the "pestilent superstition" that candles hold some "effectual power" and are themselves "meritorious sacrifices" (10:89–90). Donne goes on to demystify candles by emphasizing that we are to understand them in terms of the Apostle's call for good works "before men": our light should shine out in public, "assiduously, day by day in our Sermons . . . powerfully in the Homilies of our Church . . . actually in our many sumptuous buildings, and rich endowments" (10:93). But when he turns for a moment to an example of a "private light"—to the kind of individual illumination that is, he insists, not what the biblical text urges upon us—Donne's language is suddenly flooded by a sense of mystery so bizarre and brilliant that its enchantment seems to outshine the public exhortation of the sermon:

> We have a story delivered by a very pious man, and of the truth whereof he seemes to be very well assured, that one *Conradus* a devout Priest, had such an illustration, such an irradiation, such a coruscation, such a light at the tops of those fingers, which he used in the consecration of the Sacrament, as that by that light of his fingers ends, he coulde have reade in the night, as well as by so many Candles. (10:93)

Sight has its public significance as a metaphor for the preacher's word and, more concretely, as a kind of euphemism for the church building fund. It has its private significance as a vision of flesh miraculously illuminated against a dark background, an image, again, like Donne's gleaming fingers in the Lothian portrait, or even, in "The Relique" (pp. 62–63), like the "bracelet of bright haire" spied in the lover's grave ("And he that digs it . . . Will he not let'us alone"). Donne of course makes us aware that no one can take the story of the priest's unusual reading-light seriously save for the "pious" monks who have foisted it upon the credulous, and yet in the crescendo of "illustration . . . irradiation . . . coruscation" all doubt seems for the moment swept away. Such moments of split consciousness betray a Donne both "hither and away," at once shedding a steady "Publique" light on the errors of superstition and "Reclus'd at home," in some private room of his mind, in a fantasy about the sparkle of holy light on the fingertips. "I am not all here," Donne elsewhere confides to his congregation: "I am here now preaching upon this text, and I am at home in my Library . . ." (3:110).

For all this, as John Carey is only the most recent scholar to remind us, it would be "an exaggeration to present" Donne "as a crypto-Catholic, furtively resorting to religious practices that he would, in public, have abjured." It would be all the more an exaggeration so to present him on the basis of a mood we might like to evoke about a long-gone room, even if his writing reflects a lasting attachment to the procedures of Ignatian meditation or, in the poems just touched on, a taste for the language of the Roman breviary and the Hours of the Blessed Virgin. It would be truer to the vexing contraries of his spiritual life to regard him, in the terms of an image Donne himself finds compelling, as the product of strong magnetic forces working on him by attraction and repulsion at once. Carey continues: "His situation was less simple. On the one hand, certain aspects of Catholic devotion were second nature to him. On the other, though he had become a part of the Anglican propaganda machine, he was keenly aware of shortcomings in each of the existing churches. Writing to Goodyer about the Catholic and the reformed religions, he described them as 'sister teats' of God's graces, but added that both were 'diseased and infected.' One corollary of this critical awareness was a sense of his own isolation from the company of God's elect: he was outcast, a part of no whole." [10] An apostate, Donne had cut himself off from the Catholic teat of his childhood. He could continue to yearn for its lost comfort even as he could flay the papists in *Ignatius his Conclave* and *Pseudo-Martyr*. On the question of images, as we have seen, he could be sweetly ecumenical; he could also condemn Catholic practice in language that verges on the hysterical. In this light the calmly reasoned position of the sermon on Hosea seems less a firm conviction reached after the groping of "Satyre III" than an unstable equilibrium of charged feelings held under careful rhetorical control but ready, on other occasions, to fly apart. It is worth briefly tracing the opposite courses of these feelings in the other sermons to understand the energy they impart to Donne's verse.

Although Donne is typically not regarded as a "visual" poet, his poems are nearly obsessed with the eye—with what is reflected or contracted in it, with the erotic power of two lovers' mutual regard (the "eye-beames twisted" of "The Extasie"), with the wonder of Elizabeth Drury's heaven-bound soul growing "all eye" ("Of the Progresse of the Soule," p. 257, l. 200), even with the harsh gaze of intrusive busybodies and with his own casual ability to eclipse them with a wink. Such intense perceptual dramas seem to pack all experience into the sight, and almost to grant a fully sentient, and sensuous, life to the eyeball itself. In his sermon on 1 Corinthians 13:12 ("For now we see through a glass darkly . . .") Donne appeals to the traditional view supporting such imagery, that sight is "so much the Noblest of all the senses, as that it is all the senses." Just as the rational soul subsumes the lower vegetative and sensitive souls, so "All the senses are called Seeing; as there is *videre & audire, S. John turned to see the sound*; and there is *Gustate, & videte, Taste, and see how sweet the Lord is*; And so of the rest of the senses, all is sight"

(8:221).[11] This hierarchy of perception is metaphysical as well as psychological. For when at the resurrection we come to see God "face to face," there will be "no more working upon men, by preaching" (8:233), indeed no more spoken or audible language, so that even "the tongues of Angels, the tongues of glorified Saints, shall not be able to expresse what that heaven is" (8:231). If the "Ministery of the Gospell" is "Gods picture," in the fullness of the revelation God will "turne away that picture, and shew his own face" (8:233). The sermon ends in a celebration of that inexhaustible vision. In eternity we shall be "as glad to see, and to know God, millions of ages after every daies seeing and knowing, as the first houre of looking upon his face" (8:236).

Yet even as he exalts that final vision, Donne insists on the primacy of the word. Audible language is not merely, as one of the sermon's lines of argument proposes, a necessary limitation of our partial knowledge, "So that this day," Easter Sunday, 1628, "this whole Scripture is fulfilled in your eares; for now, (now in this Preaching) you have some sight, and then," at the last day, "a perfect sight of all" (8:219–20). From this we must suppose that Scripture as we hear it preached is but a hazy adumbration of the sight of God, superior to the light cast on the book of creatures by natural reason, as Donne tells us, but still far dimmer than the perfect vision that awaits us. But as Donne's imagination begins to pull in another direction—toward Paul's rapturous possession by the power of the word—speech and hearing no longer figure as the prelude to vision. They become instead the very medium of revelation, and then a corrective against the temptations of the eye:

> When S. *Paul* was carried up *In raptu*, in an extasie, *into Paradise*, that which he gained by this powerful way of teaching, is not expressed in a *Vidit*, but an *Audivit*, It is not said that he *saw*, but that he *heard unspeakeable things*. The eye is the devils doore, before the eare: for, though he doe enter at the eare, by wanton discourse, yet he was at the eye before; we see, before we talke dangerously. But the eare is the Holy Ghosts first doore, He assists us with Rituall and Ceremoniall things, which we see in the Church; but Ceremonies have their right use, when their right use hath first beene taught by preaching. Therefore to hearing does the Apostle apply faith. (8:228)

The smooth ascent through the senses up to the glorious vision on the top rung here yields to an agonistic model of perception in which the Devil and the Holy Ghost compete for entry through the eyes and the ears. Only when the soul has been fortified through the "doore" of the ear can it repel the danger assaulting the weaker portal of the eye. Even in the "Rituall and Ceremoniall things, which we see in the Church" the Devil stands ready to invade the eye of the Christian who has not heard their "right use." But, as Luther had observed (thinking, Erikson would argue, of the recovery of his own power of speech after the "fit in the choir"), "*Ein Woertlein kann ihn faellen*"—"a little word can overthrow him."[12]

Indeed, when Donne's text is the account in Acts 9:4 of Paul's conversion itself, he replaces the hierarchy of vision with an alternative hierarchy of the word:

> Our Regeneration is by his Word; that is, by faith, which comes by hearing. *The seed is the word of God*, sayes Christ himselfe; Even the seed of faith. Carry it higher, the Creation was by the word of God; *Dixit, & facta sunt*, God spoke, and all things were made. Carry it to the highest of all, to Eternity, the eternall Generation, the eternall Production, the eternall Procession of the second Person in the Trinity, was so much by the Word, as that he is the Word; *Verbum caro*, It was that *Word*, that was made *Flesh*. (6:216)

Carried higher and higher, Donne's imagination dwells on the sheer stunning force that descended upon Paul when, as the Scripture says, "he fell to the earth, and heard a voyce, saying, Saul, Saul, why persecutest thou me?"

> [God] speaks in his Canon, in Thunder, and he speaks in our Canon, in the rumour of warres. He speaks in his musique, in the harmonious promises of the Gospel, and in our musique, in the temporall blessings of peace, and plenty. . . . Princes are Gods Trumpet, and the Church is Gods Organ, but Christ Jesus is his voyce. . . . Man hath a natural way to come to God, by the eie, by the creature; So *Visible things* shew the *Invisible God*: But then, God hath super-induced a supernaturall way, by the eare. For, though hearing be naturall, yet that faith in God should come by hearing a man preach, is supernatural. God shut up the naturall way, in *Saul*, Seeing; He struck him blind; But he opened the super-naturall way, he inabled him to heare, and to heare him. God would have us beholden to grace, and not to nature, and to come for our salvation, to his Or-

dinances, to the preaching of his Word, and not to any other meanes. (6:217)

God's voice, like its resonances vibrating through the organ of the preacher's mouth, issues in an awesome polyphony. The opening "Canon" shot is echoed at the end of the passage in the pun on God's "Ordinances." "Thunder" resounds in the fainter rumblings of "rumour," and both join in a *concordia discors* with "promises" and "blessings." The shock of God's artillery blows the Apostle from nature to grace. Paul's blindness, we are made to feel, is more than compensated by his having heard at the same time a divine "musique" far deeper and richer than the ethereal *musica divina* of the Platonists—a cosmic performance scored for percussion, trumpet, organ, and "voyce." The "seed" planted in Paul's ears— and, through the sermon, in ours—sprouts into the "eternall Generation, the eternall Production" of the Word, filling the world with a dense foliation of sound.

The feeling here might be compared with that evoked in *The Pilgrim's Progress* when Christiana and her party find themselves refreshed in the Land of Beulah by a cacophony of bells, trumpets, and street cries. The "sharp aural images" characteristic of Bunyan's style suggest one point of convergence between the impact of Donne's preaching and the emphasis in Puritan writing—in Richard Baxter, for example—on the penetrating and quickening force of speech:

> Methinks the sound doth turn to substance, and having entred at the ear, doth possess my brain, and thence descendeth down to my very *heart*; methinks I feel it stir and work . . . Me-thinks I feel it digest as it proceeds, and increase my native heat and moisture, and lying as a reviving cordial at my *heart*; from thence doth send forth lively *spirits*, which beat through all the pulses of my Soul.[13]

Such, in "The Second Anniversary," was the "essentiall joy" that possessed young Elizabeth Drury in this world,

> Who with Gods presence was acquainted so,
> (Hearing, and speaking to him) as to know
> His face in any naturall Stone, or Tree,
> Better than when in Images they bee.
>
> (p. 264, ll. 451–54)

The pulsating force of the word is erotic and binding, carrying us up *in raptu*, as Paul was carried, into the clasp of a loving God. Indeed for Donne the very words on the page seem to twine themselves inside the text, as if they were burgeoning with the energy to pull us toward them once the way of utterance is opened: "There are words in the text, that will reach to all the Story of S. *Pauls* Conversion, embrace all, involve and enwrap all" (6:205).

If at times in Donne's writing this embrace of the word through the ear can guarantee the fidelity of the eye, at others the eye becomes a snare to faith so treacherous that the Christian must watch his every step—or glance. Such is the mood of Donne's sermon on Deuteronomy 12:30, "Take heed to thyself, that thou be not snared by following them after they be destroyed from before thee." Applying his text to the theme of safeguarding the church from Roman idolatry even after the promised land has been cleansed of its heathenish practices, Donne insists that

> A man does not ascend, except he stand. And such an ascension (an ascension without a redescent) *Moses* provides for here. First they should ascend to an abolishing of all Idolatry; And then they should stand in that state, persevere in that station, and perpetuate that ascension to themselves, by shutting themselves up against any new reentries of that Idolatry which had been once happily banished from amongst them. The inchoation of this ascension, that step which is happily made in the abolishing of idolatry, is in the beginning of this Chapter; *Ye shall utterly destroy all the places*, (which is a vehement gradation and heightening of the commandment:) It is a destruction, not a faint discontinuing of idolatry, but destruction; It is utter destruction, not a defacing, not a deferring of idolatry; and it is the utter destruction of the very place, not a seising the riches of the place, nor a slight correction of the abuses of the place, but the place it self, and (as is there expressed) all the place, not to leave the Devil one Chappel wherein the Nations had served their gods. And the Holy Ghost proceeds in the next verse with this particular vehemency, *You shall overthrow their altars, break their pillars, burn their groves, hew down their images, and destroy their names*. But all this is but the inchoation of this ascension, the first step in abolishing idolatry; The consummation of it is, in standing there; and that's in this Text, *Take heed to thyself, &c.* (4:132−33)

For the English as for the Israelites, not even the "utter destruction" of the external institutions of idolatry will suffice to stamp it out. The overthrowing, breaking, burning, hewing down, and destroying are only the "first step" in the ascent: "A man does not ascend, except he stand." The next step (*"Take heed"*) demands the continuing inward vigilance to maintain the high ground so won, "by shutting themselves up against any new reentries" of idolatry.

Hence it is, in Holy Sonnet XIV (p. 328), that even the Christian mended by the Reformation ("a faint discontinuing of idolatry"), if he would "rise, and stand," must compel God to more radical acts of destruction: "o'erthrow mee" as well as the altars of the Canaanites, "bend / Your force, to breake, blowe, burn and make me new." The verbs echoing the biblical passage (stand, overthrow, break, burn) as well as Donne's need, in the sonnet, to "breake that knot" snaring him into a betrothal with God's enemy, dramatize the conviction that the work of iconoclasm begun historically in Deuteronomy must be completed morally in the heart still drawn to the lure of "*their images*." And the "particular vehemency" of this work must go beyond the admonition of the Holy Ghost in Scripture, the sonnet suggests, to the purer "force" of God's breaking and renewing the spirit, as if the danger of "new reentries" were stronger than the power of mere persuasion to keep them out: "Reason your viceroy in mee, mee should defend / But is captiv'd, and proves weake or untrue."

The figure governing this opening passage, appropriate to a sermon preached on Ascension Day, is "our ascension in this life, (that which David speaks of, *Who shall ascend into the hill of the Lord?*)" (4:132). This invocation of the Psalmist's hill (24:3) returns us to the scene of "Satyre III." There an undiscovered "Truth stands" on that hill, and in the climb toward her, "To stand inquiring right, is not to stray." Now the poem's wise doubt of open inquiry, poised between the reluctance either to "adore, or scorne an image," hardens into a militant stand on top of a hill from which all inquiry has been barred as a threat to the victory achieved. Donne's *divisio* of the sermon, in this spirit, sounds like a posting of the orders of the day:

> Take heed you be not snared by [Idolaters]; and then by an over-curious enquiring into their Religion, *Enquire not after their Gods, &c.* And through the first, the matter of the Inhibition, we shall pass by these steps, 1. That there is no se-

curity; there is still danger, though the Idolater be destroyed. And secondly, that there is therefore a diligence to be required, *Take heed to thy self*. And then thirdly, That the danger from which this diligence must deliver us, is a snare; *Take heed lest thou be snared* (4:133).

Donne's own admonitions are actually quite restrained next to the more virulent antipapal slanders of the day. He assures us that it is according to God's plan that the idolaters should be allowed to remain among us—otherwise we might grow too confident of our spiritual security and so "remove all diligence" (4:136). It would be wrong to go so far as to take up arms against them, and yet you must take heed to yourself lest your perhaps natural curiosity about their practices ensnare you in their errors. It would also be prudent not to enroll your sons in foreign universities. The idolaters have, however, set an especially dangerous snare "for thy wife"; and as Donne exposes this one, all the jaunty anxiety about unfaithfulness that had run through the *Songs and Sonets* comes to the surface of the sermon:

> Her Religion, say they, doth not hinder her husbands preferment, why should she refuse to apply herself to them? We have used to speak proverbially of a Curtain Sermon, as of a shrewd thing; but a Curtain Mass, a Curtain *Requiem*, a snare in thy bed, a snake in thy bosome is somewhat worse. I know not what name we may give to such a womans husband; but I am sure such a wife hath committed adultery, Spiritual Adultery, and that with her husband's knowledge. (4:138–39)

Again, to regard the particular vehemence of this sermon as final or typical would be to disregard the constant habit of Donne's inconstancy. And yet his emphasis on the "husbands preferment," on the intimate world of the bedroom revealed, as in "The Sunne Rising," through curtains, and on the religious split within families, seems to touch the central nerves of Donne's life and poetry. The tangled snare coupling idolatry with adultery and fornication is both traditional in the literature of iconoclasm and deeply personal for Donne. Its use as material for Donne's imagination remains to be considered.

The apocryphal Wisdom of Solomon regards the "idols of the heathen" as "snares to the souls of men," for "the devising of idols is the beginning of fornication" (14:11–12).[14] While in the grip of the "frenzied revels" associated with the worship of images, men cannot "keep their lives, or marriages pure, / But one man waylays another and kills him or grieves him by adultery" (14:23–24). The worship of idols is thus the "beginning and cause and end of every evil"—of the "Defilement of souls, confusion of sex / Irregularity in marriage, adultery, and indecency" (14:26–27). Those who know God are not led astray by any "artful device of men . . . / Nor the fruitless labor of scene-painters, / A figure smeared with varied colors, / The appearance of which leads to desire in fools, / And they long for the lifeless form of a dead image" (15:4–5).

After clarifying the point that "the Scriptures use the sayd two words (idols and images) indifferently for one thing," the Elizabethan *Homilie against perill of Idolatrie* (1563) calls special attention to this apocryphal text as proof that images are an "abomination, a temptation unto the soules of men, and a snare for the feet of the unwise," and that "the invention of them was the beginning of spirituall fornication" (pp. 12, 15, 60).[15] The *Homilie* bases its condemnation of all such snares in church ritual on the argument that

> the nature of man is none otherwise bent to worshipping of Images (if hee may haue them, and see them) then it is bent to whoredome and adulterie in the company of harlots. And as unto a man giuen to the lust of the flesh, seeing a wanton harlot, sitting by her, and imbracing her, it profiteth little for one to say, Beware of fornication, GOD will condemne fornicatours and adulterers: for neither will hee, being ouercome with greater inticements of the strumpet giue eare or take heede to such godly admonitions, and when hee is left afterwardes alone with the harlotte, nothing can follow but wickednesse: euen so, suffer Images to bee set in the Churches and Temples, ye shall in vaine bid them beware of Images, as Saint John doeth, and flee Idolatrie, as all the Scriptures warne us, yee shall in vaine preach and teach them against Idolatry. For a number will notwithstanding fall headlong unto it, what by the nature of Images, and what by the inclination of their owne corrupt nature.
>
> Wherefore as for a man giuen to lust, to sit downe by a strumpet, is to tempt GOD: So is it likewise to erect an Idole in this pronenesse of mans nature to Idolatrie, nothing but a tempting. Now if any will say that this similitude prooueth nothing, yet I pray them let the word of GOD, out of the which the similitude is taken, prove something.

> Doeth not the worde of GOD call Idolatrie spirituall for-
> nication: Doeth it not call a gylte or painted Idole or Im-
> age, a strumpet with a painted face: Bee not the spirituall
> wickedness of an Idols inticing, like the flatteries of a wan-
> ton harlot: Bee not men and women as prone to spirituall
> fornication (I meane Idolatrie) as to carnall fornication[?].
> (p. 61)

For us the fornication and adultery have become "spirituall." No longer the carnal orgies of the biblical idolaters, our abominations are perhaps less colorful but more insidious, catching our very souls in the wiles of a wanton harlot. The psychological process implied here is the consequence of the principle of interpretation brought to the passage of the Old Testament describing the decking of the Temple: "S. Ierome teacheth the sumptuousnesse amongst the Iewes to be a figure to signifie, and not an example to follow, and that those outward things were suffered for a time, untill Christ our Lord came, who turned all those outward things into spirit, faith, and trueth" (p. 68). Just as ritual has turned inward to adorn the new temple of the heart with spirit, faith, and truth, so its corruption is now similarly bred within—a furtive lust of the eye no less wicked than the lust of the flesh, as Matthew 5:28 confirms in its exposure of the adultery of the heart. Despite the preacher's warnings, our own "corrupt nature" is such that, once left alone with an image, we are prone to fall "headlong" into its—her—embrace. In this drama of temptation the nature of the image has also changed. In the Apocrypha the image "leads to desire": it provides the occasion and the spark for grieving another man by adultery. When the Scripture, in one of the several places here cited by the *Homilie*, warns the children of Israel against "whoring after" strange gods (Lev. 20:5), its intent is to forbid the actual adultery, incest, bestiality, and other profanations imagined to pollute the religious practices of Israel's neighbors. In the *Homilie*, however, and in the iconoclastic polemics it condenses and authorizes, the emphasis shifts so that the image itself becomes the object of desire, a "strumpet with a painted face." The man who gives himself to an image by that very act betrays his spouse.

As the *Homilie* amplifies this point through the contrast between the true church as the spouse of Christ and the "idolatrous Church" of Rome, its language becomes the sounding board for Donne's holy sonnet, "Show me deare Christ." Like Spenser's Duessa, the Catholic church is a

foule, filthie, olde withered harlot . . . and understanding
her lacke of nature and true beautie, and great lothsome-
nesse which of her selfe shee hath, doeth (after the cus-
tome of such harlots) paint her selfe, and decke and tyre
her selfe with gold, pearle, stone, and all kinde of pretious
iewells, that the shining with the outward beauty and glory
of them, may please the foolish fantasie of fonde louers,
and so entice them to spirituall fornication with her. . . .
Whereas on the contrary part, the true Church of GOD, as
a chaste matron, espoused (as the Scripture teacheth) to
one husband, our Sauiour Jesus Christ, whom alone shee is
content onely to please and serue, and looketh not to delight the eyes of phantasies of any other strange louers, or
wooers is content with her naturall ornaments, not doubt-
ing, by such sincere simplicitie, best to please him, who can
well skill of the difference betweene a painted visage, and
true naturall beauty. (p. 69)

Donne's sonnet echoes the phrasing of this passage—the "richly
painted" church on the other shore, the "pleasing" spouse—and
dramatizes its argument. Again, as in "Satyre III" there are hills to
be climbed, "travaile" to be endured, in the search for a church
"most trew." But measured against the obvious and complacent
choice offered in the *Homilie* (and in related texts like John Bale's
The Image of Both Churches [c. 1548]) Donne's poem (p. 330) travails
through a complicated swerve of feeling on its way to the abrupt
paradox of the closing couplet:

> Show me deare Christ, thy spouse, so bright and clear.
> What! is it She, which on the other shore
> Goes richly painted? or which rob'd and tore
> Laments and mournes in Germany and here?
> Sleepes she a thousand, then peepes up one yeare?
> Is she selfe truth and errs? now new, now outwore?
> Doth she, and did she, and shall she evermore
> On one, on seaven, or on no hill appeare?
> Dwells she with us, or like adventuring knights
> First travaile we to seeke and then make Love?
> Betray kind husband thy spouse to our sights,
> And let myne amorous soule court thy mild Dove,
> Who is most trew, and pleasing to thee, then
> When she'is embrac'd and open to most men.

The "spouse, so bright and clear" cannot be the "richly painted"
woman "on the other shore." She only shines, we know, with the

"outward beauty and glory" of her paint and jewels. But where we would expect the poet, like the homilist, to turn from the whore to the "chaste matron . . . content onely to please and serue" her husband, Donne finds instead one "rob'd and tore" who "Laments and mournes"—an image that glances not only at a reformed church violently stripped of adornment, but at a woman violated and wounded. The unhappy choice seems to be between two spouses chaste in neither case, the one flaunting herself, all too eager to be shown, the other no less exposed, as if the iconoclasm of the Reformation were itself a kind of sexual tampering.

This unsatisfactory choice only spurs the need to see a clearer spouse, until the increasingly explicit "amorous" longing at the end of the poem seems to cast doubt on the very motives of the search underway. If we seek her "like adventuring knights" then we seek her for the sake of conquest. The opening "Show me . . ." now reappears in the harsher "Betray . . ." of line 11, where the wish to have the true church palpably exposed "to our sights" barely conceals the desire to wrest her away from her husband, to commit spiritual adultery—"and that," as Donne remarks in the Ascension Day sermon, "with her husbands knowledge." That she should be "most trew, and pleasing" to her husband when she is "open to most men" recalls the "sincere simplicitie" and the "true naturall beauty" of the homilist's chaste spouse. But the lusty snicker in the word "open" marks the difference between Christ's true church—universal, welcoming, open to the embrace of faith—and the speaker's demand for a vision of that church pleasing to him. It betrays the failure of the traditional language of the "bride of Christ" to accommodate the mysterious body of the church to our perception. Just as the wit of the love poems often depends on our ability to cut through a web of fallacious comparison, this sonnet confronts us with what Donne, in the sermons, calls the "awful discrimination of Divine things from Civill."[16]

What is "most trew" to God turns into a blasphemous falsification when we push the metaphor of the "bride" from concept to image; and our recoil from the blunt impact of that discovery reinforces the irony that to seek her in this way is to lose her all the more, the closer we seem to approach. The "Show me" of line 1 generates the poem's quest for an image to embrace. That image appears only in sullied forms that at once disappoint the eye and rekindle its longing for an object "bright and clear." The poem thus evokes the urgency of the speaker's desire while it reveals the idolatrous, and adulterous, contamination of that desire to "make love" to the image it seeks. In so doing, it confirms the severe teaching of the *Homilie* on the "corrupt nature" of man, but it also contains an implicit critique of the homilist's procedure—for if we are susceptible to a chronic lust after images, then the image of the "chaste matron" can be no better for our spiritual health than that of the "withered harlot."

All the crosscurrents of attraction and repulsion flowing through Donne's preaching on the image are channeled into this sonnet, but their force is felt throughout his poetry—often so powerfully that the making and breaking of images becomes Donne's figure for registering the deepest conflicts of his imagination. A man split between the Roman and the Reformed church, Donne would seem to have absorbed both sides of the iconoclastic controversy into the language of his little world, where their antagonism remains fully charged. When he is dead of love in the *Songs and Sonets*, Donne's curious friends will find his lady's picture in his heart—to their regret, since her image, like a concealed infection, breeds "a sodaine dampe" that will prove no less fatal to those who "survay each part" of his corpse than it was to him (p. 63). Or, in the Elegies, he offers the lady his own portrait—"Here take my Picture"—in a gesture combining affection and faint contempt: "Tis like me now," he observes, "but I dead, 'twill be more / When wee are shadowes both, then 'twas before" (p. 86).

The mutual reflection of the lovers' pictures in their eyes, the safekeeping of the lover's picture in the heart, become for Donne the virtually sacred emblems of their fidelity, as in the "Epithalamion" ("Thou art repriv'd old yeare," p. 137) where he praises the bride:

> Still in that Picture thou intirely art,
> Which thy inflaming eyes have made within
> [the bridegroom's] loving heart.

But the lover's "picture" in Donne's poems is also associated with death, with the decoration of corpses, and with images of the self— as in "Witchcraft by a picture" (p. 45)—captured and consumed by those inflaming eyes:

> I Fixe mine eye on thine, and there
> Pitty my picture burning in thine eye,
> My picture drown'd in a transparent teare,

> When I looke lower I espie;
> Hadst thou the wicked skill
> By pictures made and mard, to kill,
> How many wayes mightst thou performe thy will?

The lady's ability to burn and drown his picture suggests the "wicked skill" of murder by effigy, while the rhyme of "skill," "kill," and "will" reinforces the sense of the lethal authority embodied in her art. "By pictures made and mard": the phrase catches in brief the twin impulses of Donne's own witchcraft as a poet, and the shifts between them carry the tone of many of his poems through an ambivalent regard for the artifacts he imagines.

As perhaps Donne's most celebrated "picture," the "stiffe twin compasses" of "A Valediction: forbidding mourning" (pp. 49–51) provide a very clear example of an emblematic image marred in the making. Students will often remark that despite the apparent geometrical "firmnes" of their construction, the compasses cannot really be visualized at all: if the moving foot "comes home" it must rejoin the "fixt foot" at the center of the circle and cannot at the same time inscribe a "circle just" by completing the circumference. The convenient solution is to dispose of the problem by arguing that, as a *concetto*, a figure of thought, the compasses are not intended to be visualized at all (any more than Marvell's vast "vegetable Love" in "To his Coy Mistress" is intended to call forth visions of gigantic cabbages). But this shortcut overlooks a crucial function of the compasses in the poem's own argument. They first tempt us to visualize the love praised in the poem by an appeal to "sense," offering the kind of pictorial representation that even "Dull sublunary lovers" can perceive. The "failure" of that image suggests the mystery of a love "so much refin'd" that the appeal to sensual analogues (here, with telling irony, to instruments of measurement) cannot encompass it. A version of the poem's master paradox ("two soules . . . which are one"), the two incommensurable motions of the compasses weld "sense" and "Absence," reveal one aspect of love and conceal its essential mystery—and so negotiate the rhetoric of "tell[ing] the layetie our love" in a kind of *Biblia pauperum* for the illiterate while securing it finally from the "prophanation" of vulgar eyes.

The same ambivalent regard for the image, in a similarly playful sacred context, appears in "The Relique" (pp. 62–63). Here the notorious "bracelet of bright haire about the bone" is intended, Donne tells us, as a "device" to reunite him with his lover at the "last busie day." But it may well be mistaken for a relic if his grave is "broke up" in some superstitious age, for where "miracles are sought," miracles will be found even in such a modest token. But then, because they have "lov'd well and faithfully," the bracelet figures a love more truly miraculous than "mis-devotion" can understand—unless taught, not by the "bright" image in the grave, but by "this paper" on which the poem itself is written.

So too with that "subtile wreath of haire, which crowns" Donne's dead arm in "The Funerall" (pp. 58–59). Keeping his "limbes . . . from dissolution," the bracelet is "The mystery, the signe you must not touch." But, it appears, the bracelet may have actually been intended by the lady for his torture, "that I / By this should know my pain, / As prisoners then are manacled, when they'are condemn'd to die." What then is the meaning of the "signe"? Is it a magical preservative, a unifying symbol which because "These haires . . . upward grew" threads the body and the soul? Or is it the mark of the condemned prisoner that Donne would take with him into the grave only for revenge, "That since you would save none of mee, I bury some of you"? Donne dismisses his sign, an image made and marred, in a gesture that yet preserves its aura of mystery:

> What ere shee meant by'it, bury it with me,
> For since I am
> Loves martyr, it might breed idolatrie,
> If into others hands these Reliques came.

He is "Loves martyr," and in the martyrology of love appropriated from the religion of his childhood, he is entitled to his "Reliques." But his unfaithfulness had denied him, except in fantasy, the opportunity of martyrdom, and had led him to condemn those who were manacled and condemned to die for their religion's sake as pseudomartyrs. And so for others to discover his relics "might breed idolatrie," just as the lady's picture exhumed from his heart had bred a pestilential damp.

In the divine poems this tainted image of the lady in his heart must be repudiated, his own history effaced. Donne's spiritual autobiography, as he now constructs it, turns on the contrast between the "sighes and teares" he wasted on his mistresses "In mine Idolatry," and "this holy discontent" (p. 323), between an earlier "prophane" self now buried and the contrite Christian struggling through these poems—a contrast blurred, to Donne's vexation, when he finds his contrition "As humorous . . . / As my prophane Love, and as soone forgott" (p. 331). Because the corpse of that former life threatens to rise up—spangled, we might imagine, with its bracelets and wreaths of hair, all its dissolute humors resisting dissolution—the sincerity of the divine poems would seem to depend all the more on their making a clean break from the idolatry of the love poems. To be made new on the Pauline and Augustinian model demands that the old self and its idolatrous artifacts, the old self *as* an idolatrous artifact, be marred—broken, blown, burned. Image-breaking thus offers Donne a pattern for what the sermon on Deuteronomy 12:30 calls "utter destruction" (4:132–33) and a pattern for self-renewal as the temple is swept clean of the fragments of an old life and an old poetry. This is the pattern originally set for Donne by the crisis of his apostasy. Then an idolatrous Catholic self was rejected, its residual attachment to Roman ritual and imagery relocated in the private amatory religion of the *Songs and Sonets*. Now the love poet who is seen to have painted his fornications in holy colors—the idolatrous celebrant of all those erotic canonizations and ecstasies and martyrdoms—must be toppled as well. But as before there is not a clean break but a displacement. For the picture of the mistress, Donne substitutes a new image as the focus of his purer devotions: "Mark in my heart, O Soule, where thou dost dwell, / The picture of Christ crucified" (p. 328).

Harboring such an image against not only the suspicions of the radical reformers but against the authoritative pronouncements of Ridley, Jewel, and the homilist, Donne must go on the defense:

> Since Christ embrac'd the Crosse it selfe, dare I
> His image, th'image of his Crosse deny?
> Would I have profit by the sacrifice,
> And dare the chosen Altar to despise?
> It bore all other sinnes, but is it fit
> That it should beare the sinne of scorning it?
> Who from the picture would avert his eye,
> How would he flye his paines, who there did dye?
>
> (ll. 1–8)

Donne's elaborate conceit here, in "The Crosse" (pp. 331–33), will demonstrate that we cannot in fact avert our eye from the cross, since it is to be seen wherever we look—in swimmers (doing the breaststroke), in the masts of ships, in flying birds, in the lines marked on globes, even in the "sutures" of the skull, "which a

Crosses forme present" (l. 56). The "chiefe dignity" belongs to the "spirituall" cross of therapeutic tribulation (l. 26); its embrace not only reveals "th'instrument / Of God, dew'd on mee in the Sacrament" (ll. 15–16), but virtually transforms its bearer into Christ himself, and so validates the image absolutely by closing the gap between it and its prototype:

> For when that Crosse ungrudg'd, unto you stickes,
> Then are you to your selfe, a Crucifixe.
> As perchance, Carvers do not faces make,
> But that away, which hid them there, do take;
> Let Crosses, soe, take what hid Christ in thee,
> And be his image, or not his, but hee.
>
> (ll. 31–36).

Nevertheless the "Materiall Crosses" Donne finds everywhere in nature are also "good physicke" (l. 25), and the poet's eye delights in discovering the cruciform traces of the passion in the unlikeliest spots. If the world is a hieroglyph of the cross, then any individual cross must be honored as the epitome of a vast sacred pattern.

Harboring such an image, however, Donne must also reassure himself—if we consider the whole of the sonnet touched on before—that his embrace of "Christ crucified" is disentangled from that of his "profane mistresses":

> What if this present were the worlds last night?
> Marke in my heart, O Soule, where thou dost dwell,
> The picture of Christ crucified, and tell
> Whether that countenance can thee affright,
> Teares in his eyes quench the amasing light,
> Blood fills his frownes, which from his pierc'd head fell.
> And can that tongue adjudge thee unto hell,
> Which pray'd forgivenesse for his foes fierce spight?
> No, no; but as in my idolatrie
> I said to all my profane mistresses,
> Beauty, of pitty, foulnesse onely is
> A signe of rigour: so I say to thee,
> To wicked spirits are horrid shapes assign'd,
> This beauteous forme assures a pitious minde.

The structure of the sonnet (p. 328) seems to pivot on the contrast between "this present . . . night" of holy meditation and those past nights full of "all my profane mistresses"; between the "picture of Christ" and the "idolatrie" now forsworn; between what Donne says to his soul now and what he said to his lovers then. The turn itself seems at first to carry all the force of a rebuke to that former self: "No, no." On such a structure, with the last judgment his theme, we might imagine Donne praying for salvation by virtue of the image of Christ in his heart, reborn there in its "beauteous forme" after the crucifixion of the old, idolatrous Adam. By the process of spiritual sculpture imagined in "The Crosse," everything in Donne that hid that beauty would be carved away, leaving him not Christ's "image . . . but hee." Instead, unexpectedly and disturbingly, Donne would convince Christ to be merciful by addressing him in the cocky, self-assured voice of the *Songs and Sonets*, and by trying out on him the same argument he had once used to snare his profane mistresses: "as . . . / I said" to them, "so I say to thee."

The difference between the "pitious"—which is to say, pliable, and therefore even pitiable—mind of the mistress, and the "forgivenesse" of Christ tips the comparison toward blasphemy. What in *The Courtier* would be an artful compliment to the lady, that her "beauteous forme assures a pitious minde," becomes an attempt to seduce Christ into granting an assurance of mercy. This strange collapse of Donne's grave meditation into the rubble of amatory rhetoric is, for Carey, the symptom of "the incompetence of the polluted mind."[17] Donne himself seems to reflect on such a moment in Sonnet XIX: in "flattering speaches I court God" (p. 331). Similarly flattered, the picture of Christ seems to merge with the idolatrous image of the profane mistress—although its "beauty," we feel, is shadowed by the terror of judgment also reflected in Christ's face. For the picture of Christ seems to shift, even as Donne tries to fix it, between the image of pity he hopes to find there ("Teares in his eyes . . . Blood . . . that tongue . . . Which pray'd forgivenesse") and the image of awesome suffering and wrath ("frownes . . . pierc'd head . . . adjudge thee unto hell") he sees but would wipe away. And insofar as "that countenance" that "can thee affright" lingers on to the end of the poem as a kind of afterimage, line 13 takes an ominous twist: "To wicked spirits are horrid shapes assign'd." The horrid shape Donne would *not* see reasserts itself as the image rightly "assign'd" to him, as a reflection of the idolatry that continues to dwell in his heart, and as a judgment upon it.

Inevitably (in both Grierson's and Gardner's ordering of the Holy Sonnets) this poem is followed by "Batter my heart" (p. 328), where the assurance of mercy crumbles before the ram of God's power, where "Reason," which had just proven its way to that factitious assurance, "proves weake or untrue," and where, interestingly, the gender roles in the drama between Donne and God have been re-assigned. First feminized as the tearful and piteous mistress dwelling in the poet's heart, God now emerges as the jealous lover, the overmastering destroyer and creator, implored to expel his "ene-mie" from that heart, and to enthrall a feminized supplicant. This is an absent, even an adversary, God characterized by his "force" rather than his picture. He is a "three person'd" mystery, myste-riously both loving and violent in his assault on the hard heart, working upon it (as in the Protestant heart emblem) rather than within it. Thus, although we are likely to think of it as the exem-plary sonnet isolated in anthologies, "Batter my heart" might bet-ter be regarded as the companion piece to the previous sonnet ("Marke in my heart . . ."), the one poem shattering a devotional image that the other had set up.

The pull between these two poems makes itself felt all the more strongly in "Goodfriday, 1613. Riding Westward" (pp. 336–37). This masterful and wholly individual meditation on the crucifixion contains all of Donne's divided impulses in the tense, almost bru-tally physical bonds it dramatizes between the poet and the image of Christ "upon the tree":

> Let mans Soule be a Spheare, and then, in this,
> The intelligence that moves, devotion is,
> And as the other Spheares, by being growne
> Subject to forraigne motions, lose their owne,
> And being by others hurried every day,
> Scarce in a yeare their naturall forme obey:
> Pleasure or Businesse, so, our Soules admit
> For their first mover, and are whirld by it.
> Hence is't, that I am carryed towards the West
> This day, when my Soules forme bends toward the East.
> There I shoould see a Sunne, by rising set,
> And by that setting endlesse day beget;
> But that Christ on this Crosse, did rise and fall,
> Sinne had eternally benighted all.
> Yet dare I'almost be glad, I do not see
> That spectacle of too much weight for mee.
> Who sees·Gods face, that is selfe life, must dye;
> What a death were it then to see God dye?
> It made his owne Lieutenant Nature shrinke,
> It made his footstoole crack, and the Sunne winke.

Could I behold those hands which span the Poles,
And turne all spheares at once, peirc'd with those holes?
Could I behold that endlesse height which is
Zenith to us, and our Antipodes,
Humbled below us? or that blood which is
The seat of all our Soules, if not of his,
Made durt of dust, or that flesh which was worne
By God, for his apparell, rag'd, and torne?
If on these things I durst not looke, durst I
Upon his miserable mother cast mine eye,
Who was Gods partner here, and furnish'd thus
Halfe of that Sacrifice, which ransom'd us?
Though these things, as I ride, be from mine eye,
They'are present yet unto my memory,
For that looks towards them; and thou look'st towards mee,
O Saviour, as thou hang'st upon the tree;
I turne my backe to thee, but to receive
Corrections, till thy mercies bid thee leave.
O thinke mee worth thine anger, punish mee,
Burne off my rusts, and my deformity,
Restore thine Image, so much, by thy grace,
That thou may'st know mee, and I'll turne my face.

These are meditations in an emergency; they reflect the trials of a spiritual life lived on the run rather than in the cloister. We are indebted to Carey for observing that this springtime poem—written evidently "in transit," while Donne was riding the sixty-five miles westward from Sir Henry Goodyer's estate at Polesworth, in the Forest of Arden, to Montgomery Castle—is oblivious to "what has become one of the most poetically renowned landscapes in the British Isles. . . . Warwickshire and Shropshire, with their rivers, birds, trees and sizeable populations, have been obliterated—as, for that matter, has Donne's horse. It is no earthly terrain he passes across. The poem's geography is surreal. He moves like a planet away from a giant crucifix, the landscape's only feature, which he dare not look at, and on which Christ hangs, watching him. In all the two counties, Donne and Christ are the sole figures." [18]

This very striking sense of what the poem blots out helps us to feel how intensely all the energy of vision in it is focused on what Donne "should see"—"There," in the east on this Good Friday— the "spectacle" of the crucifixion. The "should" in line 11 knots together the opposing forces straining Donne's vision. The actual scene of the crucifixion—the muddy mix of dust and blood, the torn flesh, the "miserable mother"—is long past but vividly "present yet unto my memory," present to the exclusion of all else, and so compelling as almost to persuade us that Donne would see it if he dared to look over his shoulder. It is present for the meditator using the resources of memory, in the first step of his spiritual exercises, to compose the "place" of his meditation; present, too, in the sense that Christ's sacrifice occupies an eternal moment in the design of salvation history; but present above all in the imagined setting of the poem, where Christ, looking toward the meditator, seems to anticipate the final prayer by burning the image of the crucifixion into the back of Donne's skull.

Yet even as his "Soules Forme bends toward" the cross, Donne is "hurried," "whirld," and "carryed" from it, and not just by the "forraigne motions" of pleasure or business. Against the pull of the image Donne pulls back, recoiling from its terror: "Yet dare I'almost be glad, I do not see" what he nonetheless does see, "That spectacle of too much weight for mee." This anguish is reflected in the series of questions that propel Donne through the middle of the poem: could he behold "those hands . . . that endlesse height . . . that blood . . . that flesh"? Durst he cast his eye on Christ's "miserable mother"? The answer, as A. B. Chambers has suggested, is no, and yes: "The self-questioning must take the form it does because only thus can Donne simultaneously affirm the impossibility and the inevitability of seeing what he cannot and yet must see." Every detail sketched into this vision, each more painful than the last, only adds to the crushing "weight" of that spectacle—until Donne himself, stretched between east and west, seems to have taken on all the tortures of the cross. From this impasse, Chambers goes on to argue, the poem moves toward a resolution in the understanding that "one must ride to Last Judgement in the West to receive an oriental resurrection."[19] Since only through suffering the mortification of Christ's passion can the Christian heart be opened to the vivification of grace, the poem's strain is relieved in the paradox Donne elsewhere finds both witty and comforting—that in matters of faith as well as cartography, "East and West touch one another and are all one" (2:199). Donne does of course find the reassurance, as he turns to the final colloquy, that God's anger is restorative. But the fear of not being worth that anger, the hunger for punishment, and the fleeting resentment of "I turne my backe to thee," all leave the end of the poem no less jarring than the middle.

We might remark here the difference in tone between Donne's encounter with Christ's image and an otherwise very similar moment in Nicholas Sander's *A Treatise of the Images of Christ*. Deflecting the hammer blows of Bishop Jewel, the recusant Sander explains that "God should be contrary to himself" if he were to forbid the making of an image:

> For he hath so made us, that we cannot learne, know, or understand any thing, without conceiuing the same in some corporal Image or likeness. Our knowledge commeth by the senses, of yᵉ which our eies are the chefe. They see visible Creatures, and heare soundes by voices, whereby the common sense being informed with such images as it is able to cōceaue, offereth the same to our phantasie or imagination, whēce the mind beginneth to gather knowledge & to print (as it were) or to graue in it self that, which is powred into it by the senses.
>
> And so ofte as the mind will either use or encrease his knowlege, it alwaies returneth to those images and figures, which it receaued and laied up, to thend it might have wherewith to occupie or to delight it selfe, when occasion should require.
>
> If then at what time I reade that Christ died with his hands stretched and nailed vpon the woode of the Crosse, I may and necessarily must deuise with my self an Image which sheweth so much (otherwise I can neuer vnderstand yᵗ which I read) how can a wise man doubt, but that thing may be laufully set furth in an outward Image, which must be necessarily conceiued in an inward Image?[20]

Donne's poem shares the belief that we "may and necessarily must" devise an internal image in order to conceive of Christ at all, but having devised it, the eye in the poem internalizes it more radically than Sander's epistemology envisions, and suffers under its intolerable "weight." If Christ's death made the earth "crack," and Nature "shrinke," the poem shows how the more fragile sphere of the soul in meditation—unable to contain the space between "those hands which span the Poles"—also cracks under the internal pressure of Christ's image. What would it be like, the poem asks, to push the meditative act so far as to "deuise with my self" not the flat, conventional image of Christ "nailed vpon the woode of the Crosse," but one so full of the horror and wonder of that event as actually to represent the death of God? Far from presenting me with a figure "wherewith to occupie or to delight" myself, it would be an image on which I should not dare to look. It would turn the art of meditation into a terrifying exercise in negative theology, stunning me with the sense of God's incomprehensibleness rather than bringing me closer to him in imaginative participation with his suffering. Donne's "Could I behold . . ." signifies the necessary absence of an adequate image of the crucifixion even as it suggests the force of that image in the middle of his poem.

The result is a poem which applies all its formal ingenuity toward an effort to control a structure through which the imagined experience of the crucifixion threatens to explode. The structure is suggestively emblematic. The "hands which span the Poles" of the cross stretch across the middle line of the poem, and as these are the hands of the cosmic Christ spanning the poles of the world, they also seem to stretch across the space of the text, catching Donne's errant soul as it whirls out of its orbit and bending it back toward the east. We know from "The Annuntiation and Passion" that God's "embleme" is the circle—in him, "As in plaine Maps, the furthest West is East" (pp. 334–35). So, in the metaphysical geometry of "Goodfriday," what we experience as linear distance in texts and in the world, in God's design circles back on itself; and so the soul must be instructed, in the end, that through the paradox of grace turning one's back on Christ can turn into a way of approaching him. This circular movement, turning around the poles of the cross in the middle, bends the beginning and the end of the poem together like the text circumscribing a roundel, or like the wreath formed by the seven sonnets of "La Corona," at whose "end begins the endlesse rest" of a meditation circling endlessly around its "changing unchang'd" God (p. 318). The language of the *Songs and Sonets* is helpful here, for in them as in "Goodfriday" Donne centers the formal "patterne" ("The Canonization," p. 15, l. 45) of his celebratory poems on a crucial image in the middle line—the Phoenix of "The Canonization," the "one little roome" of "The good-morrow" (p. 7), here, the hands of Christ—around which the structural "firmnes" of an emblematic imagination "makes my circle just, / And makes me end, where I begunne" (p. 51). "The Canonization," like "Goodfriday," turns the hurried sprints of pleasure or business, those strings of raw experience that elsewhere run through Donne's bitterest lines—"I have lov'd, and got, and told" (p. 39), "I spring a mistresse, sweare, write, sigh and weepe" (p. 56)—into a "well wrought" and enduring form. If, in "The good-morrow," "love, all love of other sights controules" (p. 7), in "Goodfriday" it is the sight of Christ, the "Sunne" setting and rising on the cross at the center, that controls the emblematic firmness of the poem.

As the poem's formal cause, all the poet's visual artistry—the conceit of the spheres, the emblematic circularity of the text, the imagined spectacle of the crucifixion—are necessary to give the devotion its shape. But it is to Christ, the poem's final cause, that Donne must at last yield responsibility for perfecting the text: it is Christ's hands that "turne" (and "tune") "all spheares at once," including the sphere designed by the hands of the poet. The final "corrections" Donne turns his back to receive are not merely the lashes of Christ's anger. They include the more subtle corrections of Christ's mercy—the readjustment of the vagrant "motions" of Donne's soul, and Donne's poem. The poem enters on its circle with Donne postulating the terms of the encounter with a kind of Euclidean arrogance: "Let mans Soule be a Spheare . . . and then . . . Hence is't." Now it closes with Donne, humbled like the Christ he imagines, putting the weight of his salvation on the one back strong enough to bear it. What matters in the end is not that I may know thee, but that "thou may'st know mee." The end of the poem thus corrects the beginning, a movement punctuated by Donne's emphasis on the soul's "forme," which, even as it "bends toward the East," is governed in its movement by the stronger opposing pull of worldly affairs. The failure to follow his soul's "naturall forme" is, as the end acknowledges, his "deformity." In this way the formative, constructive motions of the mind that go into the making of Donne's devotion come implicitly under the poem's own scrutiny.

From this final perspective, the image of Christ formed by the poet must itself be regarded as a deformity, a scum of rust that must be burned off before the untarnished image of Christ can be restored—restored, paradoxically, by the artisan uniquely qualified for his craft by having submitted himself to be deformed on the cross, just as Donne had imagined him. The making of the poem thus requires a joint effort, Donne creating the materials of his devotion ("Let . . . be"), the image of Christ on which, so convincingly has he done his imaginative work, he "durst not looke"; Christ, in anger and in mercy, correcting the deformed image of, and in, the meditator, and restoring his own. Yet the future tense of the last line leaves the circle broken: the crucial "turne" toward a face-to-face knowledge of God is reserved for a higher sphere even than Donne's masterpiece. In death the glorified soul, like Elizabeth Drury's in "The Progresse of the Soule," "Peeces a Circle" (p. 266, l. 508); but this world and its productions, to the anatomist's eye in "The first Anniversary," are "all in peeces, all cohaerence gone" (p. 237, l. 213). The emphasis on the "deformity" of Donne's devotions—on the deformity of the poem, formed with such care, in which the course of those devotions is traced—pushes its way through the emblematic integrity of the text. Shrinking and cracking, the circle refuses to close. Donne does not turn his face. Christ looks "towards mee" silently, so far withholding anger and mercy alike. The structure thus made and marred by the poet responds to the particular vehemence of the Holy Ghost's command, as Donne understands it in the sermons, to "hew down" the idolatrous "images" within the self. Such contrition may or may not be rewarded "by thy grace." Donne "bends toward" Christ, both by shouldering the imaginative weight of the crucifixion and by enduring the painful correction of his own poem. Will Christ piece the circle by bending toward Donne? The tone of the final lines is as much bold as submissive: even as he begs to be punished Donne lays down for his savior the conditions on which he will agree, we are almost made to feel, to turn his face. The force of the ending depends not only on the absence of the Christ whose loving punishment must be so fervently implored, but on Donne's assertive presence; on the kind of power Donne exerts over Christ by the very refusal to face him. "I turne my backe to thee" carries a harshness, even an effrontery, only partially softened by "but to receive / Corrections." The line, and the poem, suggest how strongly the voltage of Donne's piety flows across the gap between "I" and "thee," and how central to that turbulent piety is the confrontation between the poet's image of God, and God's.

The works of George Herbert and Richard Crashaw, each tapping the current of Donne's divine poems, will provide a final contrast. Donne's followers, if we remind ourselves of a drastic but perhaps useful simplification, settle the issue of iconoclasm in different but equally comfortable ways—comfortable because the solution in each case results in the taming of the obdurate self inherited from Donne. At crucial moments of intense dissatisfaction—we have seen his anguish, in "Sinnes round," at reconstructing the tower of Babel in the three emblematic "stories" of that poem—Herbert submits, as Donne never can, to the reassuring presence of the divine voice. He is content to imagine the church monuments "fall down flat," and content to see the light shining through the church windows as a metaphor of the "eternall word" shining through the holy preacher. His poetry is pieced together like a "broken Altar," and however artfully he may pile its stones into emblems, hieroglyphs, and verses of various shapes, however firm an architectural design *The Temple* may suggest, he is content to survey the collapse of his own "painted" fictions before the loving admonition of a friend. His image of the poet is the scribe, the "Secretarie of thy praise," copying out a "sweetnesse readie penn'd" in Scripture.[21] Crashaw, on the other hand, makes his submission to the power of the eye. He is not only content but often deliriously happy to dissolve himself in the swirling visions of hearts and darts and wounds and milk that flood through his imagination. His image of the poet, as of the mystic Saint Teresa, is the "sweet incendiary," heating language to the flashpoint where it will explode into a vision that numbs everything but the reader's wonder. His image of the book—here, "Mr. G. Herberts booke . . . sent to a Gentlewoman"—would have astonished Mr. Herbert most of all:

> Know you faire, on what you looke?
> Divinest love lyes in this booke:
> Expecting fire from your eyes,
> To kindle this his sacrifice.[22]

For both Herbert and Crashaw—and despite the complexity of feeling we have recently come to appreciate, especially in Herbert —the crisis of poetic, as of religious, authority is resolved, whether in submission to an ideal of childlike obedience to the father's voice, or in absorption into the baroque fantasies of the mother church. Donne's spirituality stands isolated, spanning the poles of Crashaw's visual Catholicism and Herbert's aural Protestantism, unable to support his weight on either one, unable to let go. The craftsman whose poetry hangs on that cross would have to suffer the agon of making and marring spared his disciples, with the one hand forming sacred images that the other hand deforms as profane.

6

Milton's Contest
"'Twixt God and Dagon"

The failure of Milton's visual imagination had until recently been so entrenched a critical commonplace that even those who would isolate a "pictorial" quality in his work were thrown on the defense. Dr. Johnson, objecting that Milton's "images and descriptions of the scenes and operations of Nature do not seem to be always copied from original form, nor to have the freshness, raciness, and energy of immediate observation," also reminds us of Dryden's opinion, that Milton "saw Nature . . . *through the spectacles of books*, and on most occasions calls learning to his assistance."[1] For Coleridge Milton was "not a picturesque but a musical poet"—a balanced judgment at least, but one that tips toward cruelty in Leavis's characterization of the poet's "sensuous poverty," and even more so in Eliot's chilly autopsy report that Milton suffered from a "hypertrophy of the auditory imagination at the expense of the visual and tactile."[2] Milton's defenders who, like John Peter, choose to argue on the same grounds can only conclude that by managing "bold and broad impressions, where the density given by detail is not needed," Milton did about as well as can be expected of the blind.[3]

Yet there is also the very different Milton whose poetry, as Hazlitt remarked, "is not so barren of resources." This is the poet in whom D. C. Allen, Wayne Shumaker, Louis Martz, and Jeffry Spencer find a strong visual sense; the poet in whose descriptions Arnold Stein discovers so careful an arrangement of "depth and chiaroscuro" that "the final effects may approximate those of painting"; and the poet whose imagination, for John Demaray, is so richly colored by *sacre rappresentazioni*, masques, and pageants that his *Paradise Lost* must be regarded as a "theatrical epic."[4] Roland Frye's massive collection of Miltonic analogues in the visual arts supports his argument, which otherwise remains circumstantial, that this poet

149

must not only have seen the great monuments of Renaissance and Baroque art during his Italian visit, but recalled them so clearly that the poems written during his blindness would make frequent and expert gestures toward history painting, landscape, and architecture as well as emblems, mosaic, enameled work, and stained glass.[5] This is also the poet whose last, iconoclastic drama must nevertheless be understood as Milton's final engagement with theatrical spectacle: *Samson Agonistes* may never have been intended for the debauched Restoration state of the 1670s, but it is, as Anthony Low maintains, "still essentially the kind of play Milton wanted those in authority to produce in some public theater of the 1640's."[6]

Criticism gives us at once a visual and a verbal Milton, with the split between them all the wider for the fact of Milton's blindness. The two can surely be reconciled as the several facets of Milton's talent—he of all poets was not barren of multiple "resources"—or admired as paradox. The "energy of immediate observation" may be blocked but still be felt to flow through Milton's later poetry, the poet standing like his own Samson "amid the blaze of noon, / Irrecoverably dark" (80–81).[7] Yet I would want to add, especially with a view toward *Samson* at the close of Milton's career, that the relationship between the two Miltons is agonistic in a more complex and interesting sense defined ultimately by that drama, but apparent also as it takes shape in the prose and in *Paradise Lost*. By ruining the Philistine "spectacle" Samson will soberly destroy an audience of his captors "Drunk with Idolatry" (1670). In the language of *Areopagitica* (1644), written in the years when Milton first had such a drama in mind, Samson will be the exemplary impure man purified by trial, and "triall is by what is contrary." Here Milton suggests the connection to be completed eventually in *Samson Agonistes*, between his own ideal of the "true wa[r]faring Christian"—he "that can apprehend and consider vice with all her baits and seeming pleasures, and yet abstain"—and Spenser's temperate iconoclast Guyon, whom that "sage and serious Poet" brings "through the cave of Mammon, and the bowr of earthly blisse that he might see and know, and yet abstain" (4:311).[8] To "see and know, and yet abstain": the phrase foreshortens a pattern of engagement and triumphant withdrawal that will inform Milton's drama as Samson proves, like the Phoenix, to be "vigorous most / When most unactive deem'd" (1704–5). Confronting the temptations offered by a procession of false comforters, Samson will affirm himself a "person separate to God" (31) by abstaining—vigorous most in the end, with a "force of winds and waters" (1547) to match the Spenserian "tempest" of Guyon's "wrathfulness" (2.12.83)—from what he had once seen and known all too well. This pattern also describes Milton's own agon as over the course of his career he confronts the baits and seeming pleasures of his own pictorial forms with the obligations, over and above, of writing as a militantly reforming Christian.

To approach Milton's iconoclasm in this way is to risk invoking what Edward W. Tayler has called "the Schizoid Axiom," that the "Puritan Moralist unconsciously distrusted the Humanist Artist."[9] The aim is rather to explore how Milton worked quite knowingly to resolve the divergent claims of craft and conscience, and in our doing so to move beyond the easy discovery of a "striking contradiction between Milton the poet and Milton the religious thinker," or the tidy conclusion that, as both a "Puritan" who "rebelled against sensuous worship" and a "poet" whose "mind was inveterately plastic and creative," Milton the "iconoclast is at the same time an idolater."[10] William Madsen, who cites these passages, is one of several critics who take pains to remind us that, even for rigid Calvinists, the abolition of images in worship does not necessarily entail a whitewashing of the imagination either in preaching or in poetry devoted to sacred themes. On the contrary, Calvin encourages ministers of the Gospel to make men "see Christ crucified," and he praises those capable of such imaginative preaching as "painters." Both Perkins and Baxter distinguish between the blasphemous crucifixes and pictures of the Roman church and the vibrant images of divine things that display themselves inwardly to the eye of faith: "get the liveliest picture of them in thy mind that possibly thou canst."[11] The Word spoken by the preacher, the Word planted in the faithful, carries its own radiant visual potential; properly "seen," it not only compensates for the loss of pictures as a help to devotion, but also satisfies the imagination so fully that only those mired in the carnal would still have resort to external images.

Such conciliatory reflections, however, are not typically Milton's. Quite apart from the hazard of tying his poetry to one or another authoritative pronouncement (his own included), we know that Milton characteristically chose to cast ideas in adversary roles. In what might be regarded as an ongoing interior drama of the poetry written during his blindness, the presence of the eye in his language is neither celebrated unequivocally nor spurned outright, but put to trials no less severe than those faced by Adam, Christ, and Samson. If the "Celestial Light" invoked in *Paradise Lost* responds to Milton's plea to "Shine inward" and "plant eyes" in the mind, the sightless poet will have been granted the gift of a luminous, prophetic vision, the power to "see and tell / Of things invisible to mortal sight" (3:51–55). But even here, the force of the invocation comes from a poignant, even bitter, awareness that the plea has as yet not been answered ("thee I revisit . . . but thou / Revisit'st not these eyes, that roll in vain" [3:20–22]). The invocation begins with a quiver of guilt. Can the poet presume "unblam'd" upon a realm of "unapproached Light" that is God's alone (3:3–4)? It ends, when the narrator resumes the "telling" of *Paradise Lost*, by reopening the gap between divine sight and human knowledge that had seemed momentarily bridged by the conjunction of "see and tell." The Father "sits / High Thron'd above all highth" (3:57–58). His eye commands a view of the whole creation "at once," and from "his sight" the angels receive "Beatitude past utterance" (3:59,61,62). The focus shifts from "things invisible" as the object of a privileged human vision, things seen and then translated into discourse, to God himself as the one qualified seer whose gaze confers a joy above translation. From this divine perspective, the urge to "see and tell" may look like a bold assault on God's "prospect high" (3:77). God, having "bent down his eye" (3:58), observes his adversary "bent . . . / On desperate revenge" (3:84–85). The remark refers directly to Satan, but as critics note, it seems for the moment also to reflect upon a poetic aspirant suffused in the glow of Neoplatonic desire and bent on a direct and steady illumination of mind and language—bent, even, on tapping a source of vision power "coeternal" (3:2) with God. This power the God who here presides over Milton's invocation "from above" (3:56) seems indisposed to grant.

To the extent that the urge to see, however inwardly and purely, is not severed from the frustration of actual blindness—and nowhere in the invocation is there a clean break—the poet cannot rest secure in what the Milton of the antiprelatical tracts had praised as a "*faith* needing not the weak, and fallible offices of the senses" (3:1). Again and again in the polemics of the 1640s (and as late as the 1670s, in his final tract, *Of True Religion*) Milton batters away at the "grossenesse, and blindnesse" of those who would return to the "new vomited Paganisme of sensuall Idolatry,"

> that they might bring the inward acts of the *Spirit* to the outward, and customary ey-Service of the body, as if they could make *God* earthly, and fleshly, because they could not

make themselves *heavenly*, and *Spirituall*: they began to draw downe all the Divine intercours, betwixt *God*, and the Soule, yea, the very shape of *God* himselfe, into an exterior, and bodily forme. (3:2)[12]

Here and elsewhere Milton inveighs against the "Idolatrous erection of Temples beautified exquisitely to out-vie the Papists," against the "snares of Images, Pictures, rich coaps, [and] gorgeous Altarclothes" (3:54), and against those who, like the impious Jews of Ezekiel 23, "go a whooring after all the heathenish inventions" because they crave a "religion gorgeously attir'd and desirable to the eye" (3:355). Although Milton cheers on those stalwart early bishops who "threw the Images out of *Churches*" (3:43), the danger lies not so much in the images themselves, which he might otherwise be willing to regard as "things indifferent" (3:12). It lies rather in a pustulant disease that breaks down the membrane between the inner and the outer self: "fixt onely upon the *Flesh*," the superstitious man "renders likewise the whole faculty of his apprehension, carnall, and all the inward acts of *worship* issuing from the native strength of the SOULE, run out lavishly to the upper skin, and there harden into a crust of formallitie" (3.3).

The same distinction between the inner and the outer man serves Milton in the divorce tracts when he insists that the true satisfactions of marriage must proceed from the mind rather than the body. Marriage as a physical union alone "can be no human society, but a certain formality; or guilding over of little better then a brutish congresse." Where a marriage is outwardly chaste but inwardly barren or turbulent, to oppose divorce is to "make an Idol of mariage, to advance it above the word of God" (3:423). Milton is intent upon arguing further that as the scriptural ground for divorce, "adultery" must itself be taken to signify not only the "trespas of the body" but also "any notable disobedience, or intractable cariage of the wife to the husband." The point depends on the biblical connection between adultery and idolatry. Just as, in Numbers 15:39, "willfull disobedience to any the least of Gods commandments is call'd fornication," and just as God therefore calls idolatry fornication, so in divorce proceedings fornication must be interpreted in as wide a sense as idolatry to include a "constant alienation and disaffection of mind" (4:179). Put to such uses, "idolatry" in Milton's writing expands beyond a veneration of images in worship or even an undue concern for outward formality and "ey-Service of the body" at the expense of "inward acts of the *Spirit*." These are the

symptoms of a lust for the visible and the tangible that can so con-
taminate the inner man as to render "the whole faculty of his apprehension, carnall." The part of that faculty which is inward and
mental is no less disastrously susceptible to idolatry than the bodily
eye, especially since the disease can fasten there unseen until it
breaks out in a poxy scum.

When this disease grips the body politic, as Milton believed it had
with the publication of the *Eikon Basilike* in 1649, iconoclasm becomes the necessary instrument of public health. When Charles I
was beheaded on January 30, 1649, advance copies of the "King's
Book" had already begun to circulate. This "Pourtraicture of His
Sacred Majestie," as it announced itself, was to become the most
effective piece of Royalist propaganda of the Civil War. It sparked
what Hughes calls an "explosion of pity" for the martyred king and
soon provoked a spate of attacks and vindications.[13] Apologists for
the regicide found themselves up against the extraordinary influence of a book that, they reported, was received with a kind of
"Idol worship" even by some who had been indifferent to the king's
fate.[14] Milton himself complains in *Eikonoklastes*, published in October 1649, that the "blockish vulgar" have set it "next the Bible,
though otherwise containing little els but the common grounds of
tyranny and popery, drest up, the better to deceiv, in a new Protestant guise, and trimmly garnish'd over"; and he adds that the king's
friends, "by publishing, dispersing, commending, and almost adoring it" have made it the "chiefe strength" of their cause (339–40). It
was bad enough that in the "superstitious rigor of his Sundays
Chappell" (358) Charles himself was an idolater—a charge that
Milton loses no opportunity to repeat. Now his parasites, whose
study was to "imitate him exactly" (351), have fashioned him into
an idol.

As Milton recognizes, the strong appeal of the *Eikon Basilike* lay
as much in the celebrated frontispiece designed by William Marshall
(fig. 18) as in the hash of polemic, chronicle, and meditation that
follows. Marshall, the engraver of Quarles's *Emblemes*, had also been
responsible for the unfortunate portrait of Milton published four
years earlier as the frontispiece to his *Poems*. For the *Eikon Basilike*
that "good-for-nothing artist" (as Milton calls him in a Greek squib
appended to the 1645 portrait) had created an image of the king at
prayer—the earthly crown at his feet, the crown of thorns in his
hand, the heavenly crown, shortly to be his reward, now the object
of his steadfast gaze. The background of the engraving is studded
with conceits appropriated from the emblem books for the honor

Figure 18. *Eikon Basilike* (1649), frontispiece

of the royal martyr. George Wither, who shared Milton's horror of idolatry, may well have been discomfited to find at the upper left a version of his own emblem of the "mighty Rockes" unmoved by wind and wave: it was now, in Wither's (misappropriated) language, the "firm foundation" of Charles's character that "bides the dread-full shockes" of fortune and envy (218).[15] The king must surely be venerated for that "manly constancy of mind" not tossed by opinion that Henry Peacham, with a marginal reference to Lipsius, had found in the same emblem.[16] It was now Charles in his undaunted courage who must also be seen to embody the very "pow'r of *Truth*" that Wither had discovered in the emblem, at the lower left, of the encumbered but resilient palm tree:

for as this *Tree* doth spread,
And thrive the more, when weights presse down the head;

So, *Gods* eternall *Truth* (which all the pow'r
And spight of *Hell*, did labour to devoure)
Sprung high and flourished the more, thereby,
When Tyrants crush'd it, with their crueltie.

(172)

From Milton's point of view it can only have been a grim irony that a device so resolutely anti-tyrannical in the emblem literature should itself be pressed into the eye-service of a tyrant.

With such motifs clustered around the pious figure of the king, the frontispiece becomes a rich pictorial synopsis of Charles's Christ-like virtues. It is his *Eikon* in a more nearly devotional than representational sense, and it intends to engage the viewer in a kind of sacred vision, *clarior é tenebris*, analogous to the king's own. Just as Charles can see more clearly through the darkness of his affliction, so the viewer sees not only the essence of the royal spirit revealed in the rocks and trees, but through the king's eyes—indeed, projected from the king's eyes—a manifestation of the crown of glory itself. This is the illuminated monarch celebrated in the Stuart masque as both the focus and the source of all ennobling visions. He is brought low but still (as Ben Jonson said of Charles's father) "placed high": "His meditations to his height are even, / And all their issue is akin to heaven." [17] Raised by his humility, we ourselves can say with him, and because of him, *Coeli Specto*. As if to emphasize the intensely visual mode of this experience, Charles seems not at all distracted by the book on the table before him, or attentive to its message, "In your Word is my hope." His vision, transfixed by beams of holy light, pierces the heavens to reveal things invisible to mortal sight.

Milton in reply scoffs at "the conceited portraiture before his Book," dismissing it as a piece of cheap manipulation "drawn out to the full measure of a masking scene, and sett there to catch fools and silly gazers" (342). But he is also compelled to admit its power, for "now, with a besotted and degenerate baseness of spirit," all too many Englishmen "are ready to fall flatt and give adoration to the Image and Memory of this Man" (344). In his *Tenure of Kings and Magistrates*, Milton had just exposed Charles as a tyrant. Against this new peril—Charles reinvested in the imagery of a saint—Milton defines his own role as an iconoclast:

[T]he Picture sett in Front would Martyr him and Saint him to befool the people. . . . But quaint Emblems and devices begg'd from the old Pageantry of some Twelf-nights entertainment at *Whitehall*, will doe but ill to make a Saint or a Martyr. . . . In one thing I must commend his op'ness who gave the title to this Book, Εἰκὼτ Βασιλικὴ, that is to say, The Kings Image; and by the shrine he dresses out for him, certainly would have the people come and worship him. For which reason this answer also is intitl'd *Iconoclastes*, the famous Surname of many Greek Emperors, who in their zeal to the command of God, after long tradition of Idolatry in the Church, took courage, and broke all superstitious images to peeces. (343)

Their courage must now be Milton's own, for "the People, exorbitant and excessive in all their motions, are prone ofttimes not to a religious onely, but to a civil kinde of Idolatry in idolizing their Kings: Though never more mistak'n in the object of their worship" (343).

Milton's tactics are implied here in the wry observation that those who have laid an image at the start of the king's book to "catch fools" have themselves been justly caught in the snare of language at the end. For there they have attached a Latin tag in praise of Charles—*Vota dabunt quae Bella negarunt*—which, says Milton, they would have us believe to mean, "That what hee could not compass by Warr, he should atchieve by his Meditations," but which might better be rendered in a completely opposite sense: the "Latin Motto in the end, which they understand not, leaves him, as it were a politic contriver to bring about that interest by faire and plausible words, which the force of Armes deny'd him" (342–43). As this tiny confrontation between the image and the word demonstrates, and as Milton will go on to argue at length, the king's language is no less idolatrous than his portrait.

Anyone not "fatally stupifi'd and bewitch'd" who compares the king's "fair spok'n words" with his "own farr differing deeds, manifest and visible to the whole Nation" will see them exposed as "bare words" (346–47). Just as a king's words are substantial only in "the authority and strength of Law, so like *Sampson*, without the strength of that *Nazarites* lock, they have no more power in them then the words of another man" (545–46). Well might Charles have bemoaned "the *pulling down of Crosses* and other superstitious Monuments" (535). Milton's *Eikonoklastes* will enjoy "the honor belonging to [God's] Saints: not to build Babel . . . but to destroy it" (598). As he topples the king's book, argument by argument over hundreds of pages, he will regard Charles's text as a "rott'n building newly trimm'd over" (377). Trimmed, as Milton will say, by the mere "outward work of devotion" (362), the king's life and his book are so false to the very "foundation, and as it were the head stone of his whole Structure," that it betokens "the downfall of his whole Fabric" (350).

Milton's iconoclasm at this particular moment in 1649, strident as it is, might for that very reason be dismissed as a polemical tour de force provoked by the heat of the regicide debate and by the fear that an "image-doting rabble" would flock like Circe's victims to the "new device of the Kings Picture at his praiers" (601). What remains important for the later Milton, however, is that this attack on idolatry coincides with a lasting change in Milton's own prose style. Thomas Corns has now demonstrated statistically what many readers of Milton's prose have felt, that the regicide tracts of 1649–50 mark a change from the "flamboyance and linguistic innovation of his anti-prelatical pamphlets" to a "more sober style, a plainer medium of expression." After 1649, a sparer Milton will use "fewer and terser images," an imagery that "loses the luxuriance that characterizes it earlier." In his handling of biblical imagery, for example, Milton would no longer feel free to embellish a verse, but would maintain a scrupulous regard for accurate quotation and citation. Where the anonymous *Eikon Alethine* had chosen to attack the king's book in language as colorful as its opponent's "painted grapes," Milton chose to abstain. The words he used to throw down an idolatrous book would themselves be purified by the same trial. By some measures the cost was high. As Corns concludes (with some exaggeration), Milton "dismantled what was possibly the most exhilarating and inventive prose style of the seventeenth century and replaced it with a spare functionalism."[18] After *Eikonoklastes*, Milton's own prose would have to observe the same standard of unadorned truthfulness that the "Stage-work" of the king's prose had so spectacularly flouted.

In the problematic shift from vision to narration in Book 12 of *Paradise Lost*, Milton applied the same standard to his poetry as in the regicide tracts he had applied to his prose. Ever since C. S. Lewis dismissed the last books of the epic an an "untransmuted lump of futurity," more sympathetic readers have shown that Michael's history lesson is less lumpish than Lewis was willing to grant.[19] Within the overall symmetry of a "world destroy'd" in Book 11 and a "world restor'd" in Book 12, a number of subtler designs have been detected in the Archangel's account of what shall come in future days: the emergence of a line of greater men singled out to carry the burden of salvation history, the unfolding of the traditional six ages of the world, or of progressive manifestations of the Covenant, or of the pattern of three temptations.

The test of all these defenses, as Raymond B. Waddington notes, continues to be their ability to explain Milton's emphatic shift to narration.[20] Waddington himself accounts for it by urging that just at the time foreseen in Book 12, that is, at the Flood, the "historical Adam" must be supposed to have died ("I perceive / Thy mortal sight to fail"), so that Milton's Adam is told, as a matter of decorum, only those things he will no longer witness. Milton's readers, however, will appreciate above all that the "objects divine" (12:9) to be related in Book 12 are the flowers of Adam's germinating paradise within, and as such must be planted deep in the mind by that "new Speech" (12:5) which alone reveals the mercies of a "God who oft descends to visit man / Unseen" (12:47). This knowledge does not so much reveal itself to Adam directly through anything he sees as take root in his gradual understanding of the words of the *Protevangelium* of Genesis 3:15—that Eve's "seed shall bruise" the Serpent's "head" (10:181).[21] The external, spectacular (and spectacularly turbulent) history of Adam's progeny conceals an inner history of the Word growing smoothly to fruition, a process to be nourished by a few faithful men in every age "Laboring the soil, and reaping plenteous crop" (12:17). As Barbara Lewalski has shown in detail, "Adam's shift from vision to non-vision is related to a pervasive pattern of sight imagery throughout the prophecy," all of it, however, reinforcing the Pauline insight that "we walk by faith, not by sight."[22]

In the long view of Milton's career, the "new Speech" of Book 12 is all the more striking because it breaks from the highly visual dramatic treatment of the Fall that he had first sketched out in the early 1640s. "Adam Unparadiz'd," the last and most specific of four such outlines preserved in the Trinity College manuscript, begins with "The angel Gabriel, either descending or entering" (18:321). This detail echoes the opening stage direction in *Comus*—"The Attendant Spirit descends or enters"—and suggests that a descent would be preferred if the stage allowed. Thus we may imagine the angel "descending" like one of those celestial figures lowered onto the masquing platform at Whitehall in an Inigo Jones cloud machine, or like the figure of "Peace" in Milton's "On the Morning of Christ's Nativity," who makes her masque-like entrance "softly sliding / Down through the turning sphere" (ll. 47–48). It ends when

the Angel is sent to banish [Adam and Eve] out of paradise
but before causes to passe before his eyes in Shapes a mask
of all the evills of this life & world [This "mask" the third
outline had envisioned as a procession of twelve "mutes,"
"praesented" by the angel and identified as "Labour,"
"grief," "famine," "Death," and so on (18:230)] he is
humbl'd relents, dispaires. at last appeares Mercy comforts
him promises the Messiah, then calls in faith, hope &
charity, instructs him he repents. . . . (18:232)

Hinting as they do at the spectacular motions of English masquing
and pageantry, as well as at Italian *trionfi* and *sacre rappresentazioni*,
Milton's notes point toward the fuller elaboration of these effects in
Paradise Lost. Pandemonium springs up, to a musical accompani-
ment, like those gilded and outrageously ornate canvas palaces of
the masque, with which it has long been compared. Adam in Book
11 is dazzled by the "wonder strange" (11:733) of the visions pass-
ing before him. Incorporating such motifs, the overall design of
the poem, with its careful juxtaposition of demonic and heavenly
scenes, is even more strongly reminiscent of the "antithetical" structure of antimasque and revel, and these elements of theatrical spectacle are often more conspicuous than the epic conventions under
which they have been subsumed.[23] Behind this artistry lies Milton's
conviction, expressed in his comment on Tertullian's *De Spectaculis*,
that patristic objections to pagan games should not deter a "wary
and prudent Christian from venturing to witness a dramatic poem,
artistically composed by a poet no wise lacking in skill" (18:207).

But the wary spectator of *Paradise Lost* will also realize that illusions are the property of Satan. By 1660 Milton was all the more
bitterly persuaded that the art of the corrupt prince, like that of
his demonic archetype, lies in setting "a pompous face upon the superficial actings of the State, to pageant himself up and down in
progress among the perpetual bowings and cringing of an abject
people, on either side deifying him and adoring him for nothing
don that can deserve it," and that sustaining this mere appearance
of virtue requires, among the other instruments of illegitimate
power, "masks and revels, to the debauching of our prime gentry"
(6:121,247). The abject people gulled into submission by such theatrics will have lost to Satan the power of reasoned choice: they will,
in the language of *Areopagitica*, have become the descendants of
"a mere artificiall Adam, such an *Adam* as he is in the motions"
(2:527). By the decade of *Paradise Lost*, too, Milton had developed

the metaphysical position from which the earlier polemical attacks against idolatry could be more rigorously defined.

In the subordinationist Christology of the *Christian Doctrine*, the Son is not of the same essence as the Father but *paternae gloria imaginem*, "the image of the glory of the Father" (14:251), just as man, "though in a much lower sense," is also said to be the image of God (14:275). Man in his fallen state bears "some remnants of the divine image" (14:29), God having "imprinted on the human mind so many unquestionable tokens [*clara indicia*] of himself . . . that no one in his senses can remain ignorant of the truth" (14:25). Indeed, like Raphael's lesson on accommodation in *Paradise Lost* (5:570–76), Milton's comment on Genesis 1:26 leaves open the possibility that heaven and earth are "Each to other like, more than on Earth is thought":

> If God is said to have "made man in his own image, after his likeness," Gen.1.26. and that too not only as to his soul but also as to his outward form (unless the same words have different significations here and in chap. V.3. "Adam begat a son in his own likeness, after his image") and if God habitually assigns to himself the numbers and form of man, why should we be afraid of attributing to him what he attributes to himself, so long as what is imperfection and weakness when viewed in reference to ourselves be considered as most complete and excellent when imputed to God? (14:35)

Still, any encouragement such an argument might seem to offer for a fleshly representation of God must be checked by a right understanding of Christ's unique role as the mediating image. As Christ is "the image, as it were by which we see God, so is he the word by which we hear him. But if such be his nature he cannot be essentially one with God, whom no one can see and hear" (14:401). The only true image we have of God is true by virtue of its not being "one with God": grounded in difference, in a necessary falsification, the true image allows us only to understand that God is not like that.

With even the image of God in Christ to be understood in this carefully delimited way, idolatry—which Milton defines here as "the making, worshipping, or Trusting in *idols*, whether considered as Representations of the true God, or of a false one" (17:135)—becomes all the more radical a denial of God. By the working of grace, "THE OLD MAN BEING DESTROYED, THE INWARD

MAN IS REGENERATED BY GOD AFTER HIS OWN IMAGE,"
but "REGENERATION IS THAT CHANGE OPERATED BY THE
WORD AND THE SPIRIT" (15:367). The "conformation of the
faithful to the image of Christ" (15:315) is mediated inwardly and
verbally. Anything that feeds the eye, "Even the brazen serpent, the
type of Christ, was commanded to be abolished, as soon as it became an object of religious worship, 2 Kings xviii 4 'he brake in
pieces the brazen serpent that Moses had made'" (17:141). Hence,
"the papists err in calling idols the laymens books; their real nature
whether considered as books or teachers appears from Psal. cxv. 5,
&c. 'they have mouths but they speak not . . . they that make them
are like unto them, so is every one that trusteth in them,'" and
hence, "we are commanded to abstain" (17:143). In a vicious parody of the "conformation" of the faithful, the idol debases the
faithless into its own image, a vanity compelling to the eye, but lacking the power of the Word.

The opposition of Christ and Satan in *Paradise Lost* is in the same
way, as John Steadman has argued, the difference between image
and idol, the "*eikon* and the *eidolon* of heroic virtue."[24] The Son is
the image of the Father's glory; Satan, in his "Sun-bright chariot," is
the false appearance or phantasm of that image, the "Idol of Majesty Divine" (6:100–1). His fallen legions, left free to wander the
earth after the Fall, will inaugurate the history of idolatry in the
shape of "various Idols through the Heathen World" (1:375), and
their polluted rites will become the type of Catholic mis-devotion
and of the political idolatry of the Stuart court. This distinction between idol and icon, which Steadman traces back through Bacon's
critique of the "idols" to Plato's *Theatetus* and *The Sophist*, also set
the terms of the debate in Italian criticism between Mazzoni and
Tasso—the one maintaining that poetry is "phantastic," a sophis-
tical art of fallacious appearances only, the other that poetry is
"eikastic," an art of likeness and probability related to dialectic and
more directly reflecting the truth it images. The topic is epitomized
in Sidney's *Apologie*, where it is illustrated by analogy with the sister
art of painting:

> For I will not denie, but that mans wit may make Poesie
> (which should be *Eikastike*, which some learned haue de-
> fined, figuring foorth good things) to be *Phantastike*: which
> doth, contrariwise, infect the fancie with vnworthy obiects.
> As the Painter, that shoulde giue to the eye eyther some ex-
> cellent perspectiue, or some fine picture, fit for building or

fortification, or contayning in it some notable example, as *Abraham* sacrificing his Sonne *Isaack, Iudith* killing *Holofernes, Dauid* fighting with *Goliath,* may leaue those, and please an ill-pleased eye with wanton shewes of better hidden matters.[25]

An idolatrous poetry infects the fancy and pleases the eye. An eikastic poetry illuminates the desire for "good things." It too can appeal to the eye, but as Sidney's notable examples suggest—all of them Old Testament histories, often represented in Protestant art, against which no charge of idolatry could be leveled—its highest aim is to move the soul to virtuous action, to the sacrificing, killing, and fighting performed by the faithful in response to God's word.

With the "new Speech" of Book 12, it is almost as if Milton had commanded himself to abstain from completing the design envisioned, in his greener years, in "Adam Unparadiz'd." The earlier notation of a "mask of all the evills of this life & world" accurately describes the series of visions set before Adam in Book 11. These are an extension onto the human stage of those "mute signs in Nature"—the dire "Signs, imprest / On Bird, Beast, Air"—which Adam has already divined before the angel's arrival as the "Forerunners" of God's purpose (11:194–95). Like those hieroglyphs, the visions revealed to Adam disclose only a partial, or even a misleading, aspect of the truth. As the commentators have remarked, Adam more than once mistakes what he sees, or he draws premature conclusions that must be corrected by the Archangel. The scenes of the primal murder, the lazar house, and the "spacious Plain" of erotic love move Adam to wonder and compassion, but in the last instance also to a recognition of the "bent of Nature"—the tug of Sidney's phantastic impulse—that draws him into the same "amorous Net" (11:597, 586). Adam is implicated in a receding visual and moral perspective of watchers watching watchers. Like the men he observes eyeing the "Bevy of fair Women" on the plain, Adam has let his "eyes/ Rove without Rein" (11:580–86). With the vision of the Flood Adam has learned that he must ask the angel to "unfold" (11:785) by explanation the last of what has otherwise been a series of fascinating, but perplexing and disjointed, pageants lacking what Calvin had called the "thread" of the Word that guides man through the labyrinth of history (*Inst.* 1.6.3). As Georgia Christopher aptly notes, "Adam does not really 'see' the dumb shows until the Angel's verbal account has been interposed, like a theatrical scrim, between the pupil and the visible vision." It is "a mark of his spiritual growth that the Angel can dispense with the spectacle and move into a purely literary presentation in Book XII."²⁶

"Dispense" is, however, too weak a term to catch the note of triumphant repudiation sounded in the transition to Book 12, as the angelic voice pauses for a moment before raising Adam above his visual captivation by a "world destroy'd." Here, where the early notes in the Trinity College manuscript had foreseen a conclusion in the same mode, Book 12 replaces the figures of "Mercy," "faith, hope & charity" with the voice of Michael. Speaking now openly as the mediator of Christian truth, he, like Moses after him, will "report" the will of God, his mission "to introduce / One greater, of whose day he shall foretell" (12:241–42). In the movement of biblical history the events chronicled in the two books are continuous, and in the progress of Adam's education the visual tableaux are a preparation for the higher wisdom of Book 12. Both in their chronological and their psychological dimensions, as Madsen says, such "images, like the types of the Old Testament, represent a stage in the history of man's religious development; their function ceases with the coming of Christ, who is the true image of God."²⁷ But they also embody a more sharply agonistic competition for Adam's attention between the claims of sense and spirit, an opposition caught in Adam's thanks to his heavenly instructor for the "gracious things" that have been revealed to him: "now first I find / Mine eyes true op'ning, and my heart much eas'd, / Erewhile perplext" (12:273–75). It is an exhilarating and liberating moment, one linked ahead to the promised resurrection, and behind to that moment in Book 4 when Eve had resisted the phantastic fate of Narcissus (and Satan) by following the eikastic voice of her own instructor Adam as it pulled her away from adoring her own reflection in the lake:

> There I had fixt
> Mine eyes till now, and pin'd with vain desire,
> Had not a voice thus warn'd me, What thou seest,
> What thou there seest fair Creature is thyself . . .
> . . . What could I do,
> But follow straight, invisibly thus led?
>
> (4:465–76)

Invisibly led by his own teachers in the art of the epic, Milton no less than Spenser before him uses the pictorial resources of his language in these books with a full awareness of their hazards as well as their power. Adam's final education proceeds in three stages. In the first, he is granted a "prospect" on the kingdoms of the world from the highest hill in Paradise: "His Eye might there command wherever stood / City of old or modern Fame" (11:385–86). Milton is, however, careful to sketch the boundaries of this initial vantage point:

> Not higher that Hill nor wider looking round,
> Whereon for different cause the Tempter set
> Our second *Adam* in the Wilderness,
> To show him all Earth's Kingdoms and thir Glory.
>
> (11:381–84)

The "different cause" is Satan's temptation of Christ through the eye. The similarity of the two prospects lies in their both being limited, as Christ's refusal to be tempted will confirm, to a topographical survey of earthly "Fame" and "Glory." Michael remains silent while Adam's eye sweeps out the great circle from the "seat of *Cathaian Can*" in the east to the "Realm / Of *Congo*, and *Angola* fardest South" to Europe and America on the west (11:388–411). The greatest world surrounding the local action of the epic is thus revealed to Milton's hero as it had been to Homer's on the circlet of Achilles' shield.

But now, in preparation for "nobler sights," Michael removes the tempter's "Film" from Adam's eyes, purges the "visual Nerve," and instills three drops from the Well of Life (11:411–22). In the transition to a purer mode of sight Adam, "now enforc't to close his eyes," sinks "down . . . intranst." He moves "down" from the high hill of his original vision, but since the descent, like the angel's therapy, sinks inward to the "inmost seat of mental sight," Adam can be "rais'd" again to a new vision in which history up to the Flood unfolds, like the history of Rome on Aeneas's shield, in a vast prophetic landscape.[28] Vision, in this second lesson, now extends to encompass the dimension of time. As Michael tells Adam, however, even the eye so clarified can discover only "Th' effects which thy original crime hath wrought, / In some to spring from thee" (11:424–25). It is as if (to complete the analogy that the angel's ophthalmological precision here suggests) the ill "effects" to "spring" from Adam to his children were now also to pass between his eye and the objects of his vision, for whose "corruption" he is himself responsible. Adam's seminal spirits and his visual spirits are alike contaminated, their issue the "Sight so deform" (11:494) that moves Adam to tears at the vision of the lazar house. The Fall, Adam learns, was the original iconoclastic act, by which men defaced their "Maker's Image" in themselves (11:510–25). It will have to be repaired by the destruction of those idolatrous images they have put in its place. This lesson like the first sums a circle, though now one drawn typologically through the arc of time: with the Flood Adam's descendants are punished as he had been, the human race reduced again to one man. A "World devote to universal rack" (11:821) will be effaced, the Flood offering only its own "wide wat'ry Glass" to the gaze of the "clear Sun" (11:844). The eye returns at the end of Book 11 to the hill from which it began, knowing now that even this original vantage point will be undermined by the very cataclysm Adam has foreseen and engendered:

> then shall this Mount
> Of Paradise by might of Waves be mov'd
> Out of his place, push'd by the horned flood,
> With all his verdure spoil'd, and Trees adrift
> Down the great River to the op'ning Gulf,
>
> . . . .
>
> To teach thee that God attributes to place
> No sanctity, if none be thither brought
> By Men who there frequent, or therein dwell.
>
> (11:829–38)

The high "place" that had secured Adam's vision is "push'd . . . Down" in time to teach him the lesson of sanctity. Milton's version of the destruction of the Bower of Bliss, this anticipated destruction of the Mount of Paradise breaks the image of God's creation and the poetic image of Paradise so lovingly created by Milton himself in Book 4.

Equipped only to perceive the ruins of his own making in a "world destroy'd," Adam's "mortal sight" must fail and give way to his hearing the "new Speech" of a "world restor'd." In the third part of his lesson, Michael fully reveals the lineage of the second Adam by narrating it: "Henceforth what is to come I will relate, / Thou therefore give due audience, and attend" (12:11–12). This "transition sweet" between Books 11 and 12 marks the final movement from vision to speech, one understood as restorative both medically and musically. Michael's bitter "prospect" on a fallen world fades into the sweet "prediction" (12:553) of its renewal, while Adam's impaired phantastic imagination yields before the therapeutic music suited to the new knowledge.

Michael's pedagogical method in this passage recalls Milton's own in *Of Education*, where the "end . . . of Learning" had similarly been "to repair the ruines of our first Parents by regaining to know God aright" (4:277). There he had offered to conduct Hartlib "to a hill side where I will point ye out the right path of a vertuous and noble Education; laborious indeed at the first ascent, but else so smooth, so green, so full of goodly prospect . . ." (4:280). The sentence opens out into description, offering a glimpse, perhaps, of the "spatious house and ground" (4:280) that Milton is about to imagine as the setting for his ideal academy. In both epic and treatise, the student's ascent to virtuous knowledge at the hands of a guide—however broad the allusion to Bonaventura or Dante— seems more directly modeled on the descriptive technique of the *Table of Cebes*, one of the several ancient "Book[s] of Education" (4:281) that Milton specifically recommends for elementary pupils. Itself a brief, late-classical digest of mainly stoic and Platonic precepts, the *Table* enjoyed a wide reputation in dozens of Renaissance editions and translations, not only because it was mistakenly ascribed to a contemporary of Socrates, but also because it stood as an exemplary piece of ekphrastic composition: the journey through life appears, we are told, on a painting whose winding allegorical landscape is described and interpreted to a group of eager young men by a fatherly instructor.[29] Whether or not Milton may have known one of the numerous Renaissance illustrations of this text (fig. 19, for example), he begins to sketch the "right path" for Hartlib in an explicitly, and conventionally recognizable, pictorial mode—but only to dissolve the image, as Michael does, in an appeal to the ear: "so full of goodly prospect and melodious sounds on every side, that the Harp of *Orpheus* was not more charming" (4:280). If, as Milton says earlier in the essay, the limitations of "our understanding . . . in this body" force us to approach the invisible knowledge of God by "orderly conning over the visible and inferior creature" (4:277), his curriculum makes it clear that such knowledge is to be conned first through a text that lends itself to visualization, but then through the sweeter melodies of language.

This one sentence from *Of Education* may only record an unpremeditated movement of Milton's mind in a direction natural to it. Yet insofar as it moves through and beyond the language of *ut pictura poesis* it epitomizes the larger movement at the end of *Para-*

Figure 19. Engraving of the *Table of Cebes* by Erhard Schön (1531), published with Hans Sachs's German translation (Nuremberg, 1551)

dise Lost—especially since, in the same way, Adam's lesson emulates but finally declares its difference from the famous culminating ekphrases in the works of Milton's ancient teachers. The epic of sacred history recapitulates the history of the epic. In Achilles' shield Homer offers a model for an extended survey of the concentric world enclosing, and enclosed by, the geography of the text. Closer to Christian revelation, Virgil next offers a model for representing the generations of Adam in a simultaneous prospect just as Vulcan, one "not unskilled in prophecy," had "set the generations of / Ascanius, and all their wars, in order."[30] But from the Christian perspective, these must be regarded, and finally rejected, as flawed anticipations—beguiling images in the pool of literary tradition from which the poet must allow himself to be called away if he is not to be the mere reflection of his predecessors in the epic. The "transition sweet" of Book 12 marks a final shift in poetic allegiance, foreshadowed by the first invocation, from Milton's *pietas* toward his pagan instructors to his inspiration by the new speech of a greater teacher: "O Spirit . . . / Instruct me, for thou know'st" (1:17–19). The pictorial mode sponsored by Homer and Virgil and honored in the Renaissance aesthetic of the *pictura loquens* recurs in Milton as a visual prelude to the more "advent'rous Song" of the second Adam.

And yet, as the complex rising and falling movements of Milton's ending also suggest, the stages of Adam's education do not simply record, in the supersession of Homer and Virgil by Christian song, the fading of vision into speech as an ascent toward truth. For Michael's lesson after the Fall replaces Raphael's before it, when Adam's first angelic instructor had been able to "delineate" to him "what surmounts the reach / Of human sense" (5:571–72), and when Adam himself had been able, he tells Raphael, not only to name the animals at sight but to see God (8:295–356). "God is Light": the invocation to Book 3 above all may remind us that the fruit of Adam's sin is his deprivation of that light—his punishment by a fall into the darkness of language which the progressive darkening of Michael's discourse reenacts. Adam having fed on the fruit, the blind poet must now be content to "feed on thoughts" (3:37), however much he may hunger for visions. For the race as for the poet who "Sings darkling" (3:39), language is both the punishment of blindness and the compensation for it. The attempt to "reascend" must be undertaken through a language that disinfects the eye of its own fallen images, but one whose purpose is finally to "plant eyes" in the mind, "that I may see and tell / Of things invisible to mortal sight" (3:54–55).

The order of "see and tell" for which the poet prays is the order of Adam's unfallen account of the "Presence Divine" to Raphael. Now Adam must be content to walk "As in his presence" (12:563). The vantage of direct sight having been lost, Adam's re-education after the Fall must aim at recovering that order by reversing it: Michael, the "Seer blest," offers Adam the "prediction" that will lead him to see again in the end. For the theorists of the sister arts, Homer and Virgil could open access at least to the shadow of an original pictorial language, conceived at the *fons et origo* of poetry, and luminously delineated in a style to which the latter-day poet can only aspire. For the reformer of images, the very vividness of such a style touching on sacred matters condemns it as the product of a factory of idols and risks transforming the poet into the *eidolon* of what he adores. Working at this crossroads, Milton is concerned in *Paradise Lost* to accommodate the speaking picture of the epic tradition to an ampler Christian view of the relationship of "see and tell." This concern finds its last, and most acutely self-conscious, expression in Milton's tragedy—in that form he had praised as offering better than any other "a survey at a single glance of the hazards and changes of human life" (18:207).

Oedipus and *Lear* aside, there can be few plays that so intensely evoke the mood, and the rage, of blindness as *Samson Agonistes*. "O loss of sight, of thee I most complain" (67): Samson's lament echoes everywhere in a drama almost obsessively attentive to things seen and unseen. The angel who foretold the hero's birth "at last in sight / Of both my Parents" ascended to heaven (24–25). Samson, who can only hear the approach of the Chorus in the "tread of many feet," suspects that his enemies have "come to stare" at his affliction (110–12). Manoa refuses to follow his son to the Philistine temple "Lest I should see him forc't to things unseemly" (1451). His worst fears are both realized and transcended by the "horrid spectacle" (1542) that ensues. From a long list of such examples, Anthony Low observes that Milton never lets us forget that "Samson is a blind man among people who see." With much of its action "subtly mediated to the reader as if he perceived [it] through the blind Samson's senses," the play creates a feeling of "claustrophobic closeness and frequent hypersensitivity." Here is the "narrow, tortured world of the blind Samson, a world where the other senses are magnified, where footsteps echo, where seeing is constantly spoken of, and sensed, and used metaphorically, yet little can be directly seen."[31] Like a lens stopped down to ever-narrowing apertures and admitting less and less light with every click, the scene of Milton's last works diminishes from the broad vistas of *Paradise Lost*, to the desert "with dark shades and rocks environ'd round" (1:194) that is the featureless setting of *Paradise Regained*, to the prison yard of *Samson Agonistes*—and then, within the play, to the even more radically dark confinement of "Prison within Prison" (153), where Samson is his own "Sepulcher, a moving Grave" (102). To read the last two works as companion poems is to drop from the "highest pinnacle" of the temple at the end of *Paradise Regained* (4:548) to a dungeon "close and damp" at the beginning of *Samson* (8), a descent, as Balachandra Rajan says, from a "point of ultimate disclosure" to "the blindness of experience in the valley below."[32]

As in *Paradise Lost*, the recompense for blindness is a superior inner vision: "though blind of sight," Samson stands between the pillars "with inward eyes illuminated" (1687–89). Once "Irrecoverably dark" amid the "blaze of noon" (80–81), the hero finishes heroically at noon, his enemies, always blind to the inner strength of God's champion, now cast into darkness. The perception of these reversals will lead us to feel that we have been dismissed by the drama, if not with perfect "calm of mind," at least with the consolations of a providential irony. Yet Samson's has also been, as the Chorus acknowledges, a "dearly bought revenge" (1660). The play's vast reserves of anger and frustration are unleashed at the end in the destruction of the temple of idolatry. But that one climactic moment may well be felt as the last blow in a more general revenge against the sighted world, including not only the Philistines (and their English counterparts), but implicitly the "audience" of *Samson Agonistes* and the form of tragedy itself insofar as that kind of dramatic poem offers an audience the satisfactions of spectacle. The "contest . . . / 'Twixt God and *Dagon*" (461–62) extends well beyond its immediate biblical arena. It results first in the slaughter of a pagan foe "Chanting thir Idol" in defiance of "our living Dread" (1672–73), but then no less directly in the condemnation of that "choice nobility and flower" (1653) of play-going aristocrats, their hearts filled with "mirth, high cheer, and wine" (1613), exulting in the restoration of an idolatrous English monarchy. As Samson transfers the fault of his nation's servitude onto "*Israel's* Governors" (242), the play also issues a wider indictment of a people grown so corrupt as to desert its hero and "to love Bondage more than Liberty" (270). It is this "righteous ferocity" of the play that makes it, for Kenneth Burke, "a kind of witchcraft, a wonder-working spell by a cantankerous old fighter-priest who would slay the enemy in effigy."[33]

The play's revenge turns (as so often in the Baroque drama which *Samson* parallels at least in this respect) on the relationship between an internal and an external audience. Each is denied the spectacular entertainment it had been led to expect. Onstage, Samson's performance in the "spacious Theater" (1605)—Milton is apparently unique in so describing the Philistine "house" of Judges 16:27–sets off a chain of ironies connected by Milton's play on the word "obscurity." The better to see the show, the illustrious Philistines sit under the pillared vault, where they are obscured, in shade. They will see, or rather fail to see truly, a hero obscured by blindness, who will nevertheless work his glorious revenge. The Messenger who reports all this managed to escape death because, along with the vulgar who were too obscure to get the good seats, he "obscurely stood" (1611) in the noonday sun, "under Sky" (1610). The "choice of Sun or Shade" proposed to the hero at the beginning of the play has unravelled, like one of Samson's own riddles, into a surprising solution.[34] The irony reflects equally on the audience "offstage." We have been in one sense, through the Messenger's account, intimate witness to the spectacular catastrophe, but in another—since we know it only by report—we have been denied even an obscure glimpse of it. By barring our direct entry to a violent spectacle, Milton at once succeeds in preserving the decorum of classical tragedy and in frustrating a desire, aroused by our forced confinement in the drama's blindness, to see the events of that tragedy. Like the Messenger's, our own salvation depends on an act of abstinence: in our role as readers or auditors we must stand "aloof" (1611) from the temptation to see up close. In our role as imagined spectators at the drama, we are nevertheless drawn by that very temptation. The "true experience" afforded by "this great event" (1756) thus makes itself felt in part as the experience of humiliation, as if we were forced to sit through a play with our eyes closed, or to watch a "play" staged entirely behind the curtain. From the opening line—"A little onward lend thy guiding hand"— we are cast into an obscurity that only deepens as the play unfolds: who's that? a compassionate warden? a child appointed to be Samson's guide? the unseen hand of God?

The experience I have been trying to suggest presumes that *Samson Agonistes* is neither simply a script for performance in the usual sense, nor simply the closet drama that Milton's critics often suppose when they conclude that it "was never intended for the stage and is a forerunner of symbolic drama like *Manfred* and *Prometheus Unbound*."[35] Milton's famous disclaimer of any intention to stage his biblical drama might well be taken, not without a note of sarcasm, to mean that it could hardly have been destined for production in a time when, as Anthony Low remarks, "the cry was for such plays as Wycherley's *Love in a Wood*."[36] Milton's tone betrays the hint that audiences addicted to lascivious comedies get exactly what they deserve when a drama like *Samson* is withheld from their worthless gaze. But even his emphatic "never" cannot conceal the fact that the play, though likely written late, was laid down along the lines of those early dramatic projects (including a "Gideon Idoloclastes") envisioned in the more propitious climate of the 1640s, when there can be no doubt that Milton was planning works for the stage. There is nothing in the play itself or in the history of its conception insofar as we know it that would lead us to conclude, even from Milton's point of view, that the play could not be staged.[37]

Neither a drama nor a nondramatic poem, the text of *Samson* occupies a liminal space between two genres. From one side, it is a blind, and blinding, "antiplay"—the term is Northrop Frye's, from an essay in which he contrasts our experience of Milton's tragedy with "the very intense visual experience" of a Greek play, "with its masks and amphitheater setting." In *Paradise Lost*, "Adam was surrounded by a visible paradise, but what the forbidden Tree primarily forbids is idolatry, the taking of the visible object to be the source of creative power." Now, in *Samson*, "the Word continues to operate in society as an iconoclastic force, in other words a revolutionary force, demolishing everything to which man is tempted to offer false homage."[38]

From the other side, however, *Samson* seems to retain at least the shadow of visual experience, not only in whatever performance the reader may imagine, but in the several other distinctively visual contexts the play evokes. The feats of Samson were among the most frequently illustrated biblical episodes in the Renaissance. The Wittenberg Old Testament of 1524 offers a series of five Samson woodcuts (the only such illustrations chosen by Luther himself), including a full-page synoptic view of the hero's career, and ending, like Milton's play, with Samson in the Philistine temple.[39] Among the other exploits recalled by Milton's Chorus, the motif of Samson carrying off the gates of Gaza reappeared in many later versions and proved all the more intriguing for the parallels the image suggested to Atlas and Hercules, as well as to Christ breaking through the gates of death at his resurrection. For some readers, *Samson* has also been strongly reminiscent of the masque, unfolding as it does not by dramatic development but by sudden disclosures, and exposing the hero to the "antimasque" challenges of his visitors before revealing his power in a revel that "with amaze shall strike all who behold" (1645).[40] There is, finally, the "all-embracing emblem of the fiery Phoenix, the image of Samson's regeneration." For one critic the Phoenix, because it "holds in suspension all the important thematic and structural motifs" of the drama, supplies the ultimate pictorial focus of a sightless play.[41]

Yet even here, two implications of the Phoenix "emblem" need to be addressed. One is that, as a singularly miraculous bird, the Phoenix "no second knows nor third" (1701). In this she parallels Samson, both in his Nazarite breeding as "a person separate to God" (31) and in his radical withdrawal from all human attachment over the course of the play. But between two such uniquely incomparable creatures as Samson and the Phoenix, what correspondence can there be? Even as the Chorus asserts that Samson is "Like that self-begott'n bird" (1699), the odd illogic of the comparison of incomparables implies that Samson no more resembles the Arabian bird—that his inner illumination or his sacrifice is no more "like" the Phoenix's holocaust or its conventional image in so many Renaissance emblems—than the angel Raphael resembles the *"Phoenix"* that he "seems" to be "to all the Fowls" who observe his descent in Book 5 of *Paradise Lost* (5:271–72). The picturing of Samson's mysterious regeneration by the Phoenix or by any such image as the play may suggest declares its own inadequacy.

The second implication arises from the word "embost":

> Like that self-begott'n bird
> In the Arabian woods embost.
>
> (1699–1700)

The usual gloss regards it as a synonym for "embosked," a "word originally applied to hunted animals."[42] The Phoenix is thus "sheltered" or hidden in the woods, a detail that reflects again on the private quality of Samson's spiritual drama and reminds us, perhaps, that his "intermission" between the pillars has been a last, momentary refuge from his persecutors. So understood, "embost" conveys the feeling of something covert and unseen, but in its most common Renaissance uses it implies just the opposite: it refers to images all the more striking to the eye because they are carved or molded in relief.[43]

In this sense, the word occurs in pejorative contexts to characterize overly sumptuous images. The *Homilie against perill of Idolatrie* regrets that "Images came into the Church, not now in painted cloths only, but embossed in stone." Such images appear in their hardest, most tactile form—a connotation preserved in the technique later called "embossed printing," in which letters are raised on the page for the benefit of the blind. The word also suggests the bulging of a tumescent disease—Prince Hal calls Falstaff an "emboss'd rascal" (*1 Henry IV* 3.3.157), while Lear calls Goneril a "plague-sore, or embossed carbuncle" (2.4.224). Used figuratively of a swollen style, it can glance, as it does in Holinshed's *Chronicle*, at an "embossed speech" artfully studded out to "tickle the eares and harts of the yoong" (2:163). In the early tracts Milton had praised the "sober, plain, and unaffected stile of the Scriptures" and taunted those prelates who scurry into the refuge of deceitful traditions because they "feare the plain field" of the Word: such men "seek the dark, the bushie, the tangled Forrest, they would imbosk" (3:35). The idolatrous architecture of Pandemonium in Book 1 of *Paradise Lost* is distinguished in all these senses by a "frieze, with bossy Sculptures grav'n" (1:716). Shadowed by these associations, the Phoenix "emblem," as a memorial to Samson embossed in the text, anticipates Manoa's projected "Monument" to his fallen son, which will be designed to "inflame" the breasts of "all the valiant youth" to "matchless valor, and adventures high" (1734–41). As if to declare its difference from the Phoenix, the monument, though hung "with all his Trophies," will be most conspicuously decorated by language alone, Samson's "Act enroll'd / In copious Legend, or sweet Lyric Song." Yet from the larger perspective Manoa does not share, it will be a stony thing that only petrifies the outward features of Samson's "adventures."

In a passage already charged by the oxymoron of the Phoenix's "ashy womb" (1703), it is doubly paradoxical that Milton should choose to gather up the threads of his play into an appropriated "emblem" so vivid as to make the whole text seem like an extended epigram attached to this triumphant illustration—and that he should choose at the same time to emboss the Phoenix with a word that questions the integrity of this brilliant creation. It is as if we are asked once again to see (the image of the Phoenix) and know (its significance for Samson), and yet abstain (from dwelling upon it or accepting it uncritically insofar as it may claim to embody and envision a mystery lodged only in the experience and in the language of blindness). In a moment of destruction and re-creation like the Phoenix's own, Milton revives an image only to discard it in the service of a higher truth which it cannot represent. The bond between the image and the word which had seemed complementary stands revealed in the end as agonistic—our knowledge of their connection "vigorous most" in our perception of their divergence.

In the broader contest 'twixt Milton and the genres of pagan an-

tiquity, the Christian poet similarly chose to recast his Greek tragedy into a form cleansed of its appeal to the eye. His comment on
Tertullian, while it ends in praise of "noble tragedy," still concedes
that the "corrupting influences of the theater ought to be elimi-
nated" (18:207). The warrant for such a purification could indeed
be found in Aristotle himself. Several passages of the *Poetics* observe that the element of spectacle, though it has an "emotional attraction of its own," is the "least artistic" and the most dispensable
part of tragedy, "for the power of tragedy, we may be sure, is felt
even apart from representation and actors." Elaborating a point
that Parker believed could not have been lost on the author of
Samson, Aristotle argues that

> Fear and pity may be aroused by spectacular means; but
> they may also result from the inner structure of the piece,
> which is the better way, and indicates a superior poet. For
> the plot ought to be so constructed that, even without the
> aid of the eye, he who hears the tale told will thrill with hor-
> ror and melt to pity at what takes place.[44]

Milton could write a tragedy, as Mary Ann Radzinowicz says,
"stripped of spectacle," and "composed of encounters which, as debates, are metaphors or metonymies for serious inward change."[45]
Yet with Aristotle available as a kind of proto-Protestant advocate
for the "inner" value of tragedy, he could bring about a reformation that would redeem and not supplant the ancient art. Samson
was to be an actor in a Philistine revel; under his direction, the
Philistines become the actors in a sacred drama that Milton's preface allows us to connect with the "Tragedy" of "*Revelation*." In the
terms, once again, of the note on Tertullian, Samson has chosen to
participate in the most corrupt form of spectacular theater, "the
pagan games." His role will be at once to ruin that drama and to
transform it into a typological dress rehearsal for the "Last Judgment," one of those "better spectacles . . . of a divine and heavenly
character" that "a Christian can anticipate" (18:207).

The "ashy womb" at the end of *Samson* thus reflects the paradoxical standing of the play itself in the history of tragedy. For Milton
the womb is the place where gestation contends with ruin, where
time destroys its own creations: "Fly envious *Time* . . . / And glut
thyself with what thy womb devours" ("On Time," ll. 1–4). It also
symbolizes that agnostic arena where Milton's major poems have
been generated, like Samson's final performance, by "trial." *Paradise*

Lost was a broken epic, just as *Comus* before it had been a broken masque and "Lycidas" a broken pastoral. In each case Milton does not so much revise or adapt an inherited form as dismantle it.

Again and again, acts of iconoclasm overthrow the idols of genre and clear a space for renewal. The narcissistic fantasies of the court masque are chastened in Milton's masque by "the sage / And serious doctrine of Virginity" that "must be utter'd" and not seen, though the false enchanter Comus has "nor Ear nor Soul to apprehend" it (784–87). Where the court masque turns on the revelation of a scenic wonder, Milton's "brothers rush in with Swords drawn, wrest [Comus's] Glass out of his hand, and break it against the ground" (814). In "Lycidas" the conventions of pastoral elegy, and in particular the comforting but delusive spectacle of the hearse strewn with beautiful flowers, are exposed as "false surmise" (153), while, through the water myths of Alpheus and Arethuse, the inspiration of classical pastoral must be "sunk low" like Lycidas himself before being "mounted high" again "Through the dear might of him that walk'd the waves" (172–73). *Paradise Lost* shatters the conventions of epic heroism, as well as much of the pictorial machinery associated with those conventions, by transferring them to Satan, while the Christ of *Paradise Regained*, it might be added, repeatedly affirms his faithfulness to the word of the Father by dispelling the "specular" temptations conjured by his adversary. In each of these performances between the pillars of received genres, Milton enacts for the reader what Samson will finally declare aloud to his own audiences—to the pagans, to the Christian reader, and to God: "such other trial / I mean to show you of my strength, yet greater" (1643–44). Milton's major works are all born with "horrible convulsion to and fro" (1649), the ashes of what he has ruined mysteriously sparking "Some rousing motions in me which dispose / To something extraordinary my thoughts" (1382–83).

With Milton the iconoclastic impulse of the Reformation is amplified and transmuted into a revolutionary aesthetic that replaces the filial piety of *imitatio* with the sharper antagonism of a trial of strength. Its consequences will reach far beyond the locale of Protestant polemics. It will define for Milton's successors a conception of poetry and of literary history either to embrace or to reject, one ultimately our own when we speak, in a variety of critical idioms, of a poet's "iconoclasm."

Conclusion

In a sense, this study can only have an inconclusive conclusion—
one reflecting what Quarles might have called the "unresolv'd resolves" of the authors themselves. The preceding four chapters on
Spenser, Quarles, Donne, and Milton have fallen into no very clear
pattern of development. They have not (as might perhaps have
been hoped of a survey moving, conventionally, from Spenser to
Milton) revealed the gradual flowering of a theme or a literary
mode. Instead they have observed each writer working out his own
strategy for managing a confrontation none of them could avoid
between the image and the word. For Italianate theory, *Pictura* and
Poesis are sisters joined in the service of the poet's language to
produce high and hearty inventions that speak to the eye as well as
the ear. Together they can extend the reach of poetry not only into
the spatial dimensions of the visual arts, but into the realm of hieroglyphic mystery and sacred illumination. For the English Reformation, the dominant metaphors for the same relationship tend to be
military and erotic. *Pictura* remains feminine, but she can appear in
the guise of the seductress, the enchantress, the Whore of Babylon.
Poesis, struggling to escape her snares, draws his strength from the
masculine authority of the divine voice invoked by the Elizabethan
homilist: "Doeth not the worde of GOD call Idolatrie spirituall
fornication: Doeth it not call a gylte or painted Idole or Image, a
Strumpet with a painted face?" At the extremes, the poet's language faces the choice of polluting itself by coupling with its own
idolatrous desires, or of rising up as the weapon of the warfaring
Christian to cleanse the temple of the heart and throw down the
high places of the imagination: Donne's God "speaks in his Canon,
in Thunder," and the poet's voice echoes with the same destructive
report.

The individual tactics have varied. Spenser releases a *Doppel-
gänger* into the text of *The Fairie Queene*, an "arch-imager" who must
be restrained but cannot be defeated because his plastic impulses
are the poet's own. Quarles adapts and partially subverts a body of
devotional imagery, turning the reading of his *Emblemes* into a
drama of visual seduction and verbal reprimand. Donne harbors
an image of Christ that, because it cannot be disentangled from the
image of his profane mistresses, must be broken by an iconoclastic

God before it can be renewed. Finally, Milton writes a drama that can succeed in vanquishing the idolatrous spectacle of Dagon only by blinding itself. The overall strategies, however, have been crafted in response to a common dilemma, and they have been remarkably alike. In each of these Reformation poets, an alliance between image and voice is put under severe strain, and in each a powerful charge of creative energy is absorbed in embodying, accommodating, exploiting, or warding off the conflict. At the crossroads, a conception of the text as imaginative space—as pattern, spectacle, emblem, hieroglyph, enclosure—is pitted against an adversary conception of the text as action—questing, pilgrimage, riding westward, ruining bowers, and shaking pillars. In setting the agonistic scene of this writing, and in trying to register the anxiety it provoked, I have argued nonetheless that the impact of iconoclasm on an iconic poetry was to strike a vital spark. Yet if iconoclasm posed a "problem" for the literary imagination, then these poets were not able to find a "solution." The "rigour pittiless" unleased by Guyon against the Bower of Bliss resounds in the "horrible convulsion" that shakes the pillars in *Samson Agonistes*. Early and late in the period, these two moments of ambiguously triumphant demolition do not so much suggest a resolution as a desire to be free of the problem altogether—to break the bondage of the eye at any cost. For the Reformation poet as for Milton's Samson, blindness is a superior gift, but not one joyfully received. His hard task is to "see and know" all the pleasures of the image lurking in the bower of his own art, "and yet abstain."

By the time *Samson Agonistes* was published in 1671, both the controversy over idolatry and its literary reflections had begun to fade. The word "iconoclasm" would lose its literal force but retain its currency in the language to describe a political or artistic attitude for which the Reformation had supplied the model. The word "image" would take on a growing and more general importance in aesthetic discourse but would never quite shed the implication attached to it by the Reformers as the object of idolatrous veneration. Indeed, it was the "opposition of verbal and visual representations"—an opposition so forcefully posed in the iconoclastic debates—that would be the starting point of the entire newly developing philosophy of aesthetics in the eighteenth century.[1] As we have seen, iconoclasm flared one last time in England during the twenty years of civil war, and it added its heat to much of the writing that would ensue far beyond the arena of frontline theological combat over the decoration of churches.

In 1651, for example, Hobbes devotes the bulk of a chapter near the end of the *Leviathan* to an exposure of idolatry that must stand as a kind of palinode to his praise of the poet in the *Answer to Davenant's Preface*, published the year before. There he had seen the poet as a "Painter" who "should paint Actions to the understanding with the most decent words, as Painters do Persons and Bodies with the choicest colours to the eye," and he had gone on to observe that one of the virtues of a heroic poem "consists in the perfection and curiosity of Descriptions, which the ancient writers of Eloquence called *Icones*, that is, *Images*."² Now, in the *Leviathan*, the word appears in a darker shading as he concludes, in language familiar since the earliest Zwinglian reforms, that "as Hezekiah brake in pieces the brazen serpent, because the Jews did worship it, to the end they should do so no more; so also Christian sovereigns ought to break down the images which their subjects have been accustomed to worship" (p. 431).³ The most obvious usefulness of the topic for Hobbes—aside from the occasion it provides for a spirited attack on the Catholic church as the "Kingdom of Darkness"—lies in the evidence that the history of image-worship offers for his critique of the imagination as "decaying sense" (p. 8). Thus, as a "relic of Gentilism," the veneration of images is the worship of "those appearances that remain in the brain from the impression of external bodies upon the organs of [the] senses, which are commonly called *ideas, idols, phantasms, conceits*, as being representations of those external bodies which cause them, and have nothing in them of reality, no more than there is in the things that seem to stand before us in a dream" (p. 423). Religion itself, born of "anxiety" and perpetual "fear of death, poverty, or other calamity," invents "some *power* or agent *invisible*" as the cause of "good, or evil fortune"—an agent which it then makes visible in "apparitions" that "are nothing else but creatures of the fancy . . . as the Latins called them *imagines*" (pp. 70–71). Perhaps a subtler motive behind Hobbes's attack arises from a need to protect his own iconic project by a strong offense, since the Commonwealth as he imagines it (and especially as it is pictured on the title page of his book) is "but an artificial man" reminiscent of the cosmic Christ whose hands span the poles in Donne's poetry, and the *Leviathan* is designed to "describe the nature of this artificial man" (p. 5).

Through the influence of Hobbes as well as of the older polemical debate that Hobbes inserts into a new philosophical context, Locke's empirical psychology performs its own iconoclastic act on a venerable conception of the mind. A *tabula rasa* scoured of all received ideas, the mind at birth is now supposed "to be, as we say, white paper, void of all characters" and ready to receive "that vast store" of confused images "which the busy and boundless fancy of man has painted on it."[4] Kant, himself regarded by a later age as "the great iconoclast," would argue that his postulated "schemata, and not images, be at the foundation of our pure sensuous conceptions," and that without the mediation of the schema—a "pure synthesis" that transcends the imaginative faculty—no "image which I can set before myself can ever reach to the universality of the conception."[5] The schema thus connects the empirical imagination with the realm of the a priori, but it also circumscribes it and contains its dangerous power in a way that leaves the higher sphere of "pure" ideas uncontaminated by any Hobbesian association with "idols" and "phantasms." Kant sees a need to "moderate the impetus of an unbounded Imagination," but he also finds in the feeling of the sublime, "which is quite negative in respect of what is sensible," a means by which an effaced imagination can soar free: "for the Imagination, although it finds nothing beyond the sensible to which it can attach itself, yet feels unbounded by this removal of its limitations; and thus that very abstraction is a presentation of the Infinite, which can be nothing but a more negative presentation, but which yet expands the soul." It is a significant moment in the latter-day history of Reformation iconoclasm as well as in the history of the sublime that Kant should at this point be reminded of the second commandment: "Perhaps there is no sublimer passage in the Jewish Law than the command, 'Thou shalt not make to thyself any graven image . . . etc.' This command alone can explain the enthusiasm that the Jewish people in their moral period felt for their religion."[6]

Perhaps the most crucial aftershock of iconoclasm for literary criticism first makes itself felt in the curbs and bounds that neoclassicism would place on the poetic imagination by drawing up "rules," very much as the early reformers had done, for keeping a sinful tendency under restraint. Sir William Temple—who finds that he can "easily admire Poetry, without adoring it"—accounts for its great "Force" over the passions by explaining that "in it are assembled all the Powers of Eloquence, of Musick, and of Picture, which are all allowed to make so strong Impressions upon Humane Minds." But compared with music and eloquence, whose powers are largely therapeutic, "Picture" immediately brings to mind all the notorious examples of men "fallen down right in Love with the Ravishing Beauties of a lovely Object drawn by the Skill of an admirable Painter"—including that of the young unfortunate who "pined away and dyed for being hindred his perpetually gazing, admiring, and embracing a Statue at *Athens*."[7]

In the eighteenth-century English arts, it is possible to see Swift and Hogarth especially, but even Gay and Fielding, as "iconoclasts" ranged against Dryden, Pope, Reynolds, and Johnson in a latter-day secular reenactment of the image debate. Iconoclasm has now been absorbed deep into the culture and may be taken to describe a temperamental, moral, and political stance, a general frame of mind rather than a specific doctrinal position. Thus, both Hogarth and Swift confront a creaking but still idolized artistic tradition with an art (as Ronald Paulson argues) that "regards itself as an act of iconoclasm": they force a "break" with the past "in order to reconstitute an English art of the contemporary, local and commonplace."[8]

Hogarth's career in particular forces us to dwell on the seeming paradox that we have already glimpsed in the mixed motives of early Protestant graphic art, the iconoclastic image-maker. An image like the first illustration to his treatise *The Analysis of Beauty* (1753) betrays Hogarth's lingering affiliation with the Renaissance tradition of *ut pictura poesis* (fig. 20). Generically, this engraving—at one level, an image from the life taken at a contemporary sculpture yard in Hyde Park Corner—may also be regarded as the visual embodiment of a classical ekphrastic text. Just as Botticelli, in his *Calumny of Apelles*, had recreated the lost, ancient painting discussed in Lucian's dialogues, or just as artists from the sixteenth to the eighteenth centuries had illustrated the philosophical allegory of the *Table of Cebes*, so Hogarth now envisions the scene described in a passage of Xenophon's *Memorabilia* translated for him by the Reverend Thomas Morell: in Xenophon, Socrates discourses on the theory of beauty while visiting the yard of Clito the statuary, and he uses the marbles exhibited there, very much as Hogarth uses the figures in the plate, to illustrate the topics of his argument.[9]

Perhaps the one aspect of Hogarth's definition of beauty most forcefully represented by the plate itself is variety, evident especially in the border running around the central panel with its bizarre collection of cactuses, candlesticks, and corsets. Suggesting the artist's taste for the odd, the unsymmetrical, and the disproportionate, these disparate images, of course, have nothing whatever to do with one another in the logical scheme of Hogarth's book, where they serve as a mere compilation of visual footnotes to the text, each little vignette as well as most of the elements in the main

Figure 20. William Hogarth, *The Analysis of Beauty* (1753), Plate I

panel keyed by number to the relevant portion of the treatise. Yet to a Renaissance eye of a certain esoteric cast—to the devotee of emblems and *imprese*, of hieroglyphics and Neoplatonic commentaries on the image—Hogarth's plate might well recall a Ficinian appreciation of Egyptian picture-writing, which "presented the whole of the discursive argument as it were in one complete image" [10] Such an image would overcome the temporal dispersion of thought in the text, unify its multiplicity, and present a dense and instantaneous visual epitome of its contents.

In this sense, the image absorbs and supersedes the text, reinforcing the claims for the painter over the writer that figure in Hogarth's treatise as late echoes of the Renaissance *paragone* between the arts. Thus the painter enjoys a direct access to beauty beyond the reach of "mere men of letters" (3) who can only resort to "pompous terms" (23) and "fashionable phrase[s]" (7) to describe it. [11] The connoisseur's feeble *je ne sais quoi* as a definition of beauty only reveals the failure of language to penetrate a realm luminously expressed by the image—and there, indeed, inscribed in a purer language whose essential grammar Hogarth himself claims to have discovered as a student, when he devised a private shorthand system of linear notation to capture the "Ideas" of a figure without the labors of wholesale copying.[12]

In its intricate, even riddling, effect, Hogarth's plate would also seem far more capable than the text's consecutive exposition of engaging the "active mind" whose "pleasing labour," says Hogarth, is to "solve the most difficult problems." Answering to an instinctual "love of pursuit" that Hogarth sees as key to a psychology of art, intricacy of form "leads the eye a wanton kind of chace" along wandering paths from goddesses to pineapples to parsley leaves to dancing masters—all these details no less capacious (if far more bizarre) than the enclosing text (41–42). The playful dance of the mind through the "Mazes intricate" (160) of such a plate—Hogarth here glances at Milton's description of the angelic dance in *Paradise Lost*—must be contrasted with the straightforward paths laid out for the mind by the draftsman's ruler. This is a tool for which Hogarth reserves a special scorn in the text, and which, in the plate, he places in the hand of a mournful *putto*. In Hogarth's mind, the notion of constricting linearity extends, one would guess, beyond a formal preference for S-shaped curves or an artist's impatience with "mere men of letters" to a deeper suspicion of letters themselves for enticing the mind down the "beaten path" (4) of conventional wisdom. This may help to explain why Hogarth is not a writer, and it certainly sheds light on the discrepancy between the tight prose of the published text of *The Analysis* as it was "improved" by Morell, and the defiantly meandering style of Hogarth's manuscript drafts. Engaging movements of perception and feeling beyond the range of the accompanying text, Hogarth's image does not so much illustrate the word as animate it. As language cannot, the image affords the pleasures that Hogarth remembered from his childhood, of the "eye eagerly pursuing a favourite dancer through all the wanderings of the figure" (45).

With the image so apparently privileged in Hogarth, Paulson's emphasis on the artist's iconoclasm may come as a surprise, but it is an insight borne out everywhere in Hogarth's writing—in his remarks on the age's idolatrous veneration of classical models (105), in his wry account of his own apprenticeship, when, he will now "confess," he grew so "profane" in his admiration of nature as to question the "devinity of even Raphael Urbin . . . and Michel Angelo," and perhaps most sharply in a published letter of 1737 attacking the importation of "shiploads of *dead Christs, holy families, Madonnas*, and other dismal dark subjects" from the Continent (xxiii). This sentiment carries over into the *Battle of the Pictures*

(1745)—a Swiftean conceit engraved as the admission ticket to an auction of Hogarth's works—in which an army of foreign paintings, including in the van a St. Francis and a Mary Magdalen, launch an attack against Hogarth's own studio. The sight of the Magdalen speared into the bedchamber plate of *The Harlot's Progress* reminds us by the juxtaposition of Hogarth's parodic and "profane" appropriation of the very devotional imagery now bent on an even more destructive revenge. A similar connection holds between the classical canon and the broken, dispirited castings jumbled together in Hogarth's sculpture yard. Dominated in the foreground by the headless and limbless classical figure known as "Michelangelo's Torso," these statues are no more than ironic reminiscences of some lost iconographic program, no more than fragments of a dead tradition waiting to be sold.

The significance of such an image is deeply ambiguous. As Paulson maintains, it may be seen as a turn toward an art free of classicizing constraints, toward a greater degree of naturalism or "sacred realism"—"transforming the mystified object into (or returning it to) its original, common form, its material use," its human equivalent. If idols are desacralized by the iconoclast, common objects are conversely "invested with spiritual value." [13] In this view (of iconoclasm, as it were, as a form of georgic), destruction clears the ground for renewal, and Hogarth's career defines a crucial moment of artistic transition. The image whose meaning was once delimited by, and fully disclosed within, a rigid conventional code now cracks itself free; the old meaning is drained (but residually present, to act as counterpoint), the image now opened to an invigorating sense of contemporary life.

Yet this funereal sculpture yard may also be seen as one marker along Hogarth's road to a more darkly iconoclastic view of his own art. For if *The Analysis* gives the image a privileged place, it is also shot through with the ironies of representation to which the iconoclast would be especially attuned. Even if salvation of a sort seems to lie in the transparent procedures of taking images "from the life," so that a "Waterman on the Thames" may serve as a better model for the figure of Charon than some antique statue (100), Hogarth knows that there is no unmediated image, no uncontaminated percept not already prejudged or rectified by the mind. At the most fundamental levels of perception, without the prior intervention of the mind between the eye and the natural world, we would see "a fly upon a pane of glass as a crow," and "all things double and upside down" (119). So Hogarth cautions us that the figures in his plate are never to be imagined as "placed there by me as examples themselves, of beauty or grace, but only to point out to the reader what sorts of objects he is to look for and examine in nature, or in the works of the greatest masters" (21). These images are thus not natural but indexical, pointing toward what they cannot represent, and signifying by their difference from that unattainable prototype as much as by their resemblance. In an ironically receding ontological perspective, Hogarth's own images of the gods in this plate are after all copies of copies of copies, and the plate itself no less a bargain item, a cheap substitute for the real thing, than the lead castings warehoused at Hyde Park Corner. The end of the road for Hogarth's art lay in the *Tail Piece* (1764). This is Hogarth's final work, the image intended as the last in a set of his complete engravings, and the one he finished just days before his death. The engraving—whose motto, "The Worlds End," appears on a teetering inn-sign showing the destruction of the world by fire—is modeled in part on Dürer's *Melencolia I*, and it is both littered with things broken, cracked, and blighted (including the artist's palette), and filled with a final sense of despair.

Rather than in a rejuvenation of the image, a more rigorously iconoclastic solution to these dilemmas might arguably lie in Hogarth's desire, if not to disown, then to rejoin or subordinate his imagery to the power of the word. Hogarth's self-portrait rests on the works of Shakespeare, Milton, and Swift. As Fielding did, we also tend to regard his pictures, particularly the series of engravings, as a species of narrative. Hogarth's interest in a grammar of drawing, and in an aesthetics of movement rather than static composition, might now be seen not as an attempt to subsume language into the visual arts but to resubmit the image to the condition and authority of writing and channel it back into the stream of narrative flow: "Action is a sort of language which perhaps one time or other, may come to be taught by a kind of grammar-rules" (149). "Subjects" he "consider'd as writers do" (290), and his writings refer perhaps as often to the novel, the epic, and the drama as to painting and sculpture. In the *Tail Piece*, a passage of text appears below the crumbling image as if to suggest that the collapse of that image will be undergirded or survived by the word; and the two quotations offered, from Tacitus and Maximus Tyrius, reaffirm the argument of *The Analysis of Beauty*.

Lessing's *Laocoon* was published in 1766, two years after Hogarth's death. *The Analysis of Beauty* had already been translated into German in 1754 by a friend of Lessing and favorably reviewed by the famous critic and playwright. Although Lessing quotes Hogarth at length on the Apollo Belvedere and the Antinous (both statues are pictured in Hogarth's plate and both are in the Vatican along with the Laocoon group itself), Hogarth remains a less explicitly influential English source for Lessing than Pope or Spence. Yet on every page, Lessing's treatise is intended to clarify just the sort of hybrid mingling of word and image that distinguishes Hogarth's art.

A reading of the *Laocoon* reveals how the Reformation's contests 'twixt God and Dagon, refracted powerfully through Hogarth, ultimately anticipate the shape of Lessing's thought, even though the terms of his argument have apparently shifted from the moral and theological to the purely aesthetic. When Lessing returns to "first principles" to assert the distinction between space-arts and time-arts, what he proclaims, as W. J. T. Mitchell remarks, has the ring of "one of those 'self-evident truths' bequeathed to us by the Enlightenment. . . . If Newton reduced the physical, objective universe, and Kant the metaphysical, subjective universe to the categories of space and time, Lessing performed the same service for the intermediate world of signs and artistic media." [14] Here was a disinterested, scientific analysis based on the necessity of things themselves, not on desire or ideology and certainly not on the dust of earlier opinion that Lessing would sweep away. Yet Lessing's zeal to cure poetry of its "mania for description" and to restore its Homeric purity of the word—to cleanse the rust of a corrupt tradition off an original truth—bears the mark of the Reformation program. The corresponding "mania for allegory" that Lessing diagnoses in painting leaves both the arts, in his view, the victims of a mutual contamination that has been allowed to breed under the cover of their presumed good fellowship.

Limited in the *Laocoon* to the representation of *körperliche Schönheit*, painting must forgo its ambition to usurp the authority of texts by carrying a discursive meaning, except insofar as the doctrine of the fruitful moment permits an image to freeze a crucial instant in a temporal process to be extrapolated from it by the viewer. Poetry has the "greater range" and the greater capacity for beauty. It also reserves to itself the quasi-magical power that the Renaissance had extended to its hieroglyphic and talismanic images, for language retains the Adamic power of naming. Like the name "Bedford" for Ben Jonson, the very name of "Urania" uttered by Lessing's poet identifies the muse of astronomy completely and instantaneously in a way that the painter can only fumble at by showing her attributes, the wand and the globe, which are his clumsy iconographic "letters." [15] As a reformation of the arts Lessing's project can be seen to have a twofold effect. It segregates poetry and painting by imposing upon them a clear but arguably reductivist difference between a temporal and a spatial art—and does so by repressing the many Renaissance senses in which language could be regarded as "spatial" apart from its capacity to describe, and in which imagery could be regarded as "temporal" apart from its capacity to allegorize. It also privileges the temporal process of which a language now blind to the temptations of the eye has become the exclusive agent.

The moral fervor of Lessing's argument has carried over in our own time in those critical positions which would alert us to the "dangers" of spatializing literature. Mitchell summarizes the warning:

> Frank Kermode and Philip Rahv argue for a connection between the spatial aesthetics of modernism and the rise of fascism, a claim which has been given its most precise formulation by Robert Weimann: "the loss of the temporal dimension means the destruction of the specific narrative effect, namely the representation of temporal processes" and thus "the ideological negation of self-transforming reality, the negation of the historicity of our world." Literary space, then, for many modern critics, has been a synonym for the denial of history and the escape into irrational reverence for mythic images. [16]

Substitute "salvation history" for "history" in the last sentence, and "saints and madonnas" for "mythic images," and the surprising congruence between the modern critics and the sixteenth-century reformers becomes clear.

Indeed if the heated theological disputations over the destruction of images in the Reformation were to be restaged at the Modern Language Association (as they have been, in some form, nearly every year), the partisans of *écriture*, engagement, and temporality would range themselves on one side of the hall, facing the defenders of spatial form and the verbal icon on the other. For American criticism the terms of this dispute were set in the exchanges between Joseph Frank and William Spanos, whose existentialist attack on the spatializers and the worshipers at the well-wrought urn issued from a moral stance as much reminiscent of Lessing and the reformers as of Sartre. Spanos's critique would be endorsed, at our imaginary meeting, by a loose coalition numbering among its mem-

bers Walter Ong, Stanley Fish, Wolfgang Iser, and Roger Shattuck—
all of whom would deploy the dynamics of reading and the sound
of the human voice in motion to break down the walls of what they
regard as a petrified reification of the text.

Now as in the first incarnations of this debate the reformers have
prevailed, at least insofar as the presuppositions of criticism since
Frye have progressively filtered our idea of the text of any pictorial
residue. In the *Anatomy of Criticism* the archetypes that form a hidden or deep pattern somewhere below the surface of literature are
nevertheless still imagined to be "there" in the text. You are likely to
emerge from a reading of Frye not so much with an argument in
hand as with an intricately detailed image of the literary cosmos—
one subsuming all books but also inscribed within any one book—
that would seem familiar to the Renaissance reader of Fludd or
Kircher; an anatomy is, in one sense, a laying open to the eye of the
body of literature. In structuralist criticism, however, the focus of
inquiry shifted from the text to an "abstract" model built typically
on the principle of binary opposition and following Levi-Strauss's
definition of a model as "not related to empirical reality" but "constructed according to that reality." [17] Frye's relatively visualizable designs "in" the literary work have since been replaced in poststruc-
turalist writing by critical fictions set next to or against the work,
fictions whose purpose is often to wrest meaning from the text by
dispelling the possibility of determinate meaning itself as an ideology or an iconolatry in which the text would entrap us. In this
criticism, the text as composition crumbles back into the process of
the composition of the text, and the writer's books dissolve into the
more fluid category of his "writing." A preference for the writing
over the writer is one dogma shared by critics today and the generation of Ransom and Brooks. But in other ways the sons must now
do penance for the sins of the New-Critical fathers. Rejecting any
attempt to "see" how a text coheres in some spatial dimension intrinsic to it, a reformed criticism must chisel into the pretextual and
intertextual crevices of language from which the "painted face"
of the text as an artifact is only a beguiling distraction. To be any
less vigilant is not criticism but complicity: the homilist's "spirituall fornication" has become the critical fornication of those who
would allow themselves to be enticed by the overt blandishments of
the text.

In view of the Derridean assault on the "logocentric" tradition, it
may be regarded as perverse to align deconstructive criticism with
the defiantly logocentric Protestant polemics of the Reformation,

or with Lessing's consequent valorization of the word. The very sharpness of the current attack on the authority of the literary "voice" only reveals the continuing strength of the Reformation poetic which its opponents would now silence with a very different conception of writing and interpretation. Yet the iconoclastic rhetoric of deconstruction might be seen from another perspective to carry on the work of the Reformation, for its aim is to release the mind from the text's idolatrous illusion of presence, and to expose the iconic structures projected by texts to support that illusion.

Notes

Introduction

1. See p. 12.
2. Patrick Grant's *Images and Ideas in the Literature of the English Renaissance* (Amherst: University of Massachusetts Press, 1979) runs parallel to the concerns of my own work at a number of points as he traces the gradual detachment of "images" from an Augustinian view of their ennobling participation in a realm of supersensory "ideas" to the point where Hobbes could declare that the imagination is "decaying sense." I have focused on the issue of iconoclasm, where that shift is most clearly reflected in the life of the times, and where the consequences for poetry are more immediate. James R. Siemon's admirable *Shakespearean Iconoclasm* (Berkeley and Los Angeles: University of California Press, 1984), which I did not read until this study was nearly done, opens the drama to the same concerns I bring to bear on the nondramatic literature of the period. See also A. M. Kinghorn, "Icons and Iconoclasm in the English Renaissance," *Journal of English* (Sana'a University, Yemen) 7 (1980): 14–27. John W. Erwin, in *Annunciations to Anyone: The Disclosure of Authority in Writing and Painting* (forthcoming), has chapters on Shakespeare and Milton brilliantly pertinent to any discussion of Reformation iconoclasm. W. J. T. Mitchell's *Iconology: Image, Text, Ideology* (Chicago: University of Chicago Press, 1985) pursues that discussion on a historical and theoretical level into the modern period; see also his "What Is an Image?" *NLH* 15 (1984), pp. 503–37. Huston Diehl offers a judicious and corrective account of Protestant emblematics in her forthcoming article, "Graven Images: Protestant Emblem Books in England." On the historical and theological background, John N. King's *English Reformation Literature: The Tudor Origins of the Protestant Tradition* is comprehensive, supplementing the now canonical studies of Protestantism and poetry in the seventeenth century, William Halewood's *The Poetry of Grace* (New Haven: Yale University Press, 1970) and Barbara Lewalski's *Protestant Poetics and the Seventeenth-Century Religious Lyric* (Princeton: Princeton University Press, 1979). Sanford Budick's recent *The Dividing Muse: Images of Sacred Disjunction in Milton's Poetry* (New Haven: Yale University Press, 1985) focuses on Milton's "half-interdicted images," the creations of a muse that "sets visual analogies into motion with an eye to their imminent depletion" (p. 23), and later on the "divested image" in *Paradise Lost* (Chapter 5): the sense in the epic of "a tortured rhythm of image creation

and image rejection" (p. 93), which Budick reads against a broad philosophical and theological background, is complemented by the present study of a muse (Spenser's and Donne's as well as Milton's) divided by an iconoclastic suspicion of its own promptings.

3. Lee's monograph is best known as it was reissued: *Ut Pictura Poesis: The Humanistic Theory of Painting* (New York: Norton, 1967); Jean Hagstrum, *The Sister Arts* (Chicago: University of Chicago Press, 1958); John Dixon Hunt, *The Figure in the Landscape* (Baltimore: The Johns Hopkins University Press, 1976); Stephen Orgel and Roy Strong, *Inigo Jones: The Theatre of the Stuart Court*, 2 vols. (Berkeley: Sotheby Parke Bernet and the University of California Press, 1973); Peter M. Daly, *Literature in the Light of the Emblem* (Toronto: University of Toronto Press, 1979). See also Lucy Gent, *Picture and Poetry: 1560–1620* (Leamington Spa, England: James Hall, 1981), and Norman K. Farmer, Jr., *Poets and the Visual Arts in Renaissance England* (Austin: University of Texas Press, 1984).

Chapter 1

1. Aymer Vallance, *Old Crosses and Lychgates* (London: B. T. Batsford, 1920), pp. 102, 106.

2. *Ben Jonson* [Works], ed. C. H. Herford and P. Simpson, 11 vols. (Oxford: Clarendon Press, 1925–52), 6:83, 133. All quotations from Jonson's work refer to this edition, and are hereafter cited in the text by volume number and page.

3. All quotations from Milton's poetry are taken from *John Milton: Complete Poems and Major Prose*, ed. Merritt Y. Hughes (New York: Odyssey, 1957).

4. John Aubrey, *Brief Lives and Other Selected Writings*, ed. Anthony Powell (London: Cresset Press, 1949), p. 8.

5. Thomas Cranmer, *The Miscellaneous Writings and Letters*, ed. John E. Cox, 2 vols. (Cambridge: Cambridge University Press, 1846), 2:126–27.

6. *The Reformation of Images: Destruction of Art in England, 1535–1660* (Berkeley: University of California Press, 1957).

7. E. Cardwell, *Documentary Annals of the Reformed Church in England*, 2 vols. (Oxford, 1844), 1:4–23.

8. *Sculpture in Britain: The Middle Ages* (London: Penguin, 1955; 2d ed. 1972), p. 1.

9. R. Willis and J. W. Clark, *The Architectural History of the University of Cambridge* (Cambridge: Cambridge University Press, 1886), 1:443; cited in Stone, *Sculpture in Britain*, p. 1.

10. James E. Oxley, *The Reformation in Essex: To the Death of Mary* (Manchester: Manchester University Press, 1965), pp. 151–52, 261.

11. Christopher Haigh, *Reformation and Resistance in Tudor Lancashire* (Cambridge: Cambridge University Press, 1975), pp. 83, 139, 209.

12. John Foxe, *The Acts and Monuments of the Church* (1563), ed. M. H. Seymour (London, 1838), p. 582.

13. Frances A. Yates, *Astraea: The Imperial Theme in the Sixteenth Century* (London and Boston: Routledge and Kegan Paul, 1975), p. 79.

14. Sidney Anglo, *Spectacle, Pageantry, and Early Tudor Policy* (Oxford: Clarendon Press, 1969), esp. pp. 250, 263–66, 329–30, 350–54.

15. Richard Culmer, *Cathedral News from Canterbury* (1644), p. 21; cited in Stone, *Sculpture in Britain*, p. 2.

16. Cited in Antonia Fraser, *Cromwell: The Lord Protector* (New York: Knopf, 1974), p. 103.

17. *The Shepheards Oracle, delivered in an Eglogue* (1644), p. 11.

18. See Fraser, *Oliver Cromwell*, pp. 102–3, and the sources cited by her, G. F. Nuttall, "Was Cromwell an Iconoclast?" *Transactions of the Congregational Historical Society* 13 (1933–36), and Alan Smith, "The Image of Cromwell in Folklore and Tradition," *Folklore* 79 (1968).

19. A. M. Everett, *The County Committee of Kent in the Civil War* (Leicester: University College Press, 1957), pp. 24–25; Phillips, *The Reformation of Images*, p. 187; Stone, *Sculpture in Britain*, p. 2.

20. G. F. Nuttall, quoted in Fraser, *Oliver Cromwell*, p. 105. The new outburst of iconoclasm in the 1640s was anticipated by at least one well-documented incident in Salisbury in 1632. Henry Sherfield, a solid citizen "with grey hairs upon him," was charged with defacing "an ancient and fair Window" in the Church of St. Edmonds "containing a description of the Creation." In his defense, Sherfield claimed that the window enshrined "divers falsities and absurdities," chief among them the idolatrous representation of God the Father as "a little old man in a blue and red coat." *Cobbett's . . . State Trials* (London, 1809), 3: 519, 522; as cited in George Wesley Whiting, *Milton and This Pendant World* (New York: Octagon, 1969), pp. 111–12.

21. Henry Ainsworth, *An arrow against Idolatrie. Taken out of the quiver of the lord of Hosts* (Amsterdam, 1611), p. 60.

22. John Buxton, *Elizabethan Taste* (London: Macmillan, 1963, p. 32.

23. John N. King, "Images of Truth in English Reformation Literature," p. 5, paper delivered at Special Session 515, MLA Convention, Houston, 30 December 1980. An expanded version of this passage appears in King's *English Reformation Literature*, pp. 148–49, as part of a very useful discussion of "Iconoclasm and Art," pp. 144–60. The copy to which King refers is Bodleian Library, Arch. G.b.2.

24. "Sidney and Titian," in John Carey, ed., *English Renaissance Studies Presented to Dame Helen Gardner* (Oxford: Clarendon Press,

1980), p. 1. On Sidney and Italian painting, see also Buxton, *Elizabethan Taste*, pp. 106–9. The letters to Languet appear in Albert Feuillerat, ed., *The Prose Works of Philip Sidney* (Cambridge: Cambridge University Press, 1912; rpt. 1962), 3:79–98.

25. Duncan-Jones, "Sidney and Titian," p. 4.

26. *The Poems of Sir Philip Sidney*, ed. William A. Ringler, Jr. (Oxford: Clarendon Press, 1962), p. 203 (Sonnet 74), p. 167 (Sonnet 5), and p. 165 (Sonnet 1).

27. *Phisicke against fortune* (London, 1579), pp. 57a–60a. The misrepresentation is noted in Michael Baxandall, *Giotto and the Orators* (Oxford: Clarendon Press, 1971), p. 53. The translation of Petrarch's Italian, above, is Baxandall's.

28. *A Tracte Containing the Artes of Curious Paintinge, Caruinge and Building . . . Englished by R. H.* (Oxford, 1598).

29. Gio[vanni] Paolo Lomazzo, *Trattato dell'arte de la pittvra* (Milan, 1584), pp. 4–6; my translation.

30. Haydocke, *A Tracte*, pp. 3–4.

31. See, for example, G. W. Pigman III, "Versions of Imitation in the Renaissance," *Renaissance Quarterly* 33 (1980): 1–32, and Thomas M. Greene, *The Light in Troy: Imitation and Discovery in Renaissance Poetry* (New Haven: Yale University Press, 1982).

32. The bibliography on English connoisseurship is extensive; a partial list appears in Phillips, *The Reformation of Images*, p. 169 n. 37. For a convenient survey, see Ellis K. Waterhouse, *Painting in Britain* (Baltimore: Penguin, 1953); for Rubens and the Whitehall ceiling, Per Palme, *Triumph of Peace* (Stockholm: Almqvist and Wiksell, 1956); and for the reception of Italian artistic theory in England, Lucy Gent, *Picture and Poetry: 1560–1620*. Gent's valuable Appendix (pp. 66–86) lists "the ownership and distribution of books on art, perspective, and architecture in English Renaissance libraries."

33. "An Apologie for Poetrie" (1583), in *English Literary Criticism: The Renaissance*, ed. O. B. Hardison (Englewood Cliffs, N.J.: Prentice-Hall, 1963), p. 105.

34. R. D. [Richard Dallington?], *The Strife of Love in a Dreame* (London, 1592); see the introduction by Lucy Gent to her edition of this text (New York: Scholars' Facsimiles and Reprints, 1973) for its possible influences on English poetry. For the Renaissance career of the ancient texts mentioned, see D. C. Allen, *Mysteriously Meant: The Rediscovery of Pagan Symbolism and Allegorical Interpretation in the Renaissance* (Baltimore: The Johns Hopkins University Press, 1970), and Jean Seznec, *The Survival of the Gods: The Mythological Tradition and Its Place in Renaissance Humanism and Art* (1940), trans. Barbara F. Sessions (Princeton: Princeton University Press, 1953).

35. *A Choice of Emblemes* (Leiden, 1586).

36. *Art of Making Devices* (London, 1646), p. 10.

37. *The Devout Heart* (Rouen, 1634), pp. 4–5.

38. *The Schoolmaster* (London, 1570), ed. Lawrence V. Ryan (Charlottesville: University Press of Virginia, 1967), p. 80.

39. Rudolf Wittkower, "Hieroglyphics in the Early Renaissance" (1972), rpt. in *Allegory and the Migration of Symbols* (London: Thomas & Hudson, 1977).

40. Cited in Wittkower, "Hieroglyphics," p. 116; Wittkower's translation.

41. *Emblemes* (London, 1635), Preface.

42. *Ovid's Metamorphosis* (Oxford, 1632).

43. On the iconography of the Holbein title page, see Roy Strong, *Holbein and Henry VIII* (London: Routledge & Kegan Paul, 1967), pp. 14–16; on Fludd, S. K. Heninger, Jr., *Touches of Sweet Harmony* (San Marino, Calif.: The Huntington Library, 1974), pp. 336–37.

44. Rensselaer W. Lee, *Ut Pictura Poesis: The Humanistic Theory of Painting* (New York: Norton, 1967), p. 30.

45. The Renaissance was fond of citing Ambrose's comment on the 38th Psalm: *Umbra in lege; imago in evangelio; veritas in coelistibus*—"The shadow was in the law; the image is in the gospel; the truth shall be in the heavens"; cited here from John Jewel, *Works*, ed. John Ayre (Cambridge: Cambridge University Press, 1847), 2:598.

46. *Protestant Poetics and the Seventeenth-Century Religious Lyric* (Princeton: Princeton University Press, 1979), p. 187.

47. "Apologie," p. 128.

48. Ibid., p. 111.

49. *Chapman's Homer*, ed. Allardyce Nicoll, 2 vols. (New York: Pantheon, 1956), 1:543. See also George Kurman, "Ecphrasis in Epic Poetry," *Comparative Literature* 26 (1974):1–13.

50. See Rudolf Wittkower, *Architectural Principles in the Age of Humanism* (1949; 3rd ed., rev., 1962; rpt. New York: Norton, 1971), esp. Part IV.

51. Noted in Robert Klein, *Form and Meaning: Essays on the Renaissance and Modern Art*, trans. Madeline Joy and Leon Wieseltier (New York: Viking, 1979), p. 47.

52. *Poems and Letters*, ed. H. M. Margoliouth, 2 vols. (Oxford: Clarendon Press, 1971), 1:139, 64.

53. Leon Battista Alberti, *On Painting* (1435), trans. John R. Spencer, rev. ed. (New Haven: Yale University Press, 1966), p. 90. On the tradition of the "Calumny," see Rudolph Altrocchi, "The Calumny of Appelles in the Literature of the Quattrocento," *PMLA* 36 (1921):454–91, and David Cast, *The Calumny of Apelles: A Study in the Humanist Tradition* (New Haven: Yale University Press, 1981).

54. Alberti, *On Painting*, p. 75.

55. *Giotto and the Orators*, Preface, and p. 9.

56. Baxandall, *Giotto and the Orators*, pp. 130–32.

57. Ibid., p. 44. For the connection between rhetoric and the Albertian conception of painting, see also John R. Spencer, "Ut rhetorica pictura," *JWCI* 20 (1951):26–44.

58. See Erwin Panofsky, *Studies in Iconology: Humanistic Themes in the Art of the Renaissance* (1939; rpt. New York: Harper & Row, 1967), esp. the discussion of "intrinsic" or "essential" meaning in the introductory essay, pp. 1–17. At the deepest level of interception, the work of art—understood to embody "what Ernst Cassirer has called 'symbolical' values"—is a manifestation of "underlying principles," a "symptom of something else" at the heart of the artist's culture (p. 8). The more limited procedure of isolating an "iconographical" meaning reveals the dependence of the image and its interpretation on the written record: in the fourteenth and fifteenth centuries, the new type of the Nativity showing "the Virgin kneeling before the Child in adoration. . . . means the introduction of a new theme textually formulated by such writers as Pseudo-Bonaventura and St. Bridget" (p. 7).

59. Richard Foster Jones, *The Triumph of the English Language* (Stanford: Stanford University Press, 1953), p. 145, summarizing Smith's *De recta et emendata Linguae Anglicae Scriptione, Dialogus* (Paris, 1568). That Smith's views introduced "confusion" into serious linguistics (Jones, p. 145) and awaited correction by clearer heads like Richard Mulcaster does not drain those views of their appeal in an age fascinated by the sisterhood of the arts.

60. Jones, *Triumph of the English Language*, pp. 147–48.

61. Arthur Golding, prefatory poem to John Baret's *An Alvearie or Triple Dictionarie* (1573), quoted in Jones, *Triumph of the English Language*, p. 152.

62. James Howell, *Lexicon Tetraglotton* (1660), prefatory poem, quoted in Jones, *Triumph of the English Language*, p. 263 n. 55.

63. Haydocke, *A Tracte*, p. 2.

64. For the impact of print, see the *loci classici* of modern scholarship, Herbert Marshall McLuhan, *The Gutenberg Galaxy* (Toronto: University of Toronto Press, 1962), and the works of Walter J. Ong—especially *Ramus, Method, and the Decay of Dialogue* (Cambridge: Harvard University Press, 1958), *The Presence of the Word* (New Haven: Yale University Press, 1967), and *Rhetoric, Romance, and Technology* (Ithaca: Cornell University Press, 1971)—for whom the effect of the Gutenberg revolution is widespread but largely unfortunate insofar as the printing press is seen to have stamped out the vitality of a medieval "oral culture." At the same time, Ong would argue that the effect of print is to spatialize, but not pictorialize,

thought, and his focus on the "inner iconoclasm" implicit for example in (printed) Ramist diagrams (*Rhetoric, Romance, and Technology*, pp. 104–12) will be pertinent to our discussion: see p. 44. See, more recently, Elizabeth S. Eisenstein, *The Printing Press as an Agent of Change*, 2 vols. (Cambridge: Cambridge University Press, 1979), and Martin Elsky, "George Herbert's Pattern Poems and the Materiality of Language: A New Approach to Renaissance Hieroglyphics," *ELH* 50 (1983):245–60, expanded in his *Making Words: Renaissance Language Theory and Seventeenth-Century Literature* (forthcoming). The Renaissance's sense of the "materiality" of the poet's medium—a sense strengthened by the embodiment and stabilization of that language on the printed page—encourages "an awareness of words and letters" as visible artifacts, "as physical objects to be laid out on a page" (Elsky, p. 247). It also encourages the suspicion of the iconoclast for whom the miring of words in the "material" contaminates their spiritual nature and allies them with sensual "images" carved from stocks and blocks.

65. *Elizabethan Critical Essays*, ed. G. Gregory Smith, 2 vols. (Oxford: Oxford University Press, 1904; rpt. 1959). Quotations from Puttenham are cited in the text by page number from volume 2 of Smith's edition.

66. Hoskins, *Directions for Speech and Style*, in *Life, Letters and Writings of John Hoskins, 1566–1631*, ed. L. B. Osborn (New Haven: Yale University Press, 1937), p. 116; Jonson, *Discoveries*, in *Ben Jonson*, 8:628. The sentence is originally Aristotelian (*On Interpretation*): the Renaissance substitution of "Pictures" for the more abstract "likenesses" in the classical text intensifies the visual dimension of thought.

67. "Visual Rhetoric: Chapman and the Extended Poem," *ELR* 13 (1983):36–57 (the quotation appears on p. 57). See also Rhoda M. Ribner's discussion of Chapman's "essentially emblematic technique" (p. 258) in "The Compasse of This Curious Frame: Chapman's *Ovids Banquet of Sence* and the Emblematic Tradition," *Studies in the Renaissance* 17 (1970), pp. 233–58.

68. Waddington, "Visual Rhetoric," p. 45.

69. *Francis Bacon: A Selection of His Works*, ed. Sidney Warhaft (New York: Odyssey, 1965), pp. 308, 223–24.

70. Ibid., p. 342.

71. Ibid., p. 222.

Chapter 2

1. Craig Harbison, Introduction to *Symbols in Transformation: Iconographical Themes at the Time of the Reformation*, ed. Hedy Backlin-Landman and Barbara T. Ross (Princeton: Art Museum, 1969), pp. 15–34.

2. Older studies such as Friedrich Buchholz, *Protestantismus und Kunst* (1928), and Ulrich Gertz, *Die Bedeutung der Malerei für die Evangeliumsverkündigung in der evangelischen Kirche des XVI. Jahrhunderts* (1936), have now been extended in such works as : H. F. von Campenhaussen, "Die Bilderfrage in der Reformation," *Zeitschrift für Kirchengeschichte* 68 (1957), pp. 96–128; Charles Garside, Jr., *Zwingli and the Arts* (New Haven: Yale University Press, 1966); Keith P. F. Moxey, *Pieter Aertsen, Joachim Beuckalaer, and the Rise of Secular Painting in the Context of the Reformation* (New York: Garland, 1977); Joseph Guttmann, ed., *The Image and the Word: Confrontations in Judaism, Christianity, and Islam* (Missoula, Mont.: Scholars' Press for the American Academy of Religion, 1977); and Carl C. Christensen, *Art and the Reformation in Germany* (Athens, Ohio: Ohio University Press, 1979. On Protestant biblical illustration, see James Strachan, *Early Bible Illustrations* (Cambridge: Cambridge University Press, 1957), Kenneth A. Strand, *Reformation Bible Pictures* (Ann Arbor: Ann Arbor Publishing Co., 1963), and especially Ph. Schmidt, *Die Illustration der Lutherbibel, 1522–1700* (Basel: Verlag Friedrich Reinhardt, 1962). The study of "Protestant art," once supposed almost a contradiction in terms, has profited from Panofsky's warning against the "notion that Protestantism *per se* was detrimental or even fatal to the flourishing of the arts" in Protestant countries ("Comments on Art and Reformation," in *Symbols in Transformation*, pp. 9–14); and his own work—particularly in *The Life and Art of Albrecht Dürer*, 2 vols. (Princeton: Princeton University Press, 1955), and "Erasmus and the Visual Arts," *JWCI* 32 (1969):202–227—has proved the point. One recent, and superb, study of seventeenth-century Dutch art begins by rejecting any "Calvinist influence" out of hand: "To the argument that secular subject matter and moral emblematic meanings speak to Calvinist influence, one must counter that the very centrality of a trust to images [in Dutch painting] seems to go against the most basic Calvinist tenet—trust in the Word. . . . An appeal to religion as a pervasive moral influence on the society's view of itself and the larger world of Nature seems a more fruitful direction to take than to continue to check the art against the tenets of the faith" (Svetlana Alpers, *The Art of Describing* [Chicago: University of Chicago Press, 1983], p. xxvi). Her argument (especially in Chapter 5, "Looking at Words: The Representation of Texts in Dutch Art") is that words do not show a mistrust or a deconstruction of the image but rather are given a privileged place within it: "Rather than supplying underlying meanings," words represented in Dutch pictures "give us more to look at" (p. 187). This absorption of the word by the painted image offers one happy strategy for accommodating that "most basic Calvinist tenet" to a strong pictorial tradition, but, as Alpers acknowledges, it

was not a strategy congenial to the greatest of the Dutch artists: Rembrandt, "deeply the iconoclast," rejected the characteristic trust of the Dutch that painting could be a kind of Baconian experiment in perception and that "the world and its texts were known by the eye." In a painting like *Abraham and Isaac*, the image of a conversation, it is the spoken and invisible word that Rembrandt shows to be all important (see Alpers, pp. 188 and 218, and the study by Julius Held to which she refers, "Das Gesprochene Wort bei Rembrandt," *Neue Beiträge zur Rembrandt-Forschung*, ed. Otto von Simson and Jan Kelch [Berlin: Gebr. Mann, 1973], pp. 111–25).

3. *PL* 77, cols. 1027–28, as cited in William R. Jones, "Art and Christian Piety: Iconoclasm in Medieval Europe"—a useful brief guide to the iconoclastic controversy in the medieval church—in *The Image and the Word*, p. 79.

4. *Canons and Decrees of the Council of Trent*, original texts, and trans. by H. J. Schroeder, O.P. (St. Louis: B. Herder, 1941), pp. 214–15, proceedings of the 25th session, December 1563.

5. Cited in Phillips, *The Reformation of Images*, pp. 152–53.

6. *Elements of Geometrie* (London, 1570), as cited in Roy Strong, *The English Icon: Elizabethan and Jacobean Portraiture* (New York: Pantheon, 1969), p. 54. See also John Pope-Hennessy, "Nicholas Hilliard and Mannerist Art Theory," *JWCI* 6 (1943):89–100.

7. As cited in G. R. Owst, *Literature and Pulpit in Medieval England* (Cambridge: Cambridge University Press, 1933), p. 138.

8. *Certaine Sermons or Homilies* . . . (London, 1623; facs. Gainesville, Fla.: Scholars' Facsimiles and Reprints, 1968), intro. Mary Ellen Rickey and Thomas B. Stroup, p. 40. The page number refers to *The Second Tome of Homilies* contained in this volume.

9. The phrase is Donne's; see p. 125. The eye's susceptibility to demonic captivation, a crucial theme in Milton's presentation of the Fall, was also at the heart of Puritan attacks on the theater, from Stephen Gosson's in the 1580s through William Prynne's *Histriomastix* (London, 1633). Gosson writes: "For the eye, besides the beauty of the houses and the stages, he [the Devil] sendeth in garish apparel, masques, vaunting, tumbling . . . nothing forgot that might . . . ravish the beholders with Vanity of pleasure. . . . The longer we gaze the more we Crave" (*Plays Confuted in Five Actions* [London, 1582], as cited in William Carew Hazlitt, ed., *The English Drama and Stage Under the Tudor and Stuart Period, 1543–1614* [London, 1869], pp. 192, 206). See also Alan C. Dessen, *Elizabethan Drama and the Viewer's Eye* (Chapel Hill: University of North Carolina Press, 1977), p. 10, and Jonas Barish, *The Antitheatrical Prejudice* (Berkeley: University of California Press, 1980), esp. the essays on "Puritans and Proteans" and "Puritanism, Popery, and Parade."

10. *Against the Heavenly Prophets in the Matter of Images and Sacra-*

ments (1525), in *Luther's Works*, ed. Jaroslav Pelikan and Herbert T. Lehrmann (St. Louis: Concordia, 1955–), 40:80 (hereafter cited as *LW*). For Luther's position in the iconoclastic controversy, I am indebted to the discussion in Christensen, *Art and the Reformation in Germany*, pp. 40–64.

11. *LW* 40:95.

12. *LW* 40:85, 147.

13. See p. 119.

14. Schmidt, *Die Illustration der Lutherbibel*, esp. pp. 93–112.

15. Jones, "Art and Christian Piety," p. 79.

16. King, *English Reformation Literature*, p. 146: King goes on to connect remembrance in this sense with "Augustine's Neoplatonic doctrine of memory," which leads Cranmer to identify "true images with the recovery of what mankind has forgotten as a consequence of the Fall."

17. *LW* 40: 91, 99.

18. *LW* 35: 371–72.

19. Frederick Goldin, "Luther the Translator," paper presented at the conference "Towards Luther: The Development of Dissent," Barnard College, 6 November 1982.

20. Christensen, *Art and the Reformation in Germany*, pp. 63–64.

21. Eugenio Battisti, "Reformation and Counter-Reformation," *Encyclopedia of World Art* (New York: McGraw-Hill, 1966), vol. 11, col. 902.

22. *A Piteous Lamentation of the Miserable Estate of the Church in England*, in *Works*, ed. Henry Christmas (Cambridge: Cambridge University Press, 1841), p. 52. The editor notes that in "the reign of Edward VI texts of Scripture were painted in most of the churches, particularly the second commandment, and 1 John v. 21, 'Babes, keep yourselves from images'" (p. 52n).

23. See p. 151.

24. Christensen, *Art and the Reformation in Germany*, pp. 23–24.

25. The proceedings of this disputation—recorded in *Huldrych Zwinglis Sämtliche Werke*, vol. 2 (Berlin and Zurich, 1905)—and the issues it raised are summarized in Garside, *Zwingli and the Arts*, pp. 134–50. The quotation from Jud appears on p. 134.

26. *Answer to Valentin Caspar* (1525), as cited in Garside, *Zwingli and the Arts*, p. 173.

27. Quotations from Calvin refer to the *Institutes of the Christian Religion*, ed. John T. McNeill and trans. Ford Lewis Battle, 2 vols. (Philadelphia: Westminster Press, 1960).

28. The *Treatise* appears in Christmas's edition of the *Works*, but Ridley's biographer questions the attribution. See Jasper G. Ridley, *Nicholas Ridley: A Biography* (London: Longmans, Green, 1957), p. 119n.

29. Phillips, *The Reformation of Images*, pp. 152–63, and for the queen's chapel, p. 169.

30. Maurice Merleau-Ponty, *The Phenomenology of Perception* (New York: Humanities Press, 1962), p. 235.

31. Karlstadt, *On the Abolishing of Images*, as cited in Christensen, *Art and the Reformation in Germany*, pp. 23–24; Luther, *Against the Heavenly Prophets in the Matter of Images and Sacraments*, LW 40:85; Zwingli, *Answer to Valentin Caspar*, as cited in Garside, *Zwingli and the Arts*, pp. 164–65.

32. *LW* 51:84

33. Zwingli, *A Brief Christian Introduction* (1523), as cited in Garside, *Zwingli and the Arts*, p. 148.

34. *Certaine Sermons or Homilies*, p. 61; see p. 132.

35. Nicholas Ridley, *A Treatise of the Worship of Images*, in *Works*, ed. Christmas, p. 85.

36. Henry Ainsworth, *An Arrow Against Idolatrie. Taken out of the quiver of the lord of Hosts* ([Amsterdam,] 1611), pp. 43–51. His proof texts are: Isaiah 44:9 ("The Prophet Esaias caleth mens idols their *delectable things*"), Ezekiel 23:2–5 ("Ezekiel compareth the idolaters of Israel to a woman inflamed with love"); the whore of Revelation 17:2; and the lament of Jeremiah 17.

37. *Certaine Sermons or Homilies*, p. 43.

38. *Difference of the Churches of the Separation*, as cited in William Madsen, *From Shadowy Types to Truth: Studies in Milton's Symbolism* (New Haven: Yale University Press, 1968), p. 174.

39. More's *Dialogue Concerning Tyndale* (1529) was answered by Tyndale's *Answer to Sir Thomas More's Dialogue* (1530). The quotations from Tyndale are given as cited by Stephen Greenblatt (*Renaissance Self-Fashioning* [Chicago: University of Chicago Press, 1980], pp. 112–13), who argues that for Tyndale, "at the heart of the Catholic Church . . . there is nothing else than man's own imagination idolatrously worshipped" (p. 112).

40. John Jewel, *Works*, ed. John Ayre, 4 vols. (Cambridge: Cambridge University Press, 1847), 2:660. Jewel's text includes that of Harding's *Answer*.

41. Ibid., 2:661, 662.

42. George Salteren, *A Treatise against Images and Pictures in Churches* (London, 1641), p. 2.

43. *An Arrow Against Idolatrie*, pp. 9–10.

44. *Summa Theologica* 1.84.2c

45. Walter J. Ong, *The Presence of the Word*, p. 50. For Ong, the "oral" culture of the Middle Ages suffers a tragic fall into the "visual" culture of the Renaissance—a fall from an animistic world fostering community, encounter, dialogue, and interiority into a mechanical world characterized by aggressiveness, depersonalized

relationships, anxiety, and conformity (see *The Power of the Word*, pp. 92–98, 126, 221). From Ong's point of view, Reformation iconoclasm must surely be regarded as a healthy force attempting to preserve the older orality, and in that sense, as an unlikely bedfellow of high scholasticism.

46. "A Plea for Visual Thinking," in W. J. T. Mitchell, ed., *The Language of Images* (Chicago: University of Chicago Press, 1980), p. 175.

47. Frances A. Yates, *The Art of Memory* (Chicago: University of Chicago Press, 1966), pp. 234, 298, 235.

48. For these references to Sibbes I am indebted, as for much else, to Professor William Kerrigan. On the complicated early history of the word *imago* which contributes to the Renaissance's confusion, see James Earl, "Typology and Iconographic Style," *Studies in the Literary Imagination* 8 (1975), especially the section on "The Theory of the Imago," pp. 29–33.

49. Citations by page number in the text refer to the one-volume edition of the *Acts and Monuments*, ed. M. Hobart Seymour (London, 1838). Foxe's text grew cumulatively: Originally published in Latin (Strasbourg, 1554), it was enlarged for a second Latin edition (Basel, 1559) before being expanded again for the first English edition of 1563. A second English edition, longer still, appeared in 1570. Literary martyrdom is not a calling for the short-winded.

50. *Ben Jonson*, 8:609–10.

51. Ibid., 6:282–83.

52. See the classic article by D. J. Gordon, "Poet and Architect: The Intellectual Setting of the Quarrel between Jonson and Inigo Jones," *JWCI* 12 (1949):152–78; and for a more comprehensive treatment of the masques, including the circumstances of their publication alluded to below, Stephen Orgel, *The Jonsonian Masque* (Cambridge: Harvard University Press, 1965) and Orgel's edition of the masques, *Ben Jonson: The Complete Masques* (New Haven: Yale University Press, 1969). The reference to "superfluous excesses," below, is from *Love Restored* (1612), in Orgel, *Complete Masques*, p. 192.

53. See Timothy Murray, "From Foul Sheets to Legitimate Model: Antitheater, Text, Ben Jonson," *NLH* 14 (1983): 642–64: Jonson's "efforts in the print shop illustrate his textual concerns with linguistic and rhetorical clarity, which interests favor literary standards over theatrical wonder" (p. 654).

54. *Ben Jonson*, 8:403–4.

55. Ernest B. Gilman, *The Curious Perspective: Literary and Pictorial Wit in the Seventeenth Century* (New Haven: Yale University Press, 1978). On perspective in the masques, see the introductory

essay in volume 1 of Stephen Orgel and Roy Strong, *Inigo Jones: The Theatre of the Stuart Court*, 2 vols. (Berkeley: Sotheby Parke Bernet and the University of California Press, 1973).

56. *Ben Jonson*, 8:611.

57. The quotations from Jonson's poetry (*Ben Jonson*, vol. 8) in this paragraph are from "To my Mvse," p. 48; "To Sir Robert Wroth," pp. 96–97; "To Penshvrst," pp. 95–96; "On my First Sonne," p. 41; "My Picture Left in Scotland," pp. 149–50; "To William Camden," p. 31; "To Fine Lady Would-Bee," p. 46; "Inviting a Friend to Svpper," p. 65; "An Epistle answering to one that asked to be Sealed of the Tribe of Ben," p. 220; "To William Earle of Pembroke," p. 66; "On Lvcy Covntesse of Bedford," p. 52. "*Language* most shewes . . . : *Ben Jonson*, 8:625. Cf. the Ode to Cary and Morison, where the two virtuous young men are praised, not without a strong note of envy, for having lived the perfect poem before Jonson, following their "faire example," could write the perfect life: in Cary and Morison, men "might read, and find / *Friendship*, in deed, was written, not in words" (8:247).

58. Quotations from Herbert, cited in the text by page number, refer to the *Works of George Herbert*, ed. F. E. Hutchinson (Oxford: Clarendon Press, 1941; rpt. 1970).

59. *The Writings of Henry Barrow, 1587–90*, ed. L. H. Carlson (London: G. Allen and Unwin, 1962), p. 478.

Chapter 3

1. *Spenser: Poetical Works*, ed. J. C. Smith and E. de Selincourt (London and New York: Oxford University Press, 1912; rpt. 1965). Unless otherwise noted, all quotations from Spenser's poetry refer to this one-volume edition.

2. *OED*, s.v. "depaint": to "depict," but also "To stain, distain," citing Chaucer's *Troylus* (5.1611): "I have eke seyn with teris al depeynted, Your lettre." Spenser's spelling hints at the secondary meaning.

3. "A Letter of the Authors," *Poetical Works*, p. 406.

4. Rudolf Gottfried ("The Pictorial Element in Spenser's Poetry," *ELH* 19 [1952]:203–13) summarizes this tradition (p. 204) before attacking it on grounds to be considered below.

5. Edwin Greenlaw, *Studies in Spenser's Historical Allegory* (Baltimore: The Johns Hopkins University Press, 1932; rpt. Octagon Books, 1967), pp. 86–92; Bennett, *The Evolution of "The Faerie Queene"* (Chicago: University of Chicago Press, 1942), p. 106.

6. *The Analogy of "The Faerie Queene"* (Princeton: Princeton University Press), 1976.

7. Fowler, *Spenser and the Numbers of Time* (New York: Barnes and

Noble, 1964); Fletcher, *The Prophetic Moment* (Chicago: University of Chicago Press, 1971); Aptekar, *Icons of Justice* (New York: Columbia University Press, 1969).

8. *A Preface to "The Faerie Queene"* (New York: Norton, 1962) p. 225. But cf. W. B. C. Watkins, "Spenser's Palace of Art," in his *Shakespeare and Spenser* (Princeton: Princeton University Press, 1950), pp. 223–58, for whom Calidore's vision is more nearly parallel to Mantegna's *Parnassus*.

9. On the illustrated St. George, see the edition of *Books I and II of "The Faerie Queene,"* ed. Robert Kellogg and Oliver Steele (New York: Odyssey, 1965), pp. 11–14.

10. Ibid., p. 11. Nor is Spenser likely to have seen Raphael's *St. George* (now in the National Gallery, Washington), a painting once thought to have been carried across the Alps by Castiglione in 1517 as a gift to Henry VIII, but now believed to have come into the Royal Collections at a much later date.

11. "The Structure of Imagery in *The Faerie Queene,*" *UTQ* 30 (1961):109–27; rpt. in Frye's *Fables of Identity* (New York: Harcourt, Brace & World, 1963), pp. 69–87, from which the sentence quoted is taken (p. 71). Frye has influenced a generation of critics, Fletcher among them, in his belief that Spenser works within "regular frameworks" (p. 69), attempting to build his imagery into a "structure" reflected in the sequence of significant enclosures beginning with the House of Holiness in Book 1 (p. 77), that will serve as an "imaginative home" (p. 1); and that in this sense the architecture of the imagery is "prior in importance" to the allegory (p. 72).

12. Jan Van der Noot, *A Theatre . . .* (London, 1569), sig. F3. Cf. Julia Bondanella, *Petrarch's Visions and Their Renaissance Analogues* (Madrid: Jose Porrua Turanzas, S.A., 1978), p. 82: "We do not know the exact conditions under which Spenser translated the poems . . . but it is certain that Spenser's early experience with this type of literary endeavor guided him throughout his career in both poetic theory and practice." (For this reference and for a valuable discussion of the pictorial interest of Spenser's early career that has influenced the following discussion, I am indebted to an unpublished paper on *The Shepheardes Calendar* by Christopher Martin of the University of Virginia.)

13. Helen Shire, *A Preface to Spenser* (London: Longmans, 1978), p. 13.

14. See Ruth S. Luborsky, "The Allusive Presentation of *The Shepheardes Calendar,*" *Spenser Studies* 1 (1980):29–67, for a persuasive argument that Spenser's "decision to illustrate" was "taken deliberately" (p. 41); and S. K. Heninger, *Touches of Sweet Harmony* (San Marino, Calif.: The Huntington Library, 1974), pp. 309–16, for the Pythagorean emblematics of the *Calendar*.

15. *The Works of Edmund Spenser: A Variorum Edition*, ed. Edwin Greenlaw et al. (Baltimore: The Johns Hopkins University Press, 1932–49), 9:19.

16. Barbara K. Lewalski (*Protestant Poetics and Seventeenth-Century English Literature* [Princeton: Princeton University Press, 1979], p. 187) cites this speculation of Joseph Mede, from his *Clavis Apocalyptica* (Cambridge, 1627).

17. *A Theatre*, sigs. D3–D6. For example, the Protestant interpretation of the beast from the sea (as the Antichrist and the Pope of Rome, its head wounded by the Reformation) is reflected in Van der Noot's plate, which offers both a gloss and a pictorial model for the wounding of Duessa's beast by Arthur (1.8.15–17): see John E. Hankins, "Spenser and the Revelation of St. John," *PMLA* 60 (1945): 368–69.

18. *Aeneid* 1:453ff. (the frescoes) and 8:626ff. (Aeneas's shield); to which should be added, as passages also admired and emulated in the Renaissance, 5:250ff. (Cloanthus's cloak), 6:20ff. (the wrought-iron door and bas relief), 7:790ff. (Turnus's shield), and 10:495ff. (Pallas's sword belt). For Renaissance emulations in Ariosto, Camoens, and Tasso, see George Kurman, "Ecphrasis in Epic Poetry," *Comparative Literature* 26 (1974): 1–13, esp. p. 11.

19. "A Letter of the Authors," *Poetical Works*, p. 408.

20. *A Theatre*, sig. M8.

21. *Institutes*, 3.2.6.

22. *The Marriage of Heaven and Hell*, plate 14, in *The Illuminated Blake*, ed. David V. Erdman (Garden City, N.Y.: Doubleday, 1974), p. 111.

23. *A Theatre*, sig. F3v.

24. *A Theatre*, sig. E7. Readers of Stanley Fish might conclude that Van der Noot's text enacts the process it describes, of "conuertying vnto the Lorde" (sig. E1) by consuming its own visual artifacts.

25. Carl J. Rasmussen, "'Quietnesse of Minde': *A Theatre for Worldlings* as a Protestant Poetics," *Spenser Studies* 1(1980):17.

26. *A Theatre*, sig. D2v.

27. Ibid., sigs. B3v–B4 (Petrarch's "Then heauenly branches did I see arise"); and from Du Bellay, sigs. B8v–C1 ("On hill, a frame of hundred cubites hie"), sigs. C2v–C3 ("I saw raisde vp on pillers of Iuorie"), and sigs. C1v–C2 ("Then did appeare to me a sharped spire"). Like many didactic Reformation images (cf. Cranach's "Fall and Redemption of Man" or his "Confrontation of the True and False Churches") these also embody in a kind of diptych form the division between two forces pitted in struggle, the vain arches or temples standing on the left, destroyed on the right.

28. *The Allegorical Temper*, Yale Studies in English, vol. 137 (New Haven: Yale University Press, 1957; rpt. Anchor Books, 1967), p. 218.

29. See Chapter 1, p. 8.

30. *Renaissance Self-Fashioning: From More to Shakespeare* (Chicago: The University of Chicago Press, 1980), pp. 188, 190.

31. Ibid., p. 189.

32. *Homilie against perill of Idolatrie, in Certaine Sermons or Homilies* . . . (London, 1623; facs., Gainesville, Fla.: Scholars' Facsimiles and Reprints, 1968), intro. Mary Ellen Rickey and Thomas B. Stroup, p. 61. See Chapter 5, p. 131.

33. *The Structure of Allegory in "The Faerie Queene"* (Oxford: The Clarendon Press, 1961), pp. 130–32.

34. Hamilton, pp. 131–32, quoting the trans. of *The Birth of Tragedy* by W. A. Haussmann (New York, 1924), pp. xxvii–xxviii. The interpretation of "gyon" in the *Legenda Aurea* is noticed by William Nelson, *The Poetry of Edmund Spenser* (New York: Columbia University Press, 1963), p. 180.

35. *Renaissance Self-Fashioning*, pp. 171–77.

36. A. Bartlett Giamatti, *Play of Double Senses: Spenser's "Faerie Queene"* (Englewood Cliffs, N.J.: Prentice-Hall, 1975), pp. 69–70.

37. Hamilton, p. 164, as also Giamatti, pp. 88–91: "To escape the terror and frustration of the play of double senses, the poet goes inward. He places the sources of ethical wisdom less and less in the public vocabulary of pageantry and more and more within the manageable world of the private self" (p. 90). My difference with Giamatti over the notion that the private world of the self is "manageable" should be clear from what follows.

38. *Endlesse Worke: Spenser and the Structures of Discourse* (Baltimore: The Johns Hopkins University Press, 1981). For Goldberg indeed the poem is not a "world" in the sense of being "complete" and "closed"—like a framed artifact—but a "process demanding endless doing" (p. 26).

39. *The Poetry of "The Faerie Queene"* (Princeton: Princeton University Press, 1967), pp. 9–13. Using Sidney to support this analysis of Spenser, Alpers rightly notes that in the concept of a "speaking picture" Sidney "does not attribute to poetry any formal analogies with painting" (p. 11); but it goes too far toward denying the power of the visual imagination in Sidney's poetic to conclude, as Alpers does, that the "traditional phrase" is no more than a "metaphor for the psychological effect of poetry" (p. 12).

40. *Spenser and Literary Pictorialism* (Princeton: Princeton University Press, 1972), p. 82.

41. Ibid., p. 128.

42. Ibid., p. 47.

43. Ibid., pp. 144, 146.

44. In *Spenser's Images of Life*, ed. Alastair Fowler (Cambridge: Cambridge University Press, 1967), p. 29.

45. Noted in Alpers, *The Poetry of "The Faerie Queene,"* p. 13.

46. Gottfried (p. 209) so treats the passage as an example of Spenser's "weak" pictorial composition, concluding that "nine tenths of Spenser's imagery is addressed to the ear rather than the eye" (pp. 211, 212).

47. "Ideas of Sight in *The Faerie Queene*," *ELH* 27 (1960):102–3.

48. One can only allude here to the vexed question of Spenser's doctrinal coloration—"Calvinist turned Anglican," as was once conventionally held; or "Anglican throughout," as suggested by Virgil K. Whitaker (*The Religious Basis of Spenser's Thought*, Stanford University Publications in Language and Literature 7, no. 3 [Stanford: Stanford University Press, 1950]) in view of the anti-Puritan satire in the early *Mother Hubberds Tale*; or even, despite a lingering commitment to the zeal of reform, a man capable (to judge by some passages in the *View of the Present State of Ireland*) of the kind of imaginative sympathy with Catholic rites that would later be admitted by Sir Thomas Browne in the *Religio*. This situation argues for an approach to the pictorialism of *The Faerie Queene* that can accommodate the several valences of Spenser's theology.

49. "Surprised by Puritanism," p. 2, special session 515, MLA Convention, Houston, 30 December 1980.

50. *Images and Ideas in the Literature of the English Renaissance* (Amherst: University of Massachusetts Press, 1979), pp. 57–58.

51. "An Hymne of Heavenly Beavtie," ll. 134–36, 141–45, in *Poetical Works*, pp. 587, 598; Sidney, *Apologie for Poetrie*, in *English Literary Criticism: The Renaissance*, ed. O. B. Hardison (Englewood Cliffs, N.J.: Prentice-Hall, 1963), p. 108.

52. Fletcher, *The Prophetic Moment*, pp. 130, 13.

53. *The Birth of Tragedy*, trans. Frances Golffing (Garden City, N.Y.: Doubleday, 1956), pp. 65, 39–45.

54. *The Analogy of "The Faerie Queene,"* pp. ix–x.

Chapter 4

1. *Coleridge on the Seventeenth Century*, ed. R. F. Brinkley (Durham, N.C.: Duke University Press, 1955), p. 532.

2. Rosemary Freeman, *English Emblem Books* (London: Chatto and Windus, 1948), p. 28; Mario Praz, *Studies in Seventeenth-Century Imagery*, 2d Eng. ed. (Rome, 1964), p. 163.

3. Karl J. Höltgen, *Francis Quarles, 1592–1644: Meditaver Dichter, Emblematiker, Royalist* (Tubingen: Max Niemeyer Verlag, 1978), from whom I cite the judgments on Quarles's reputation, quoted above, by Wood and Phillips (p. 340).

4. Perhaps the most important research tool for the Continental emblem has been Arthur Henkel and Albrecht Schone, *Emblemata: Handbuch zur Sinnbildkunst des XVI und XVII. Jahrhunderts* (Stuttgart,

1967; supplement, 1976). Peter M. Daly, *Literature in Light of the Emblem* (Toronto: University of Toronto Press, 1979) surveys the influence of the emblem on poetry, drama and pageantry, narrative, and much else, and acknowledges his predecessors in the field going back to Henry Green's notorious *Shakespeare and the Emblem Writers* (London, 1870). From the point of view of this chapter's concerns, too little of this critical literature deals with the emblematists themselves. The other major recent contribution in English studies, Barbara K. Lewalski's essay on "Protestant Emblematics" in *Protestant Poetics and the Seventeenth-Century Religious Lyric* (Princeton: Princeton University Press, 1979), pp. 179–212, will be discussed below.

5. Alan B. Howard, "The World as Emblem: Language and Vision in the Poetry of Edward Taylor," *American Literature* 44 (1972):384.

6. Walter Benjamin, *The Origins of German Tragic Drama* (London: New Left Books, 1977), pp. 140, 175–85.

7. See Chapter 1, pp. 15–17.

8. Joseph A. Mazzeo, "St. Augustine's Rhetoric of Silence," in *Renaissance and Seventeenth-Century Studies* (New York: Columbia University Press, 1964), p. 19.

9. There has, indeed, been at least one scholarly attempt to apply the insights of modern linguistic theory to "Reading Emblematic Pictures": see Bernhard Scholz, in *Komparatistische Hefte* 5/6 (1982), pp. 77–88.

10. A. B. Grosart, ed., *Complete Works . . . of Francis Quarles*, 3 vols. (1880–81; rpt. New York: A.M.S. Press, 1967), 3:45. All citations to Quarles refer to this edition. Grosart replaces Quarles's images (the eleventh edition of the *Britannica* labels them "grotesque") with new illustrations by Charles Bennett and W. Harry Rogers, a dubious improvement. The images included in this chapter are photographed from the first edition of the *Emblemes* in the Folger Shakespeare Library.

11. Höltgen, *Francis Quarles*, p. 342 (from Höltgen's English "Summary" of his work).

12. Louis Martz, *The Poetry of Meditation: A Study in English Religious Literature of the Seventeenth Century* (New Haven: Yale University Press, 1962).

13. *Ben Jonson* [Works], ed. C. H. Herford and Percy and Evelyn Simpson, 11 vols. (Oxford: Clarendon Press, 1925–52), 8:610. See Chapter 2, pp. 50–53. The poems cited in this paragraph appear in *Ben Jonson*, 8:52, 34, 30, 29.

14. *Protestant Poetics*, page references given in parentheses in the text.

15. Parenthetical citations refer to the 1619 polyglot edition of

de Montenay (STC 18046) and the 1631 edition of Jenner's *The Soules Solace* (STC 14494).

16. The passage in the epistle reads: "*Ad singula loca depingi figuras & typos adhiberi oportuit, nisi quod talis scultura cum sumptu oneret bene praelo nostro non convenit, nec quadrat, quia operosa & alienor est, quia exemplo caret.*"

17. *The Profest Royalist: His Quarrell with the Times* (1645); Höltgen, *Francis Quarles*, p. 267 (my trans. of Höltgen's German).

18. George Jenney, *A Catholike Conference between a Protestant and a Papist about the Church visible and invisible* (London, 1626), sigs. A3v, X4v, Y2.

19. The chief sources for the Jesuit emblems include Daniel Heinsius, *Emblemata Amatoria* (Antwerp, 1604), Otto van Veen (Vaenius), *Amorum Emblemata* (Antwerp, 1608), and Pieter Hooft, *Emblemata Amatoria* (Amsterdam, 1611). Vaenius had shown the way by spiritualizing his own earlier emblems in the *Amoris Divina Emblemata* (Antwerp, 1615). See Praz, *Studies in Seventeenth-Century Imagery*, pp. 143–49.

20. *Martin Luther: Selections from His Writings*, ed. John Dillenberger (Garden City, N.Y.: Doubleday, 1961), p. 502.

21. Quarles, *Divine Fancies* (London, 1632), bk. 3, p. 54, also in *Complete Works*, 2:237; *Divine Fancies*, bk. 2, p. 66, in *Complete Works*, 2:226.

22. *Enchyridion* (London, 1641), bk. 3, p. 9, in *Complete Works*, 1:31.

23. *Divine Fancies*, bk. 3, p. 70, in *Complete Works*, 2:238–39.

24. *Divine Fancies*, bk. 3, p. 49, in *Complete Works*, 2:236.

25. See Gordon S. Haight, "The Sources of Quarles's Emblems," *Library* 16 (1936):188–209. Quarles used the second edition of Hugo (1629).

26. On this point see Freeman, *English Emblem Books*, pp. 139–40. Christopher Harvey, *Schola Cordis* (London, 1647), and John Hall, *Emblems with elegant Figures* (London, 1658).

27. All further references to Quarles's *Emblemes*, as found in *Complete Works*, 3:43–101, are cited in the text by parenthetical reference to the book and the emblem number. Quarles's alterations in other plates seem similarly intended to heighten the emphasis on temptation and death. For example, 1:7 adds a tiny figure of death, menacing Cupid with an arrow, in the background of the engraving borrowed from the *Typus Mundi*; 1:9 adds the figure of time toppling the world with his scythe; 1:10 adds the figure of Mammon as a bowling companion for Cupid.

28. For the *via negativa* in this context, see E. H. Gombrich, *Symbolic Images* (Oxford: Phaidon, 1972), pp. 150–52, 157–60. Hall's *The Invisible World* (1652) is cited in Lewalski, *Protestant Poetics*,

p. 168: Hall urges us to "withdraw our selves from our senses . . . and make earthly things, not as Lunets, to shut up our sight, but Spectacles to transmit it to Spiritual objects."

29. *Pia Desideria*, 1:2, trans. Edmund Arwaker (1686; 3d ed., London, 1702), p. 14. Hugo's Latin (1624), p. 9:

Sed videt haec, magnus qui temperat arbiter orbem,
  Nostraque, stultitia nomine, multa tegit.
Et mea propitius deliria plurima transit,
  Multaque scit caeca dissimulanda manu.

30. Richard Sibbes, *The Soules Conflict with It Selfe* (London, 1651), p. 163.

31. The phrases "readable text" and "unreadable rebus" and the analogy between dream interpretation and emblematics are suggested by Paul Ricoeur, "Image and Language in Psychoanalysis," in *Psychoanalysis and Language*, ed. Joseph A. Smith (New Haven: Yale University Press, 1978), pp. 293–324. Commenting on a passage in the *Interpretation of Dreams*, Ricoeur notes that the "kinship" in Freud "between the task of interpreting a dream and that of interpreting a text is confirmed by the fact that analysis takes place between the story of the dream and another story which is to the first what a readable text is to an unreadable rebus, or what a text in our maternal language is to a text in a foreign language" (p. 300).

Chapter 5

1. *The Poems of John Donne*, ed. Herbert J. C. Grierson (1912; rpt. London: Oxford University Press, 1968), 1:154–58. All quotations from Donne's poetry are taken from volume 1 of this edition and hereafter cited by page number in the text (line references to quotations from the longer poems are also given).

2. For *Cebes' Tablet*, see Chapter 6, p. 167 (and n. 29). This text and its numerous Renaissance illustrations, including one by Holbein, have long been proposed—most recently by Norman K. Farmer, Jr., in *Poets and the Visual Arts in Renaissance England* (Austin: University of Texas Press, 1984), pp. 20–21—as one of a far greater number of possible sources and analogues for lines 79–83 of this satire. The other suggestions, none certain but most of them plausible, range on the literary side from passages in Hesiod and Xenophon to the *Inferno* and Petrarch's epistle describing his ascent of Mont Ventoux. On the pictorial side, connections have also been made with early Florentine painting (Louis Martz, *The Wit of Love* [Notre Dame: University of Notre Dame Press, 1969], pp. 32–34) and with emblems. The history of such conjecture is summarized by Wesley Milgate in *John Donne: The Satires, Epigrams, and Verse Letters* (Oxford: Oxford University Press, 1967), Appendix C, pp. 290–92; and, since Milgate, by Paul R. Sellin, "The Proper Dat-

ing of John Donne's 'Satyre III,'" *HLQ* 43 (1980), Appendix B, pp. 306–13. The arguments for and against the Cebes as a specific source are complex, depending in part on the differences perceived between the philosophical ascent portrayed in the classical work and Donne's climb toward Christian truth, in part on whether the mountain in the particular illustration of Cebes one has at hand may look more like Donne's cragged hill (Farmer, p. 21) or (as Sellin says of another pictorial contender) like "an earthen wedding cake" (p. 306).

Sellin himself argues in great detail that Donne's description is modeled explicitly on the reverse of a medallion commemorating the Synod of Dort. If he is right, the poem must date from 1620, not the 1590s, and my transitional paragraph on p. 118, looking forward to the sermons, should begin, "About the same time," and not "Some twenty years later." For the purposes of my argument, however, one of Sellin's most telling points against the Cebes illustrations actually works in their favor. He maintains that Donne's emphasis on the "hidden truth of Christian revelation" (p. 285)— its dazzling, mysterious, unvisualizable quality—makes the Dort medallion, over which "Jehovah hovers . . . . invisible behind a cloud inscribed with the tetragrammaton" (p. 287), a likelier source than images representing Truth or Blessedness as female figures, or God himself "enthroned above the heavenly spheres in almost idolatrous detail" (p. 307). My point is that in his poetic ascent Donne approaches, but then swerves away from, just this idolatrous prospect, evoking but then effacing the picture behind his text.

3. *Ep.* 82.i.2, as cited in Peter Brown, *Augustine of Hippo* (Berkeley: University of California Press, 1967), p. 275. I am grateful to Professor Richard Harrier for this reference.

4. *The Sermons of John Donne*, ed. George R. Potter and Evelyn M. Simpson, 10 vols. (Berkeley: University of California Press, 1953– 62). Quotations from the sermons, all taken from this edition, are identified in the text by volume and page number.

5. The texts of Donne's will is given in Appendix D (ii), pp. 563– 67, of R. C. Bald's *John Donne: A Life* (New York: Oxford University Press, 1970).

6. See John Buxton, *Elizabethan Taste* (London: Macmillan, 1963), pp. 96, 101.

7. Ibid., p. 103. For what follows on Donne and Sarpi, see John Carey, *John Donne: Life, Mind and Art* (New York: Oxford University Press, 1981), p. 36, and Frances Yates, "Paolo Sarpi's 'History of the Council of Trent,'" *JWCI* 7 (1944).

8. George Herbert, *Works*, ed. F. E. Hutchinson (1941; rpt. Oxford: The Clarendon Press, 1970), p. 304. Hereafter cited as Hutchinson.

9. On the Catholicism of "La Corona," see Helen Gardner, ed.,

John Donne: The Divine Poems (New York and Oxford: Oxford University Press, 1952), pp. 57–60, Carey, p. 51, and Louis Martz, *The Poetry of Meditation* (New Haven: Yale University Press, 1954), pp. 99, 107–8, 220.

10. Carey, pp. 51–52.

11. Donne cites Augustine's examples of the point, Revelation 7:12 and Psalms 34:12.

12. Quoted in Erik H. Erikson, *Young Man Luther* (New York: Norton, 1958), p. 233.

13. On Bunyan's "aural images," see U. Milo Kaufmann, *The Pilgrim's Progress and Traditions in Puritan Meditation* (New Haven: Yale University Press, 1966), pp. 232–33. The passage from Baxter— *The Saints Everlasting Rest*, 4th ed. (London, 1653), pt. 4, p. 254—is cited by Kaufmann, p. 244. Brainerd P. Stranahan, "Bunyan's Special Talent: Biblical Texts as 'Events' in *Grace Abounding* and *The Pilgrim's Progress*," *ELR* 11 (1981):329–43, points to the many examples of the word kindling, seizing, falling upon, or breaking in upon Bunyan as it did upon the biblical prophets (p. 333): "suddenly this sentence bolted in upon me" (*Grace Abounding*, par. 143).

14. *The Apocrypha*, trans. Edgar J. Goodspeed (New York: Random House, 1938).

15. *Certaine Sermons or Homilies . . .* (London, 1623; facs. Gainesville, Fla.: Scholars' Facsimiles and Reprints, 1968), intro. Mary Ellen Rickey and Thomas B. Stroup. Page numbers, in the text, refer to *The Second Tome of Homilies* contained in this volume.

16. Quoted in William Kerrigan, "The Fearful Accommodations of John Donne," *ELR* 4(1974):348, to whose discussion (pp. 337– 63) of the failure of accommodation in Donne's "Holy Sonnets" I am here indebted.

17. Carey, p. 47.

18. Ibid., p. 121.

19. "'Goodfriday, 1613. Riding Westward': The Poem and the Tradition," *ELH* 27 (1961):50, 51.

20. Nicholas Sander, *A Treatise of the Images of Christ* (Louvain, 1567), facs., ed. D. M. Rogers, *English Recusant Literature*, vol. 282 (London: Scolar Press, 1976), pp. 43a–43b.

21. *Works of George Herbert*, ed. F. E. Hutchinson (Oxford: Clarendon Press, 1941; rpt. 1970), pp. 65, 67, 26, 117, 103.

22. *The Complete Poetry of Richard Crashaw*, ed. George Walton Williams (New York: Doubleday, 1970), p. 68.

Chapter 6

1. "Life of Milton," in *Johnson: Prose and Poetry*, ed. Mona Wilson (Cambridge: Harvard University Press, 1967), p. 837.

2. Cited in Roland M. Frye, *Milton's Imagery and the Visual Arts* (Princeton: Princeton University Press, 1978), pp. 12–13.

3. *A Critique of "Paradise Lost"* (New York, 1960), p. 85, cited in Frye, *Milton's Imagery*, p. 15. In the same vein, see Phyllis MacKenzie, "Milton's Visual Imagination: An Answer to T. S. Eliot," *UTQ* 16 (1946):17–29.

4. Frye, *Milton's Imagery*, pp. 13–14, 17, citing Arnold Stein, "Milton and Metaphysical Art: An Exploration," *ELH* 16 (1949): 123; John G. Demaray, *Milton's Theatrical Epic: The Invention and Design of "Paradise Lost"* (Cambridge: Harvard University Press, 1980).

5. Frye, *Milton's Imagery*, pp. 20–39.

6. "Milton's *Samson* and the Stage, with Implications for Dating the Play," *HLQ* 40 (1977):313–24, p. 323.

7. All quotations from Milton's poetry are taken from *John Milton: Complete Poems and Major Prose*, ed. Merritt Y. Hughes (New York: Odyssey, 1957) and cited by line numbers in the text.

8. Except where noted, all quotations from Milton's prose are taken from *The Works of John Milton*, ed. Frank A. Patterson et al., 17 vols. (New York: Columbia University Press, 1931–42) and cited in the text by volume number and page. I have here emended "wayfaring" in the Columbia edition to the reading "warfaring," now preferred.

9. *Milton's Poetry: Its Development in Time* (Pittsburgh: Duquesne University Press, 1979), p. 41.

10. Don Wolfe and Sir John Seeley, quoted in William G. Madsen, *From Shadowy Types to Truth: Studies in Milton's Symbolism* (New Haven: Yale University Press, 1968), pp. 166–67.

11. Calvin, Commentary on Gal. 3:1; Richard Baxter, *The Saints Everlasting Rest* (London, 1650), p. 220; cited by Madsen, *Shadowy Types*, pp. 175–76, 177. See also U. Milo Kaufmann, *The Pilgrim's Progress and Traditions in Puritan Meditation* (New Haven: Yale University Press, 1966).

12. On Milton's iconoclasm, see esp. Thomas A. Brennan, "Idols and Idolatry in the Prose and Early Poetry of John Milton" (Ph.D. diss., Tulane University, 1970), and Brennan's entry on "Idolatry" in *A Milton Encyclopedia*, ed. William B. Hunter et al., 8 vols. (Lewisburg: Bucknell University Press, 1978–80), 4:52–55.

13. *Complete Prose Works of John Milton*, vol. 3, ed. Merritt Y. Hughes (New Haven: Yale University Press, 1962), p. 150. Quotations from *Eikonoklastes* only are taken from this volume of the Yale prose, and are cited in the text by page number. On the iconoclastic Milton of 1649, see Florence Sandler, "Icon and Iconoclast," in *Achievements of the Left Hand: Essays on the Prose of John Milton*, ed. Michael Lieb and John T. Shawcross (Amherst: University of Massachusetts Press, 1974), and especially David A. Loewenstein, "Milton and the Drama of History: From the Revolutionary Prose to the Major Poems" (Ph.D. diss., University of Virginia, 1985), which sees Milton's iconoclastic temperament along with his millenarianism as

crucial to his evolving sense of national history and sacred history alike.

14. *Eikon Alethine. The Pourtraiture of Truths Most Sacred Majesty Truly Suffering, Though Not Solely* (London, 1649), sigs. A2–A3v. See Philip A. Knachel's introduction to *Eikon Basilike* (Ithaca: Cornell University Press, 1966).

15. *Emblemes* (London, 1635), cited in the text by page number. See also Christopher Hill, "George Wither and John Milton," in *English Renaissance Studies Presented to Dame Helen Gardner*, ed. John Carey (Oxford: Clarendon Press, 1980), pp. 212–27.

16. Henry Peacham, *Minerva Britanna or a Garden of Heroical Devices* (London, 1612), p. 158.

17. "Oberon," ll. 258–60, in *Ben Jonson: Selected Masques*, ed. Stephen Orgel (New Haven: Yale University Press, 1970), p. 111.

18. Thomas N. Corns, *The Development of Milton's Prose Style* (Oxford: Clarendon Press, 1982), pp. 65, 57–64, 97, 101–2. Corns's "spare functionalism" cannot cover a number of passages in Milton's later prose, including *The Readie and Easie Way* and *Pro Se Defensio* (in Latin, and so not in Corns's computer).

19. *A Preface to "Paradise Lost"* (New York: Oxford University Press, 1961), p. 129.

20. "The Death of Adam: Vision and Voice in Books XI and XII of *Paradise Lost*," *MP* 70 (1972):9–21. Waddington (p. 9, n. 3) gives a bibliography of essays on the final books; see also George Miller, "Archetype and History: Narrative Technique in *Paradise Lost*, Books XI and XII," *MLS* 10 (1980):12–21, for a view opposite to mine, that Michael's shift is to a "reductive narrative" that, because it confines Adam in a fallen world of historical (rather than "archetypal") experience, becomes an "ironic reminder of how much we have lost" (p. 20). The shift from vision to speech is set into the broader context of the relationship between narrative and history in *Paradise Lost* by Marshall Grossman, "Milton's Dialectical Visions," *MP* 82 (1984):23–49 (Chapter 8 of his forthcoming *"Authors to Themselves": Milton and the Revelation of History*).

21. Georgia B. Christopher, "The Verbal Gate to Paradise: Adam's 'Literary Experience' in Book X of *Paradise Lost*," *PMLA* 90 (1975):69–76. On voice in *Paradise Lost*, see also Leland Ryken, *The Apocalyptic Vision in "Paradise Lost"* (Ithaca: Cornell University Press, 1970), pp. 130, 150.

22. "Structure and Symbolism of Vision in Michael's Prophecy, *Paradise Lost*, Books XI–XII," *PQ* 42 (1963):25–35. See also Madsen, *Shadowy Types*, pp. 143–44, 158.

23. Demaray, *Theatrical Epic*, pp. 31, 53.

24. *Milton and the Renaissance Hero* (Oxford: Clarendon Press, 1967), p. 169, and *Milton's Epic Characters: Image and Idol* (Chapel Hill: University of North Carolina Press, 1959), pp. 236–38.

25. "An Apologie for Poetrie" (1583), in *English Literary Criticism: The Renaissance*, ed. O. B. Hardison (Englewood Cliffs, N.J.: Prentice-Hall, 1963), pp. 129–30, and p. 129, n. 23.

26. Georgia B. Christopher, *Milton and the Science of the Saints* (Princeton: Princeton University Press, 1982), p. 177.

27. Madsen, *Shadowy Types*, pp. 181–82.

28. On the parallel between Michael's prophecy and the shield of Aeneas, see A. S. P. Woodhouse, *The Heavenly Muse*, ed. Hugh MacCallum (Toronto: University of Toronto Press, 1972), p. 200.

29. *Cebes' Tablet: Facsimiles of the Greek Text, and of Selected Latin, French, English, Spanish, Italian, German, Dutch and Polish Translations*, intro. Sandra Sider (New York: Renaissance Society of America, 1979). Figure 19, an engraving by Erhard Schön (1531), accompanied the German translation by Hans Sachs published in 1551 (Sider, pp. 138–39).

30. *Aeneid* 8:626–955, trans. Allen Mandelbaum, *The Aeneid of Virgil* (New York: Bantam, 1971), p. 211.

31. Anthony Low, *The Blaze of Noon: A Reading of "Samson Agonistes"* (New York: Columbia University Press, 1974), pp. 95, 107. On the play's "blind" atmosphere, see also Anne D. Ferry, *Milton and the Miltonic Dryden* (Cambridge: Harvard University Press, 1968), pp. 127–77, cited by Low (p. 107).

32. "'To Which is Added *Samson Agonistes*—,'" in *The Prison and the Pinnacle*, ed. Balachandra Rajan (London: Routledge & Kegan Paul, 1973), pp. 82–110; the phrases quoted appear on pp. 101 and 98.

33. "The Imagery of Killing," *Hudson Review* 1 (1948):151–67; p. 153.

34. See Tayler, *Milton's Poetry*, pp. 105–22.

35. Christopher, *Milton and the Science of the Saints*, p. 234.

36. Low, "Milton's *Samson* and the Stage," p. 321.

37. Ibid., pp. 320–321.

38. "Agon and Logos: Revolution and Revelation," in *The Prison and the Pinnacle*, pp. 135–63; pp. 150, 147–48.

39. Philip Schmidt, *Die Illustrationen der Lutherbibel, 1522–1700* (Basel: Friedrich Reinhardt, 1962), pp. 137, 139, 146. For examples of later Samson illustrations, see F. Michael Krouse, *Milton's Samson and the Christian Tradition* (Princeton: Princeton University Press, 1949), plate I, and Low, "Milton's *Samson* and the Stage," p. 314.

40. See, for example, George S. Peak, "*Samson Agonistes* and the Masque Tradition," *Cithara* 15 (1973):47–44.

41. Roger B. Wilkenfeld, "Art and Emblem: The Conclusion of *Samson Agonistes*," *ELH* 32 (1965):160–68; p. 164.

42. Hughes, *John Milton*, p. 592n.

43. *OED*, s.v. "Emboss," from which the examples of usage given in the text are cited.

44. *Poetics* 6:19 and 14:1, trans. S. H. Butcher, in *The Great Critics*, ed. J. H. Smith and E. W. Parks (New York: Norton, 1932), pp. 10–11, 17. See William Riley Parker, *Milton's Debt to Greek Tragedy in "Samson Agonistes"* (Baltimore: The Johns Hopkins University Press, 1937), p. 153.

45. *Toward "Samson Agonistes"* (Princeton: Princeton University Press, 1978), pp. 15–16.

Conclusion

1. Neil M. Flax, "The Presence of the Sign in Goethe's *Faust*, *PMLA* 98 (1983):185.

2. *Critical Essays of the Seventeenth Century*, ed. J. E. Spingarn (Bloomington: Indiana University Press, 1957), 2:71.

3. Page numbers in the text refer to Thomas Hobbes, *Leviathan*, ed. Michael Oakeshott (Oxford: Basil Blackwell, 1955).

4. John Locke, *An Essay Concerning Human Understanding* (2.1.2), ed. Alexander C. Fraser (1984; rpt. New York: Dover, 1959), 2:121.

5. *Critique of Pure Reason* (2.1), in *The Philosophy of Kant*, trans. John Wats (Glasgow, 1927), pp. 86–87. I take the characterization of Kant as "the great iconoclast" from J. Martineau, *Essays, Philosophical and Theological* (London, 1866).

6. *Kant's Critique of Judgement* (1.1.29), trans. J. H. Bernard, 2d rev. ed. (London: Macmillan, 1931), p. 143.

7. *Of Poetry* (1690), in *Critical Essays of the Seventeenth Century*, 3:75, 77–78.

8. "Conventional Signification and 'Natural' Resemblance in Hogarth," delivered at the conference on "Image and Text," Dartmouth College, October 6, 1984. My own view of the illustration to Hogarth's *The Analysis of Beauty* first took shape as a response to this paper. Paulson broadens the topic in his "English Iconoclasm in the Eighteenth Century" (forthcoming).

9. See Joseph Burke, "A Classical Aspect of Hogarth's Theory of Art," *JWCI* 6 (1943).

10. See Chapter 1, p. 17.

11. *The Analysis of Beauty*, ed. Joseph Burke (Oxford: Clarendon Press, 1955); quotations from Hogarth's treatise are taken from this edition and cited by page number in the text.

12. See the introduction to Burke's edition of *The Analysis*, pp. xi, xxxviii.

13. Paulson, "English Iconoclasm."

14. W. J. T. Mitchell, *Iconology: Image, Text, Ideology* (Chicago: University of Chicago Press, 1985), p. 96.

15. Gotthold Ephraim Lessing, *Laocoon* (1766), trans. Edward A. McCormick (Indianapolis and New York: Bobbs-Merrill, 1962), pp. 50, 59.

16. Mitchell, *Iconology*, p. 97. The critical positions summarized by Mitchell are collected in *Spatial Form in Narrative*, ed. Jeffrey R. Smitten and Ann Daghistany (Ithaca: Cornell University Press, 1981).

17. As noted in Karl Kroeber and William Walling, eds., *Images of Romanticism* (New Haven: Yale University Press, 1978), pp. xii–xiii.

Index

Table of Cebes, 15, 117, 167, 168, 183, 212 n.2, 217 n.29
Tasso, Torquato, 62, 162, 207 n.18
Tayler, Edward W., 151, 217 n.34
Taylor, Edward, 86, 101
Temple, Sir William, 182–83
Teresa, St., 114, 148; *Vida*, 114
Tertullian, 160, 176
Titian, 12
Trent, Council of, 32, 94
Tuve, Rosamund, 40
Twyne, Thomas, 13
Tyndale, William, 6, 42–43, 203 n.39
Typus Mundi. See College of Rhetoric of the Society of Jesus

Urmiston, Clement, 9

Vaenius. *See* Veen, Otto van
Valdesso, 56, 121
Valeriano, Pierio, 17
Vallance, Aymer, 194 n.1
Van der Noot, Jan, *A Theatre for Voluptuous Worldlings*, 63–64, 65, 67–68, 69, 70, 90, 207 nn.17, 24
Van Dyck, Sir Anthony, 14
Vasari, Giorgio, 88–89
Vaughan, Henry, 89, 114
Veen, Otto van, 211 n.19
Virgil, 24, 64–65, 72, 83, 169, 170, 207 n.18; *Aeneid*, 43
Vitruvius, 24

Waddington, Raymond B., 28–29, 159
Waller, Sir William, 9
Walpole, Horace, 85
Walton, Izaac, *Life*, 120
Warton, Thomas, 62
Waterhouse, Ellis K., 196 n.32
Watkins, W. B. C., 206 n.8
Weimann, Robert, 189
Whitaker, Virgil K., 209 n.48
Whiting, George Wesley, 195 n.20
Whitney, Geffrey, 15, 89, 90
Wilkenfeld, Roger B., 217 n.41
Willet, Andrew, *Sacrorum emblematum centuria una*, 90, 91, 92, 93
Wither, George, 85, 155
Wittkower, Rudolf, 17, 197 n.50
Wolfe, Don, 215 n.10
Wood, Anthony, 85
Woodhouse, A. S. P., 217 n.28
Word of God, 11, 22, 30, 36, 38–39, 56, 65, 88, 126, 127, 151, 159, 162, 163, 173, 175, 179
Wotton, Henry, 121
Wroth, Sir Robert, 52–53
Wycherly, William, *Love in a Wood*, 172

Xenophon, *Memorabilia*, 183

Yates, Frances, 9, 44–45, 213 n.7
Yeats, William Butler, 62

Zwingli, Ulrich, 5, 33, 38, 41